watching tv
religiously

Engaging Culture

WILLIAM A. DYRNESS
AND ROBERT K. JOHNSTON,
SERIES EDITORS

The Engaging Culture series is designed to help Christians respond with theological discernment to our contemporary culture. Each volume explores particular cultural expressions, seeking to discover God's presence in the world and to involve readers in sympathetic dialogue and active discipleship. These books encourage neither an uninformed rejection nor an uncritical embrace of culture, but active engagement informed by theological reflection.

watching tv
religiously

television and theology in dialogue

kutter callaway
with dean batali

Baker Academic

a division of Baker Publishing Group
Grand Rapids, Michigan

Published by Baker Academic
a division of Baker Publishing Group
P.O. Box 6287, Grand Rapids, MI 49516-6287
www.bakeracademic.com

Printed in the United States of America

Library of Congress Cataloging-in-Publication Data
Names: Callaway, Kutter, 1979– author. | Batali, Dean, author.
Title: Watching TV religiously : television and theology in dialogue : engaging culture / Kutter Callaway and Dean Batali.
Description: Grand Rapids, MI : Baker Academic, a division of Baker Publishing Group, [2016] | Includes bibliographical references and index.
Identifiers: LCCN 2016024903 | ISBN 9780801030734 (pbk.)
Subjects: LCSH: Television broadcasting—Religious aspects—Christianity.
Classification: LCC PR1992.8.R45 C35 2016 | DDC 791.45/6—dc23
LC record available at https://lccn.loc.gov/2016024903

In keeping with biblical principles of creation stewardship, Baker Publishing Group advocates the responsible use of our natural resources. As a member of the Green Press Initiative, our company uses recycled paper when possible. The text paper of this book is composed in part of post-consumer waste.

16 17 18 19 20 21 22   7 6 5 4 3 2 1

contents

acknowledgments

"Theological experts must unite their best insights with those of professional script writers."[1] Edward J. Carnell penned these words in 1950, long before TV became the cultural force that it is today. But in a very real sense, this book—written nearly sixty-five years later—takes his suggestion to heart. Without knowing exactly what we were getting ourselves into, Dean Batali and I (one of us a professional TV writer and the other a professional theologian) agreed to collaborate on a project exploring the theological significance of television for the contemporary world. What emerged from our countless conversations over coffee (what else?) is a final product that neither of us would have entirely anticipated when we began. As with any real dialogue, we did not always agree with each other, and sometimes our disagreements seemed intractable. But at the end of the day, our ongoing and often animated dialogue helped to produce something far more interesting and, indeed, life-giving than anything we could have created on our own. (At one point we thought we should publish the transcripts of our conversations!) So while it is often said that no book is written alone, in this case it is literally true. Although I (Kutter) wrote the bulk of what follows, every word was birthed from the kind of interaction that I think Carnell envisioned years ago—a process in which the best of my theological insights were sharpened and deepened by Dean's insights into TV storytelling and the TV industry. As a result, whatever we have done here that is worthwhile is the result of Dean's contributions. But any and all of the book's faults are of my own making. I am thankful for both his partnership and his commitment to the hard work of collaboration, but even more so for the friendship that has resulted from our time together.

Matt Aughtry joined us at an early stage in the process, serving as both sounding board and de facto consultant regarding the direction our project was heading. In addition to putting up with two fast-talking loudmouths, he fastidiously recorded the aforementioned transcripts of our numerous coffee conversations. We are incredibly thankful for his assistance, even when all we could do was pay him with coffee and pastries for his hard work. Matt also served as the teaching assistant for the Theology and TV class at Fuller Theological Seminary that I first offered in spring 2015. The students in that class read early drafts of the manuscript and offered helpful and challenging feedback. The book is a result of conversations with those students as much as it is a product of the conversations between Dean and me.

Rob Johnston and William Dyrness, the general editors for this series, offered us much-needed insight, wisdom, and encouragement along the way. They also happen to be two theologians whose work has left an indelible mark on my own understanding of theology and culture. Their influence on this work cannot be overstated.

Catherine Barsotti deserves her own line of acknowledgment for coming up with the original idea for this book, and for suggesting that the two of us work together on it. Although Dean and I were not present at the time, nor did we even know each other, it was Catherine who pointed out not only that a book of this sort needed to be a part of the Engaging Culture series but also that we were the two people to write it. We both owe a debt of gratitude to Catherine for shouting out our names in those early brainstorming sessions, which somehow led to us coauthoring this book.

Robert Hosack and the team at Baker Academic supported the project from the very start. Bob was a great advisor regarding some of the crazy ideas I kept throwing at him about transmedia content and the book's online presence. To wit: we have developed a number of supplemental resources for the book that can be found at www.bakeracademic.com/WatchingTVReligiously. Elijah Davidson of Reel Spirituality gathered together the various contributors for this project, each of whom has taken what Dean and I wrote and expanded upon it in fun and insightful ways. Of particular note are Avril Speaks, Richard Goodwin, and Matthew Pittman. We encourage readers to check out these resources as a complement to and an extension of all that is found in the book.

Dean would like to thank Chris and Kathy and Karen and Jim for discussing the bigger issues of both life and TV, and the writers of Act One and Poiema for wandering along on the journey. Thank you also to Sean and Catherine, for not falling asleep on the couch. Mostly, thanks to my wife, Beth, for watching with me, and allowing me to hit "pause" and explain to her what the writers should have done.

Finally, I (Kutter) also want to thank the women in my life who willingly endure extended periods of time in which their father or husband is either writing, thinking about writing, or planning on thinking about writing. My three daughters are growing up in a world where they are surrounded by screens of every kind, accessible at every moment. In many ways, this book is about the world we are envisioning for them. Likewise, my wife and I have always shared a fondness for TV and film stories. But as our little tribe has grown, we have discovered the beauty of domestic life, which means that our viewing habits have shifted from film to television, the location of our screenings from the theater to the living room. It is in this shared domestic space, accompanied by these four beautiful women (Jessica, Callie, Mattie, and Maeve), that something as simple as a TV show can become imbued with a meaning beyond meaning. As with all my work, this book is dedicated to them.

> Visit www.bakeracademic.com/professors to access study aids and instructor materials for this textbook.

introduction

turning us on

Season 1: Episode 1, "Pilot"

The scene opens in complete DARKNESS.

A single, four-letter word emerges from the background. The stark, all uppercase font slowly comes into focus. It reads:

LOST.

A cacophonous SOUND rises from the silence. It is more of a semi-structured noise than instrumentation per se—the relentless chaos of nature being held at bay, but always on the verge of breaking free of its sonic constraints. The text is continually moving, unmoored from the center of the screen. It twists and turns, slowly shifting to the foreground until it swallows us whole. Down the rabbit hole we go.

SMASH CUT TO:

An extreme close-up of an EYE. The eyelid OPENS to reveal a dilating pupil. First there is sight; then there is seeing. Consciousness arrives. The frame widens. The owner of the eye is wearing a suit and a tie. He is bleeding from the head. He is lying on the floor of a jungle—out of place, disoriented, and alone. Muffled sounds slowly transform into piercing screams.

The man rises to his feet, staggers, and then regains his balance. He finds his footing and begins to run. The dense trees and undergrowth fade into a blur as he races toward the sound of those crying out for help. He emerges from the forest and onto a BEACH.

He stops dead in his tracks.

Crystal-blue waves are lapping at the shore. The sand is white and untouched—serene even. The camera slowly moves along the shore of the beach, in tandem with the man's gaze. What comes into view is jarring given this picturesque tableau.

The man sees nothing but CHAOS.

The fiery wreckage of an airplane is scattered along the beach. Dead and wounded PASSENGERS are strewn about the debris. Survivors are hysterical, barely aware of themselves or others.

The man begins to assess the situation and treat the wounded. (That he is a doctor becomes evident as he administers CPR, dresses wounds, and assists a woman who is in labor.) He instructs one young man to watch over the laboring woman so that he can help someone else escape the still-exploding rubble. As the doctor turns to help another nameless stranger, the young man calls out: "Hey! What's your name?"

The man replies: "Jack."

———————

Flash forward to March 2014. A Boeing 777 with 239 passengers on board disappears en route to Beijing from Kuala Lumpur. Days turn into weeks as the search goes on, and what soon enters the public conversation about this real-life human mystery is . . . a TV show. More specifically, the prime-time TV drama *Lost* becomes almost immediately bound up with the tragic events as they unfold. Among others, newscasters, internet message boards, and daytime talk show hosts reference the popular TV series as a way of making sense of the nonsensical. Indeed, in the wake of the Flight 370 disappearance, the similarities are nearly impossible to avoid. At an event featuring the head writers from *Lost* that takes place a few days after the airplane's

Matthew Fox as Dr. Jack Shephard in ABC's *Lost*

disappearance, the moderator pointedly instructs the audience not to bring up the Malaysian flight because of concerns that it would be "in poor taste." But it is clear that everyone in the audience is already thinking about the numerous connections between this fictional narrative and these real-world events. Perhaps more important, it is also clear that a serialized television program has captured the public's imagination.

Looking back, it is perhaps unsurprising that *Lost* was able to provide a common vocabulary for people to speak of something that simply could not be. After all, everyone knows that planes don't just vanish.[1] But much like it did on *Lost*, a giant hunk of carbon fiber and aluminum alloy had seemingly evaporated into thin air. As a result, the stories about the survivors of *Lost's* Oceanic Flight 815 provided a well of resources for weaving the incomplete and sparse data from Malaysian Airlines Flight 370 into a more meaningful whole. Of all things, it was a television show that functioned as the interpretive framework through which individuals accepted and understood these events. Apparently, scientific protocols and sophisticated technologies were simply not enough, for they could neither explain away the ambiguities of the situation nor satisfy the public's collective desire for these random and muddled events to mean something more. Instead, what allowed something meaningful to emerge—some coherence in the midst of chaos—was TV.

The actual disappearance of Malaysian Flight 370 was tragic. Families were left in limbo regarding the fate of their loved ones. China alone lost 152 citizens. But the cultural conversation that surrounded this tragedy was revealing in its own right, for it gave concrete expression to two important facets of the contemporary cultural imagination that will serve as core operating assumptions for this book. First, our collective ignorance regarding the technologies that we depend upon to live, work, and travel has carved out a space for the return of the mysterious and the mystical in the modern world.[2] Although modern culture is markedly disenchanted in some important respects, contemporary persons are increasingly open to a spiritually saturated world—one brimming with enchantment. This broad interest in spirituality may have started with shows like *The X-Files*, but it is now reflected in numerous television series such as *Supernatural*, *True Detective*, *Fringe*, and *The Walking Dead*, which, in addition to *Lost*, are all concerned with the mysterious, the fantastic, the unexplained, the undead, and even the religious.

Second, and equally important, the ways in which television shows like *Lost* function in our daily lives serve as a reminder that human beings are meaning-making creatures through and through. By "meaning-making" we do not simply mean "belief" or "intellection." Instead, we are describing something far more dynamic and holistic. So here and throughout the book, we will be using the term "meaning-making" to reference the world-making capacity of television—its ability to evoke or elicit an understanding of the world that is rooted as much in our affections as it is in our intellect. Put differently, we are concerned with *how* TV means as much as *what* TV means, and this kind of "meaning" is both broader and more integrated into the fabric of our everyday existence than purely cognitivist approaches recognize.

Given that humans are constantly caught up in this dynamic process of making sense of our life and the world, it is all the more significant that one of the primary ways in which we forge a meaning-filled life is through story-telling. In fact, some have even defined "culture" itself as "the stories we tell ourselves about ourselves."[3] Because stories give shape, direction, and purpose to otherwise diverse and unrelated data, we are always in the process of locating the discrete events of our lives in a larger narrative framework. In other words, just like every culture that has preceded it, modern culture too has a mythic shape. Its deep structures of meaning cannot be accessed or understood apart from its core narratives. And if the dialogue surrounding Flight 370 and *Lost* is any indication, it is television that has emerged as the dominant storytelling medium of early twenty-first-century culture. It is both our preferred and most pervasive means for telling ourselves stories—about ourselves.

A Theology of Television

According to *New York Times* columnist Caryn James, "Anyone who does not watch television cannot possibly understand mainstream American culture. . . . We live in a vast, messy society, and television mirrors who we are in all our contradictions, complexities and uncertainties."[4] We couldn't agree more. At first blush, this claim regarding the cultural prominence of television might strike some as a bit of an overstatement—or simply out of touch with the realities of our shifting media landscape. A book about television is surely a day late and a dollar short. After all, didn't the arrival of the internet effectively announce the end of TV as we know it? It's simply common knowledge that, when it comes to the real movers and shakers in contemporary culture, television cannot hold a candle to Web 2.0. So why commit so much energy to a cultural artifact that is quickly headed toward extinction? Besides, who even owns a TV anymore, much less watches it?

These critical voices are not completely unfounded. Times have certainly changed, and so too have the media we consume. The world does not look like it did in 1964, or 1994, or even 2004. The days of *I Love Lucy* and *The Dick*

Van Dyke Show, *Saved by the Bell* and *Friends* are now distant memories. And in an important sense, this book is an exploration of how much things really have changed and why those changes matter.

But let's get one thing clear from the very start: "Television" as we have come to know it is far from dead. If anything, it is more significant than ever, and increasingly so. Rather than being a medium in decline, television is entering a time of incredible expansion and proliferation—a "golden age" even. Of course, the technology that audiences use to watch TV changes almost daily, but the simple fact remains that more TV programming is produced and consumed now than ever before. And there is no indication that things will be slowing down any time soon. Indeed, the increase in consumer demand has even brought about a shift in the medium of choice for culture's most talented storytellers. Increasingly, aspiring TV creators now start their careers by making movies in the hopes that they might ink a deal with a TV network that will allow them to explore long-form, episodic storytelling.[5] In this strange new world, movies now function as "calling cards" because, when compared with the creative possibilities of TV, the medium of film is thought to be rigid and constraining.

What is more, as the demand for the quantity of television has increased, so too has the demand for the *quality* of TV. In an age of content overload, it isn't that viewers are less interested in television. Instead, viewers are simply far less willing to invest time and energy in trite, poorly written, or aesthetically deficient stories.[6] These changing viewer practices, along with shifts in technology and the proliferation of channels, have created the necessary conditions for the emergence of a highly complex and elaborate new form of storytelling on TV. This unique narrational mode is what TV scholar Jason Mittell calls "complex TV," and has become especially prominent in the first two decades of the twenty-first century.[7] What this means is that audiences no longer tune in simply because "nothing else is on"; instead their programs of choice must meet certain aesthetic criteria that allow these complex stories to be integrated into the larger fabric of their lives. In other words, both TV production and TV consumption *mean* something to contemporary persons. And we want to suggest that this televisual meaning-making is both different and more central to contemporary life than it has ever been before.

In order to come to a fuller understanding of all this meaning-making activity, the pages that follow offer an exploration of the theological significance of the medium of TV and the contemporary practice of TV watching. By approaching TV in this way, we hope to achieve three interrelated goals. The first goal is to outline a set of analytical tools for engaging critically with television so that everyday viewers might understand and appreciate more fully the power and meaning of TV (we present these critical tools in chapters 2, 3, and 4). Second, we aim to introduce the reader to a process of theological reflection that seeks to articulate something of the presence and activity of God in this televisual world of ours (chapters 5 and 6). This process begins with a particular cultural product (e.g., a TV show like *Lost*) and the practices it fosters (e.g., fan conversations on Lostpedia) and places those into conversation with the biblical witness and the Christian tradition. The emphasis here is on lived theology—the ways in which our numerous and sometimes conflicting faith commitments find concrete expression in our daily lives. Bill Dyrness describes this approach to theological reflection in a helpful and elegant way. He suggests that theology is a matter of seeking to "develop theological categories, given to us by Scripture and tradition, in conversation with the contemporary cultural situation. It assumes that whether this is recognized or not, all living theology grows in this way."[8]

Following directly from our first two goals, the third and ultimate goal is to develop a theology of television that allows for both celebration and critique of the medium (chapter 7 and the conclusion). It should be noted that celebrating TV from a theological perspective is more than a matter of affirming overt depictions of religion that align with some abstract and predetermined notion of orthodoxy. Beyond the explicitly religious, we are even more interested in the implicit theology embedded in television programs and, by extension, the inchoate spirituality expressed in and through TV narratives and the audience's TV viewing habits. We are concerned with identifying the core impulses that compel modern persons to orient their lives around television and to derive significance from it. Thus, what distinguishes this book from others in the fields of media studies or cultural anthropology is our ultimate aim to connect the broader cultural practice of TV viewing to the presence and movement of God in the world.

Along similar lines, we are also concerned with the ways in which television is already functioning "theologically." Television has the capacity to confront audiences with questions and concerns that, although diffuse and ill defined, are nevertheless theological to their core. As Robert Johnston puts it, "Conversation about God—what we have traditionally called theology—is increasingly found outside the church as well as within it."[9] This book will argue that these exchanges are regularly happening both on TV and among TV viewers. Our hope is to chart a path for Christians to join this theological conversation in ways that are as constructive as they are life-giving.

Of course, this kind of theological project will also need to address television content that is overtly religious. Some TV narratives traffic in explicitly religious symbols, images, and themes. In doing so, they articulate certain conceptions of religious persons, communities, practices, and even the divine (e.g., *Joan of Arcadia*, *The Book of Daniel*, *The Simpsons*). In some instances, the explicit "theology *of* TV" is entirely superficial—a kind of clichéd or conventional shorthand used to evoke either laughter or a vague sense of institutionalism gone wrong. Yet other programs that feature overtly religious content move beyond generic conventions and actually offer affirming and sympathetic takes on religion and religious persons (e.g., *7th Heaven*, *Touched by an Angel*). Because these explicit religious representations are not our primary focus, we have included an appendix at the end of the book for readers who want to explore further television's overt theology. However, it is important to note here that even when TV deals directly with faith, religion, and spirituality, it cannot be assumed that its theological significance is either straightforward or simple, and a theology that seeks to celebrate what is good and true and beautiful about television must be able to account for this inherent complexity.

Thus, by "celebrate," we do not mean an uncritical embrace of all things cultural. Rather, we simply want to affirm those places where the Spirit of God is already present and active in culture, attuning our eyes and ears in a way that will allow us to discern how the people of God might collaborate with God's ongoing project in the world. We will return to this topic later, but it is enough for now to say that God has a tendency to speak in some of the most unexpected places and in unpredictable ways. Just ask Balaam (Num. 22) or Moses (Exod. 3). This is often an unsettling reality for those who prefer closed and static theological paradigms, but it is a basic assumption of this book that the God of Christian theology is in fact a God whose Spirit "blows wherever it pleases. You hear its sound, but you cannot tell where it comes from or where it is going" (John 3:8). We would like to suggest that, in and through certain television stories and even certain viewing practices, God may very well be present and active in contemporary culture, and this activity bears a striking similarity to the ways in which the Spirit once animated an angel-avoiding donkey and a rather enflamed bush.

Celebrating an overwhelmingly populist (and fiercely popular) medium like TV is not incredibly common, if for no other reason than the societal effects of TV have been called into question almost from the moment of the technology's inception. Some readers might even assume that our theological critiques are ready-made, as if the ill effects of TV are so obvious that we can simply list them as a matter of course. Television is nothing more than mindless entertainment that encourages passivity and inactivity, promotes violence and sexuality, and peddles soda and sugary cereal to already hyperactive children. Or so the story goes. But we want to turn these assumptions on their heads and suggest that the critiques that are most often leveled against television are in many cases blinding us from seeing what really matters.

We need a new vision and a new critical paradigm for assessing the ethics of television. So consumed are the many "watchdog" groups with depictions of sex, violence, and language that they have often missed the point. More important are questions concerning TV's pervasive presence within the home and its tendency to segment our viewing habits. Selective TV viewing allows individuals, whether by choice or by accident, to envision a world bereft of diversity—one where everyone looks, talks, and behaves exactly like we do. And in an increasingly globalized and pluralistic context that is filled with intertribal violence between "us" and "them," these kinds of homogenous visions have a great deal of destructive potential. Thus, when it comes to developing a theology of both celebration and critique, we are not interested in content analysis alone. Content matters, but a purely social-scientific approach to televisual meaning-making fails to take story seriously enough, much less imagination and ritual. So in distinction to many who have come before us, our constructive theological critique will be just as concerned with the overarching meaning of television narratives—its stories—and the profoundly formative nature of television viewing.

Trace Not Text

Another distinguishing characteristic of the present volume is that we are operating out of a framework more closely aligned with what might be called televisual aesthetics or philosophical aesthetics than with TV or media studies.[10] Although our descriptions and analyses will be in conversation with TV and media studies along the way, we will emphasize TV creators and TV viewers more than media theory. Part of the reason for this emphasis is that we are approaching TV primarily in terms of its artistry, which means that we are interested in the complex web of relationships that develop between TV creators, TV audiences, and TV "texts." The necessity of putting scare quotes around the word "text" is emblematic of the degree to which we depart from a pure media studies approach. "Text" is a slippery word, especially when it comes to an audience's concrete, on-the-ground experience of TV. It is commonly used to refer to the individual television program or series that is under consideration, in part because no one has identified a better option. But whatever TV may actually be, viewers surely do not encounter it as a "text." It is an irreducibly audiovisual experience that is qualitatively different from our engagement with texts such as novels, newspapers, magazines, or even webpages.

Still, there is a common thread that connects our concrete experiences with our critical analysis and our theological engagement. That unifying thread is the television program itself. However, we prefer the term "trace" instead of "text" to describe this common thread because it more accurately reflects the complex, dynamic, and ever-accruing form of meaning-making that takes place in our interaction with audiovisual media (which also include film, web videos, etc.).[11] Regardless of whether one's critical focus is on an individual episode, season, or even series, TV is consumed in a variety of settings, delivered through numerous media, and in some cases watched repeatedly. To suggest that audiences are engaging with a static "text" is not only to underplay the ways in which television programs are basically multidimensional in form but also to overlook how individual episodes are never exactly the same "text" the second or third time they are seen. Indeed, prior to the proliferation of home recording devices, TV "texts" literally disappeared after they were aired, leaving nothing but a "trace" behind. The trace element of those broadcasts only became available to the public years later when reruns of syndicated shows began to underwrite the network TV business as a whole.

Even though nearly every series in television history is now available at the click of a mouse, TV programs still leave something significant behind long after the screen goes dark. Whether it assumes the form of nostalgia, water-cooler dialogue, a fleeting memory, or a critical insight, the **trace** of a TV show is present to viewers even in its absence. The notion of a "text," however, privileges a certain kind of interpretation that hinges almost exclusively on the reading of literal texts and the writing of more texts in response. It also pictures both the artwork itself and the process of understanding art as something that is fundamentally inert rather than interactive and interpersonal. A text is fully autonomous. It is an object—an artifact even. A trace, however, is interdependent and intersubjective. In this way, the concept of "trace" embodies our concern with viewer response. Its very existence depends upon the viewer's active engagement with and embodied response to the piece of art.

Also, the concept of a TV "trace" allows us to see that every "performance" (i.e., every screening, streaming, or broadcast) of a television narrative provides yet another occasion for the ever-evolving and ongoing work of meaning-making. Yet in order to assess these numerous performances, much less make any sense of them, we need to be able to analyze what it is that brings them all together—that common object of inquiry more commonly known as a "TV show." It is for this reason that we dedicate chapters 2, 3, and 4 to outlining a basic set of analytical tools for interpreting and understanding various kinds of TV "traces."

But Why TV?

All told, we hope to demonstrate the usefulness of an engaged, participatory, exploratory, and observational approach to television and television watching. Because we are all wholly implicated in the object of our study, we cannot operate as detached observers of some distinct cultural phenomenon. Neither can we separate our theological project from the larger cultural "matrix of meanings" in which we live and move and have our being.[12] It is not incidental that this larger cultural matrix is one in which television has become a major cultural force. We include ourselves among those whose imaginations have been fundamentally shaped by the prominence of TV in our lives. And we are not alone. Indeed, the reach and influence of television almost cannot be overstated. Since its inception, television has simply captured the cultural imagination, especially in North America. Outside of working, sleeping, and eating, watching television is *the* primary preoccupation of most Americans. Individuals consume on average between four and five hours of television on a daily basis, a number that only increases when online streaming and consumption on mobile devices are taken into consideration.[13] Even in the face of radical technological change, television has adapted, continuing to exert a tremendous influence on the lives of contemporary persons. It is at once an emerging technology, a contemporary art form, a global industry, and a portal for our ritual lives. In other words, it is one of the centerpieces of life in Western culture, both reflecting and giving shape to the cultural landscape of the twenty-first century.

To be sure, TV's influence has to do in part with its ubiquity, but it is television's pervasive presence in the home that makes it a particularly significant artifact. In the span of only seventy years, television technology and programming completely transformed (and continue to transform) our habits and preferences, in large part because they situated TV as a permanent fixture of the modern household. More than being simply another appliance, TV quickly became the hub around which we oriented all our domestic life. With the proliferation of mobile devices and streaming services, television is now reorienting not only our habits but also our very notion of domestic space, in some cases collapsing the divisions between our public and private lives. The screens have simply moved from the corners of our living rooms, to the walls where art once lived, to the palms of our hands. Thus, to understand television is to understand more than a medium. Rather, it is to understand something of the contemporary imagination—the primary interpretive lens through which modern persons make sense of their lives and the world.

Given the degree to which TV is so fully embedded in the broader cultural context, it seems almost superfluous to state that people of faith—in particular the Christian faith—ought to develop the necessary skills for engaging television. Yet pastors, theologians, and lay Christian leaders have paid very little attention to developing critical methods or interpretive frameworks that would enable religious communities to thoughtfully and faithfully engage TV. And this is to say nothing of how television might provide the context for constructive theological conversations or considerations of how God might be present and active in and through the medium. Of course, some might balk at the very idea that TV has any larger meaning or theological substance, especially those whose viewing habits do not fall into the "five-hour-per-day" category or who have written off television as at best frivolous and at worst destructive. Yet even for those who have never hosted a *Big Love* viewing party or a *Glee* sing-along or a *Scandal*-fest, TV still matters. It does not simply "reflect" or "affect" culture (although it does both of these things). Television is culture creating. And it is this culture—one mediated by television—that the community of faith is called not only to understand but also to engage with wisdom, wit, and clarity. In other words, a thoughtful engagement with TV is as much about mission as it is about meaning.

In addition to this external dynamic, a theological engagement with TV has internal benefits as well, whether one is an avid TV watcher or not. For those who do have favorite shows (or even guilty pleasures), TV often serves as an important resource for our spiritual lives. Our vision of who we are, the world in which we live, and sometimes even God, can be expanded in and through TV watching. Rather than dismiss these moments of insight and, indeed, revelation, we want to consider the ways in which TV can be spiritually enlightening and energizing for people of faith.

There is also a great need within the (Protestant) Christian tradition to reconsider the value and purpose of narratives, especially as it concerns the narratives we consider authoritative for our life and faith. By developing a deeper understanding and appreciation of TV storytelling (or any excellent storytelling for that matter), we are able to approach the biblical story in ways that we might have never considered. In this respect, TV stories actually provide a framework by which we might imaginatively reengage the biblical narrative, thus allowing the story of God to find a home in the deep recesses of our hearts and minds.

Indeed, we might even go so far as to say that the biblical authors would have made good television executives. That they are already well known as storytellers is evident in the first words of the biblical witness, "In the beginning," which is like a theological version of "Once upon a time." But the stories that are recorded in the Bible can also be looked at in a more episodic way—lives and events (one might even call them "episodes") that sometimes span years and expand to multiple generations (today's television networks call those "seasons"). The person of David cannot be fully understood unless one looks at his whole life. If all we know of him is that he won a certain battle, or wrote a certain psalm, or had an affair with a certain woman, or slew a certain foe, we get a limited picture of who he was. But just as one cannot know Jack Bauer from sharing only one hour of his twenty-four-hour day, the life of David has to be seen as a whole—a "series"—that reveals who this "character" is.

Similarly, the lives of Daniel, Joseph, Ruth, Solomon, and Mary Magdalene—all their stories are not just one story. They are a series of many episodes that add up to something larger in the same way that a TV series can add up to a sum that is much more complicated and compelling than its parts. If a television series needs to be evaluated as such, so too does the biblical story. While certain moments hold special significance—the exodus of Israel or the death and resurrection of Jesus are obvious examples—the whole scope of God's story cannot be reduced to just one episode. At the same time, neither are individual episodes meaningful only as a part of something bigger. They have a narrative integrity of their own, which calls for a form of analysis that recognizes the significance of their unique contributions.

The point of the matter is this: the very nature of storytelling on television calls for a new level of dialogue. It demands a different kind of analysis and more thoughtful response from those who are at the forefront of cultural engagement. The reconciliation that happens over twenty-two minutes in a sitcom, the healing that happens in less than an hour on a medical show, and the justice that is enacted before the end of the episode on a police drama (not to mention the character arcs that are intrinsic to the life of a series) all contribute to the ways in which television functions meaningfully in the contemporary world. Television's significance is more than a matter of what is being said. It also involves how it is being said. The radically different, network-specific ways in which news organizations narrate the same current events is proof enough that how a story is told is equally as important as what the story is about. That the structure, format, limits, strengths, style, length, and—perhaps even most important—viewing methods of television all contribute to its power and meaning may seem obvious, but it has rarely been examined from a theological perspective, and it is our intent to do so with this book.

A Method to the Madness of *Mad Men*

The basic approach toward cultural engagement that we will model is dialogical—conversational even. We seek to place contemporary television into a mutually enriching, two-way dialogue with theology. By engaging in this two-way conversation, we hope to develop a deeper and richer understanding of not only TV but also our theological frameworks and language. Following Rob Johnston and Bill Dyrness, the coeditors of this Engaging Culture series, who have laid important groundwork for developing a constructive theology of culture, we describe the theological task as dialogical because it "seeks to bring together in faithful obedience the telling of our stories and the hearing of God's story."[14]

The telling of our stories involves thoughtful exploration of our concrete experiences (as both individuals and as a community), and the various cultural expressions that reflect and shape the broader culture in which we live (in this case, TV). Hearing God's story is about placing these human experiences into conversation with a few key sources—namely, the biblical witness, the historical theological tradition, and one's worshiping community. The Bible remains the central authoritative source for theology, but our ability to access the truth of the biblical text is mediated by these other sources (i.e., personal experience, culture, theological tradition, and religious community). Indeed, biblical truth is itself dialogical. It emerges as an authoritative source for faith and practice only when our stories find life and purpose within this larger, more expansive narrative. Thus, as Johnston puts it, "We read the authoritative biblical text from out of a worshipping community, in light of centuries of Christian thought and practice, as people embedded in a particular culture, who have a unique set of experiences. Here is the theological process."[15]

As with any critical methodology, there is no set procedure or recipe that, if only we could follow it meticulously enough, will somehow guarantee the production of orthodox theological formulations. Instead, our theological method functions as a framework for collaborative creativity, a set of related terms and critical questions that allow a community of interpreters not only to describe but also to see reality with greater clarity.[16] To be sure, as an active participant in this conversational to and fro, theology will eventually offer a response to television and the world it creates. But prior to articulating any sort of response, it is important to cultivate our instincts in such a way that our primary impulse is to listen rather than speak, to set aside our own agendas and presuppositions for the sake of honoring our conversation partners.

Some would challenge this notion from the very start, claiming that it is simply impossible to approach a cultural artifact without a ready-made set of assumptions that shape and, in some ways, actually determine our understanding.[17] In terms of purely analytic categories, these critics are certainly not wrong. Our preconceptions, which create the very conditions for our understanding, do "color" and to a certain degree even "limit" our awareness of the world. However, if we frame all meaning-making in this way, we run the risk of abstracting a process that, on a concrete level, is actually quite active, intentional, and relational. It is to suggest that our awareness of the world (our "worldview" as some would call it) is static and singular rather than a dynamic and multifaceted engagement with lived experience. It creates a false and unhelpful dichotomy that fails to recognize our active agency in the process and, perhaps more problematically, positions the other as fundamentally *unknowable*. It forces us to take up and even defend a position not unlike that of *Mad Men's* Don Draper—holding fast to a perspective of the world that is not only skewed by his privileged location but is also tone-deaf and violently indifferent toward those with a different outlook.

What is more, by claiming that we can only ever come to the conversation presupposition-full, these critics make the mistake of conceiving of our unique "lenses" as hurdles rather than opportunities. It is true that we see the world through tinted glasses or, as the apostle Paul put it, "through a glass, darkly" (1 Cor. 13:12 KJV). We are, after all, enculturated beings whose understanding is always shaped by the particularities of our located-ness. But it is also true that clarity does not come by resigning ourselves to the misguided notion that we have no other option but to judge the other according to the dictates of our own limited vision. Rather, clarity is something that emerges when we allow another set of lenses to augment our vision—when we willingly enter into a dynamic process in which we "try on" other ways of seeing the world. This is a fundamentally others-oriented posture, for it recognizes that each of our visions is incomplete and inadequate on its own. We need the other not simply to see but to see well, and it is only through a convergence of perspectives that we are able to gain insight into the possibilities that our world presents.[18]

Another helpful way to conceive of this dialogical approach toward theological method is to think of it in terms of a relational model. Anyone who has ever participated in an actual conversation with another human being knows that, while we each bring to the table questions and concerns that are shaped by our prehistories, a dialogue (as opposed to a monologue or a diatribe) can only take place when both parties open themselves up to the other in order to receive from that person new ways of being in the world. In order not only to see and hear but to truly understand each other, we must consciously choose to put the concerns of the other before our own. And just as it is with people, so it is with television and other works of art.

We can say more though. This approach, which recognizes that theology has something to learn from and receive from culture, is in fact motivated by our theological commitments. We might even say that, when we talk about listening and setting aside our presuppositions, what we are really talking about is the development of Christian character. This process will of course never be perfect, but if it is to be a truly Christian theology, then the practice itself must assume a Christian shape, which means that it must enact and embody kindness, hospitality, generosity, and openness toward the other in our midst. In other words, it is about cultivating friendships.[19] And if the community of faith hopes to respond to our increasingly complex world in a way that is both faithful and makes sense to late-modern persons, it must be willing to enter into this kind of ongoing, constructive engagement.

While this conscious shift toward hospitality and nurturing friendship is theologically motivated, it is also rooted in a more realistic assessment of our contemporary context. Not only is the Christian narrative merely one of a multitude of other viable options, but the Christian community is no longer in the position of cultural authority that it once was (or that it once believed itself to be) while operating in the context of Christendom. This is not to decry or bemoan the situation; it is simply to describe it accurately. But it is important to do so because knowing the location from which we speak changes everything—not just what we say or how we say it, but whether we dare say anything at all.

So Much TV, So Little Time

All of this is of course easier said than done, especially as we consider the sheer volume of television programming that exists.[20] Combining programs from the past seven decades with current and future shows, which are produced at an increasingly rapid rate and distributed through numerous portals, the landscape of contemporary TV is at best daunting and at worst impossible to navigate. Adding to the challenge of in-depth analysis is the fact that a single successful series can run for more than one hundred hours of programming. Where do we even begin? And how do we go about choosing which shows to consider and which to ignore? Do we discuss shows that we simply "like" or those that have received critical attention? Do we listen to the "masses" by focusing on highly rated broadcasts, or do we glean from the insights of passionate fans, recognizing that some of the highest-quality programming does not always garner the best Nielsen ratings?

Our selection process does not reflect an attempt to be comprehensive, as there are many shows we do not mention that might support or contradict our analyses. Neither have we set aside our own aesthetic judgments and preferences in the process. For the most part, the shows we have chosen to engage are those that we also happen to appreciate and enjoy, a methodological decision that is actually in line with other scholarship in the field of TV studies.[21] And it is for this very reason that we have created a collection of supplemental web resources. We want others to employ the critical tools we develop in the book in order to analyze shows that they deem to be culturally significant and theologically rich.

So at the outset, we want to acknowledge the inherent limitations of any endeavor of this sort. There is simply too much ground to cover in a single volume. At the same time, there is also a need to establish some reasonable criteria for our selection process so that, at the very least, we have a starting point for future discussion and consideration. For the sake of consistency and utility, the selection criteria we have established run parallel to the analytical categories we outline in ensuing chapters (i.e., form, process, practice)—modes of analysis aimed at helping us understand the power and meaning of television and TV viewing. Thus, the shows we consider exhibit certain qualities that TV creators themselves value (process), characteristics that justify their inclusion on the Writer Guild's list of "101 Best-Written TV Series." They also contain formal elements that have prompted both professional and self-described critics to describe them as excellent (form), a designation that can be found by consulting the Internet Movie Database (IMDb) website. However, because one of our goals is to understand the ways in which audiences discover and construct meaning through their daily TV viewing habits, we also include those shows that—for any number of reasons—have generated some of the larger measureable audiences in TV history (practice), information that is collected and collated by the Nielsen Company.

That being said, it will also be helpful to pause at times in order to consider those shows that don't fit into any of these categories and to ask what it is that distinguishes them from our primary collection. Again, while we must leave it to the reader and to the broader scholarly community to decide if these criteria are helpful or in need of further refinement, they serve as the starting point for our discussion.

Truth be told, determining which shows to engage in theological dialogue is simply one step in a much larger process of discerning when and where God is present and active in the medium of television. Our broader aim is to identify and affirm those moments when a contemporary cultural product like TV might actually provide an occasion for people to encounter the divine Spirit in their everyday lives, perhaps even prompting them to engage in the dangerous act of loving their neighbor.[22] We also seek to reconfigure our own notions of who God is based upon this inspired activity, recognizing that the Spirit often speaks to the people of God through voices coming from outside the community of faith, if only we had the ears to hear and the eyes to see. We are concerned with the s/Spirit that inspires our creative endeavors and animates the very basic human quest for meaning.

And this brings us back to the TV series *Lost*, which is a perfect example of both the unspoken spirituality and the core impulses that stimulate the contemporary imagination. The show was considered somewhat of a phenomenon at the time given its fractured sense of reality and nonlinear narrative, but its popularity should never have been surprising. *Lost* connected with viewers because it spoke to the core anxieties that hover over much of modern life: we are not only existentially lost but we also long to somehow redeem our broken past. Audiences did not simply watch *Lost*; they consumed it with near-religious devotion and continue to do so via the internet long after the airing of its last episode, in part because the show gives voice to the angst that plagues the contemporary situation (an angst only amplified by our technological naïveté). By doing so, it opens up avenues for engaging theologically with both the content of the program and the meaning-making associated with it. In other words, whatever *Lost* itself might mean (if it in fact "means" anything at all), it surely means something that, in order to make sense of the illogical, the unexplainable, and the mysterious elements of life, many people turned to a television program about survivors of a plane crash living on a mysterious island. We want to explore more fully avenues like these in order to discover what kind of theological fruit they might bear.

Of course, neither of us is anywhere near as striking (or strapping) as either Dr. Jack Shephard or any other character on *Lost*. And the journey we invite you to join in the pages that follow is likely not as epic as the story of the survivors of Oceanic Flight 815. But we do hope that, in some small measure, this book will spark constructive conversations that are at least as fun, enlightening, and meaning-filled as the conversations that surround so many of our favorite television shows. We may not actually be stranded on a mysterious tropical island with a bunch of strangers, but there is no doubt that we are living in an increasingly globalized cultural context that is religiously, ethnically, racially, economically, and politically plural. Generating new, life-giving visions that not only help us make sense of this world but also allow us to respond to the "other" in our midst in peaceful and loving ways has never been a more urgent task. So we are not simply offering a new perspective from which to look and listen. What we need are new eyes and new ears altogether. And it seems fitting to us that the ever-surprising Spirit of God might develop these faculties within us by breathing life into something as seemingly ordinary as television.

1

the pilot episode

what is tv?

This just in: binge-watching is good for your health. At least that's what a recent Harris Interactive poll would like the television-viewing public to believe. According to the study, which focused on the television viewing habits of US consumers, not only is binge-watching (i.e., viewing multiple episodes of a program in a single sitting) the "new normal," it turns out that most people feel pretty good about it. More than 73 percent of the respondents stated that they have "positive feelings" toward their binge-watching.[1] This of course is a completely trustworthy statistic. As everyone knows, human beings never attempt to mislead others about their unsavory behaviors, and they most certainly never try to convince anyone that what they are doing is "normal," "a purely social endeavor," or "under control." Case in point: For 79 percent of respondents, binge-watching was a welcome refuge from their busy lives; more than three-quarters (76 percent) pointed out that watching multiple episodes of a show actually made it more enjoyable; and more than half (51 percent) preferred to binge in the company of others.

It probably comes as no surprise that the company that funded the Harris poll actually has some skin in the game. According to its own publicity materials, "Netflix is the world's leading Internet television network with over 81 million members in over 190 countries enjoying more than 125 million hours of TV shows and movies per day, including original series, documentaries and feature films. Members can watch as much as they want, anytime, anywhere, on nearly any Internet-connected screen. Members can play, pause and resume watching, all without commercials or commitments."[2]

Over 100 million hours of television. As much as viewers could ever want. Anytime. Anywhere. All for one low monthly price. Welcome to the new normal.

The Netflix study is telling, and not simply because it is a somewhat transparent attempt by a multibillion-dollar company to normalize a behavior in order to bolster its primary resource engine. As one commentator put it, "Netflix's report feel[s] a bit like a pusher touting the unexpected benefits of a drug to its clients."[3] While all this heavy-handedness is surely a form of "must watch" entertainment in its own right, what is most interesting about the Netflix report is not the report at all but the actual practice that it seeks to defend. That is, for good or for ill, it is now possible to watch an endless stream of television programs by simply subscribing to an online service like Netflix—all for one low monthly price.

Of course, not everyone subscribes to Netflix, which is to say nothing of Amazon, Hulu, and other streaming services. Even fewer binge-watch TV. Patterns of contemporary television consumption are varied, and the meanings that audiences attach to their preferred programs and viewing practices are equally diverse. Nevertheless, anyone who watches television of any kind or in any way is engaged in a similar kind of cultural practice—a practice that not only draws from a shared well of symbolic resources but increasingly serves as one of the primary locations where contemporary individuals organize their everyday lives, structure their identities, and engage in meaning-laden activities. In other words, whether we view all thirteen episodes of a season of *House of Cards* in a twenty-four-hour time frame or not, when we watch TV, we are doing more than simply observing an isolated broadcast. Rather, we are engaged in an everyday ritual that is mediated by a technology and oriented around a narrative that has been produced, marketed, and delivered to us by a network of corporate conglomerates.

This combination of emerging technologies with leading-edge delivery systems such as Netflix has allowed viewers to engage television in new and, in some cases, unprecedented ways. Indeed, much of the ensuing discussion will be an exploration of the many ways in which individuals make use of and enjoy TV in the world of new media and emerging technologies. But it would be a mistake to suggest that the medium itself has suddenly become detached from that which preceded it. One of the hallmarks of television is that it borrows from both the old and the new media around it. Just as it has always done, television continues to do "some of the same things as newspapers, radio, magazines, advertisements or films while adapting what they do into its own distinctive form."[4] Put differently, the appearance of distribution platforms like

Netflix and Amazon Prime does indeed signal something new, but it is also an expression of what has always been a fundamentally hybrid and adaptive medium—one that provides many of the core resources that fuel our present-day "convergence culture."[5]

Thus, in order to engage the full breadth and depth of television's significance in the contemporary world, we must first acknowledge that TV cannot be reduced to any individual program, genre, format, or device. Rather, it is best understood as a dynamic and multilayered communication technology that opens up its own world of meaning within the contemporary cultural imagination. Television is at once a narrative art, a technology, a commodity, and a portal for our ritual practices. In part because of its near ubiquity, it also functions within the contemporary cultural imagination as the predominate lens through which individuals make sense of their everyday lives. It provides us with avenues for understanding how we relate to our selves, to one another, and to the world at large. As television historian Gary Edgerton puts it, television is ultimately a "convergent technology, a global industry, a viable art form, a social catalyst, and a complex and dynamic reflection of the American mind and character. . . . [It] contains many clues about who we are, what we value, and where we might be headed in the future."[6]

The cultural reach of television is broad, and it is with this expansive influence in mind that the present chapter seeks to identify more clearly what it is we are talking about when we use the term "television." In an important sense, this chapter fleshes out a backstory that highlights the various ways in which TV functions meaningfully in the contemporary culture. Think of it like a flashback episode on *Lost*. In order to move forward, we must pause for a moment and consider more fully how the present moment has come to be. So this chapter presses the question of what the medium of TV is at its core and, by extension, how we might understand theologically the worlds of meaning it opens up. That is, how broadly are we willing to conceive of television as an object of study, much less as a cultural artifact?

The benefits of sketching out the contours of the medium in this way are twofold. First, it charts the overall trajectory of our study by outlining some basic parameters regarding the avenues we might (or might not) explore. Second, it offers an opportunity to make our operating assumptions explicit. Any attempt to understand the cultural and theological significance of television in the modern world is based upon a series of assumptions that direct and, in some cases, determine the analytical methods one employs and the interpretations one offers. This book is no different. Rather than proceed with some misguided notion of scholarly "objectivity," we embrace the opportunities presented by the postmodern moment and lay our research interests on the table for all to see.

In this way, we are not attempting to do away with our operating assumptions (many of which are expressly theological in nature). Instead, we are naming them so that we can engage in the necessary practice of self-critique.

Due to the rapid rate at which technology and media continue to evolve in the twenty-first century, some have suggested that TV as we have come to know it is on the verge of extinction.[7] Indeed, new modes of delivery are replacing past technologies at an ever-increasing pace. Even those within the industry have no choice but to adapt to this shifting landscape. For example, members of the Academy of Television Arts and Sciences recently decided to drop the "Arts and Sciences" from the organization's formal name and even considered removing "Television" as well. They ultimately chose to keep the language of "Television" because it was decided that the word was useful as a "brand name to encompass all the delivery systems that are part of modern entertainment."[8] What the Academy's decision underscores is that the concept of "TV" still serves a significant, albeit increasingly symbolic, function in the contemporary world. Without question, the boundaries between what TV is and what it is not continue to change. Nevertheless, it is also true that many of "the distinguishing features of past television are still evident today."[9] Because television is an irreducibly hybrid medium, it is in its nature to constantly adapt and evolve. Yet something endures, and it is surely this "something" that continues to capture the contemporary imagination. Thus, while acknowledging the challenges presented by these ongoing changes, our basic suggestion is that the concept of TV is best understood in terms of four broad but interrelated categories: technology, narrative, commodity, and ritual.

Technology

Beginning with a discussion of TV as a technology might strike some as an unusual place to start, if for no other reason than because most of our daily conversations about "TV" concern what is *on* television rather than the television itself. The early adopters in our midst will always be ready to remind us of the screen size or resolution of their most recent techno-purchase, but the majority of our watercooler chatter focuses on the characters, plotlines, and narrative cliff-hangers of our most watched (and most beloved) television programs. Interestingly, what often goes unnoticed or simply unsaid during these interactions is that, as we are enjoying our favorite shows, we are engaged in a wholly mediated endeavor. Even the "immediacy" or "live-ness" of a breaking news feed is only apparent, for our ability to access or interact with television images and narratives depends upon the work of some mediating apparatus.

In this way, television relates viewers to the world, but it does so by actually distancing them from it. Herein lies the secret to some of television's formative power, for it re-presents a world to us that is both like and unlike the world as it truly is.

Before it is anything else, then, television is a communication technology. In truth, the entire history of TV could be told in terms of its evolution as a technological innovation. The original idea for television was birthed by the desire to transmit synchronized sounds and images across great distances, not necessarily to develop popular narratives for mass audiences. As the demand for episodic narratives was already being met by radio, the initial dream for TV was to develop a way of seeing faraway events as they unfolded in real time.[10] Following this historical sequence of events, it was television technology that created both the marketplace and the subsequent demand for television programming, and not the other way around. In 1939, the "first night" of US television programming, which was broadcast by the NBC network, was produced for the sole purpose of stimulating sales of RCA television sets.[11]

The emergence of television technology as an integral component of contemporary life is one of the by-products of the broader communications revolution that began in the nineteenth century. Prior to the opening of the first telegraph line in 1844, the rate at which information could be delivered was limited by the speed at which humans could travel. Yet the telegraph and its direct descendant, the radio, effectively severed the connection between transportation and communication. This separation was not without consequence, for in the short century and a half since then, the ways in which people receive, access, and make sense of information have undergone a radical transformation. In a world where the message is no longer encumbered by the limitations of the messenger, we simply engage and understand our life and the world through a different set of lenses. With more than one billion units in North America alone, television has become the primary location where modern persons access information about the world in which they live—information that, because of increasingly advanced technology, is now available almost instantaneously.[12]

Throughout much of television's history, the instant access that it offered came at a price. Television technology has always been well suited for delivering up-to-the-minute information and programming. But the trade-off was a relative lack of quality in picture and sound. As a result, questions concerning the quality of television technology (or lack thereof) have dominated conversations about not only what TV is on a fundamental level but also what its function and value are in modern society. This connection between the capacities of TV technology and public perceptions regarding its cultural function and value is perhaps best illustrated by the ways in which the television-viewing experience has so frequently been compared to its slightly older sibling, the cinema. In her study of how contemporary entertainment technologies have reshaped our understandings of film, television, and domestic space, Barbara Klinger notes,

> The big-screen performance is marked as authentic, as representing bona fide cinema. By contrast, video [on television] is characterized not only as inauthentic and ersatz but also as a regrettable triumph of convenience over art that disturbs the communion between viewer and film and interferes with judgments of quality. . . .
>
> Television in particular has often come under fire for compromising the integrity of the cinematic text. Film scholars have amply chronicled television's shortcomings as a showcase for cinema, pointing to its inferior image as well as to the broadcast industry's substantial alteration of films through "panning and scanning," editing for length or content, and commercial interruption. Further, since the televised film is watched amid the distractions of domestic space, home exhibition dispels the supposed rapture of theatrical viewing.[13]

Although Klinger's primary focus is on the growing number of people who watch movies in their homes, her summary of these broader cultural notions highlights the fact that television technology has historically been understood in terms of its relationship to film technology. The seemingly unchallenged assumption among those who draw this comparison is that the ultimate goal toward which TV is moving is the replication of the cinematic experience. We ultimately want to challenge this assumption, but in order to do so we must first take stock of the various ways in which television technology has been evaluated in relationship to film technology.

First, just as Klinger notes, those who consider film to be the primary location for contemporary cultural storytelling have conceptualized TV as an inherently deficient technology for communicating audiovisual media. Unlike the cinema, television cannot adequately "contain" certain visual content. In order to depict the full scope of the images we see on the big screen, the small screen must resort to methods that undermine the artistry of film (e.g., "pan and scan"). Second, even when it is able to contain film images, television technology still produces sounds and pictures that are inferior to those we see and hear in a theater. Indeed, until the digital revolution, television's analog signal and monophonic sound simply could not compete with cinema's towering screen and Dolby Digital surround sound. Third, the very structure of commercial broadcasting creates an environment in which economic interests trump aesthetics. According to its detractors, nowhere is television's devaluing of aesthetics more evident than in the commercial interruptions that viewers must constantly endure. Finally, and perhaps most important, Klinger points out that the quality of television technology has often been treated with suspicion, not because of the technology per se but because of the social location in which it is used: the home. Because the home is filled with constant distractions, it is simply not an amenable space for fully immersing oneself in the audiovisual experience that a film demands.

Each of these criteria takes as its starting point the ways in which television technology is comparable (or not) to film technology. Taken together, they reflect what was once a significant impulse within popular culture to conceive of the quality of TV technology as "not quite." Television screens were not quite the right size, and their images and sounds were not quite crisp enough. The artistic intentions of the television industry were not quite pure enough, and the environment that TV creates in the home was not quite focused enough. Based upon this particular conception of TV, it would seem that television is simply "less than" its more sophisticated counterpart. Worse, this narrative suggests that, driven as it is by profit margins and market shares, television does not even pretend to be concerned with aesthetics. Rather, as it elevates the "convenience" of home-viewing over the "authenticity" of cinema-going, TV actually confuses and, in some cases, blinds the viewer to issues of taste and judgment.

The irony in this line of thought is of course rich, especially when it comes to the notion that the cinema is somehow unconcerned with or untouched by economic realities. Interestingly, with the increasing accessibility and afford-ability of state-of-the-art, high-definition displays and equally advanced sound systems, an argument could easily be made that the home-theater experience has now surpassed the cinematic experience in many ways. Almost all televi-sion equipment now has the capacity to adequately handle film images. Not only do contemporary televisions allow viewers to choose between multiple aspect ratios, but every major network now broadcasts a high-definition, digital signal with these same formatting options. What is more, Netflix, Hulu, and other on-demand services such as HBO Go allow audiences to watch programs without commercial interruption.

And this is to say nothing of how TV is moving beyond not just the quality but also the capabilities of film. For example, Sony timed the release of three unique models just before the 2014 World Cup (the XBR X950B and XBR X900B Series 4k Ultra HD TVs and the Bravia W950B Series LED HD TV). They each have a feature called "social viewing." As one reviewer described it, "When the feature is turned on, tweets organized by keyword or hashtag scroll across the bottom of the screen. At the same time, a pop-up window to one side allows for real-time video chatting via Skype, so fans on different parts of the globe can watch the game as if they're in the same room. There's also football mode, which digitally alters the audio to reduce the volume of the commentators and enhance the ambient sound, better approximating the feeling of being at the game—less blabbing, more chanting."[14]

Given these and other advances, film-based criteria are surely no longer adequate for assessing the quality of television technology or judging its position or significance in the broader culture. If anything, they simply highlight the collapsing boundaries between "film" and "TV" in the contemporary imagination. To be sure, television shares a kindred spirit with film, but to judge the value (technological, aesthetic, cultural, or otherwise) of television according to criteria derived purely from another medium is to fundamentally *mis*understand it. Television is not film, nor should it be, and it is only when we free it from this all-too-common association that we will be able to understand its power and meaning in the contemporary world. However, these criteria are helpful insofar as they indicate where television both aligns with and diverges from the medium of film, thus providing us with a point of departure for more clearly identifying what TV is at its core. Like film, TV is a technology. Unlike film, TV technology is naturally inclined to adapt, evolve, and converge with other technologies and new forms of media.

So how might we best approach TV as a mediating technology operating within our contemporary culture? According to media theorist Marshall McLuhan, television, like any technology, functions as an extension of our bodies and minds, indeed the whole of our selves. Television allows us to see and hear across unimaginable distances. It thus relates us to the world by extending and amplifying our physical capacities. In doing so, it "reorganizes our imaginative lives."[15] Yet TV technology is neither value neutral nor innocuous. McLuhan suggests that, while technologies do empower us by extending our minds and bodies, they also immobilize and paralyze that which they extend. In other words, every technological gain comes with a loss. Television technology extends our ability to see and hear like never before, but it also lays bare an ever-expanding world of ambiguity and context-less information to which we are often incapable of responding meaningfully. That is, along with an expanded capacity to see and hear the world in all its diversity comes an intractable numbness in the face of its complexity.

McLuhan thus contends that, as an extension of our selves, television technology creates an entire environment—and ecology—that viewers inhabit and through which they engage in making sense of their world. Because this environment is not a passive wrapping but an active process, a fully orbed approach to new media and emerging technologies like TV must consider "not only the 'content' but the medium and the cultural matrix within which the particular medium operates."[16] Here then is the crux of the matter. Our primary focus must be not simply the content that is mediated by this technological apparatus but the entire world of meaning TV technology creates. If theology is to forge any kind of meaningful response to the "imaginative reorganization" that TV provokes, it must be concerned with more than what is "on" television. Rather, it must engage the entire matrix brought about by television technology—an extension of how we see, hear, and imagine the world to be.

Narrative

Although television technology does create an entire world of meaning, it is a world that produces its own demands—demands that can be met only by a constant stream of programming. It is therefore significant to note that this twenty-four-hours-per-day, seven-days-a-week schedule is filled to the brim with stories. Indeed, TV is obsessed with storytelling, and this is true almost in spite of the fact that the medium did not have to develop along these lines. Things could have been different. Much of the initial interest in television technology focused not on its storytelling capacities but on its ability to communicate the immediacy of live events. No longer restricted by their physical location, early TV viewers were captivated by the idea that they could see and hear a speech delivered by the president in Washington, DC, or watch their favorite sports team defeat their interstate rivals. Imagine a televisual world of this kind—one that featured an endless slate of live congressional hearings and public service announcements, a world where C-SPAN was the norm rather than the exception. As terrifying as it sounds to twenty-first-century ears, this could have been the media environment that television technology created. But it is not. Instead, both its creators and its consumers quickly recognized that storytelling was an integral part of what constitutes TV *as* TV.

That TV is a storytelling medium is a rather obvious claim, especially for those whose only experience of the world is one in which TV is an ever-present reality. As with any rule, there are of course exceptions, but on the whole, the art of television programming involves locating viewers on some point along a narrative arc. For our purposes, a "narrative" is very basically the intentional organization of temporal events into a meaningful whole. From this perspective, television bears a family resemblance to other forms of mass entertainment such as plays, novels, and films.[17] Indeed, many of the first TV series, like *Amos 'n' Andy* and *The George Burns and Gracie Allen Show*, were just revamped radio shows. So in terms of the actual form of TV storytelling and the broader context in which these stories are set, it is not the uniqueness or novelty of TV narratives that make them significant cultural artifacts. Rather, these stories are culturally significant because they have emerged as a pervasive, transmedia reality. From

Tim Moore (left) and Jester Hairston (right) as King-fish and Henry Van Porter from CBS's *Amos 'n' Andy*

sitcoms like *Seinfeld*, to daytime soap operas like *General Hospital*, to nightly newscasts like the *CBS Evening News with Walter Cronkite*, the power and meaning of TV narratives are related not only to what these stories are about but also to how these stories are told. To understand TV as a medium is thus to understand the various ways in which it gives shape to a particular kind of narrative world and in turn narrates the world in which we live.

It is significant then that these narrative worlds are generally episodic, a characteristic that distinguishes TV stories in some important aspects from other forms of contemporary storytelling. Generally speaking, the majority of films, novels, and plays feature stories with fully articulated narrative arcs. Although they do not all fit easily within a three-act structure, they almost always have a discernible beginning, middle, and end. The end may be ambiguous, confusing, or unsatisfying. The middle might come first and the beginning last. Or, as is the case with popular film series like *Star Wars*, *The Lord of the Rings*, and *The Matrix*, it may require three (or six!) separate films or books to tell a complete story. But in every case, these stories are all moving toward some kind of clearly defined end—a *telos* even.

Not so with television. What distinguishes TV from these other storytelling forms is that it is *fundamentally* episodic. Not only are the plot points of individual episodes that are broadcast on network television structured around commercial interruptions, but these self-contained episodes are themselves only one part of a larger season, traditionally comprising twenty-four episodes. For shows that either reach syndication or are distributed by a subscription-based streaming service, a single season is but one among seven or eight others. Even the language of "seasons" suggests that, within the contemporary imagination, television stories are understood to be ongoing and cyclical in nature. Just as autumn gives way to winter, so too does spring give birth to sweeps week (at least in the United States).[18]

The episodic nature of TV storytelling only adds to the complex negotiation of value and meaning that takes place between a television program and its audience. For instance, as Henry Jenkins, Sam Ford, and Joshua Green have pointed out, long-standing daytime soap operas like *The Bold and the Beautiful* have staying power because, over the course of time, they provide a storytelling universe substantially larger than the show itself. These story-worlds cannot be neatly summarized because they depend upon the audience's awareness of the show's larger history and the ritual pleasures it provides.[19] In other words, the "meaning" that viewers attach to these narratives (however we define this "meaning") is something that accrues over time and emerges in relationship to a much broader context than the story-world of any individual episode.

In contrast to the narrative complexity that emerges through the sheer volume and duration of daytime soaps, "drillable" shows pack various layers of meaning into individual episodes. Programs like *Lost* are episodic in that they spread their narratives over a number of seasons, but their run is short enough that fans are able to engage in a kind of forensic work, piecing together every last "Easter egg" (a hidden clue that sheds light on some of the show's core enigmas) they can find. Thus, "forensic fans can watch these shows repeatedly, unpacking new meanings with each viewing and revisiting old episodes once new truths are revealed in order to gain new understandings."[20] We will engage in a more detailed consideration of reception analysis in chapter 3, but insofar as the narrative dimensions of TV are concerned, the analytical categories we are addressing here are important because they reveal the inherent complexity of episodic storytelling and how its various manifestations give rise to a viewer's meaningful interactions with the medium of television.

Of course, television's propensity for storytelling (episodic or otherwise) affects more than just the content that populates prime-time lineups. It also provides the underlying shape, cadence, and coherence to the entire "flow" of network programming.[21] In this way, it is actually the network that functions as the ultimate narrator, framing every individual segment in terms of a larger and typically unseen "meta-narrative."[22] This large-scale form of narration is only implied and thus operates on the level of what some might call "discourse" rather than "narrative." However, regardless of how we define it, there is an ever-present, organizing force that directly determines which content is ultimately produced, distributed, and consumed. Consequently, television is a narrative medium not simply because it contains story-based programming, but because it is always already narrating the world to viewers. From the positioning of cliff-hangers within individual episodes, to the kinds of products advertised during commercial breaks, to the pairing of particular shows on certain days of the week, to the unbroken sequence of programming that cycles throughout the day every day, television unites otherwise discrete elements into a meaning-laden whole. It makes sense out of a series of seemingly random and disconnected events.

When we consider the narrative dimensions of TV from this global perspective, what quickly becomes evident is television's propensity for offering up not just entertaining stories but a way of understanding reality. That is, on every level of discourse, television narratives are about the discovery and construction of meaning. As others have rightly noted, "television does not just portray a social landscape, it tells stories that infuse that landscape with meaning."[23] Television thus provides modern persons with the principal narratives from which they are able to organize their lives and forge an understanding of the world in which they live. In this way, television mediates the world to the viewer and the viewer to the world, offering up not just a description of reality but a redescription of reality in terms of what is possible.[24] And television does this work in ways that are indicative of the medium itself, which sets television narratives apart from those found in other cultural forms such as films, novels, and plays. Indeed, TV narratives are far more indebted to the practices of radio broadcasting than anything else. As a result, the significance of television's contribution to contemporary life is largely rooted in its episodic, cyclical, and network-driven narratives.

By exploring television in terms not only of the stories it tells but also of how it tells those stories, we will be able to understand more fully the ways in which these episodic, cyclical narratives shape our fundamental awareness of the world. At the same time, it will allow us to return to the core narrative of the Christian tradition and consider the theological insights that might emerge along the way.

Commodity

There is an inherent risk in defining TV according to the categories we have outlined so far. Namely, the suggestion that television can be understood in terms of technology and storytelling might be taken to mean that we are primarily concerned with a series of isolated narrative "texts" or technological "objects." The problem with this conception is that television does not exist in a vacuum. No cultural product does. Rather, it is stitched into the fabric of our mundane lives, so much so that it would be an unhelpful and even misleading abstraction to approach TV as if it could be analyzed and understood apart from the broader cultural landscape in which it is set and from which it emerges. So it is critical that we keep in mind that these categorizations are largely analytical. They allow us to identify the individual parts of the medium so that we can come to a deeper understanding of the whole. However, it should never be lost on us that our primary concern is in fact this integrated "whole"—the complex and messy space where TV narratives and technologies merge with the everyday habits of modern people. The boundaries between television and our lived experiences are especially porous in the world of late capitalism, where TV is never simply a technology or a narrative. In this context, it is always also a commodity.

For American viewers especially, the commercial element of television is so fully ingrained in our conception of the medium that it is almost transparent. Yet what is perhaps most interesting about the apparent "naturalness" of commercialized television broadcasts is the common (mis)perception regarding *what* is being sold to *whom*. As early as 1950, prominent voices within American Protestant Christianity were already noting that television was an "advertiser's dream." Indeed, Edward Carnell, president of Fuller Theological Seminary at the time, observed the following,

> TV will proceed a long way in dictating the purchasing habits of the masses. The goal of the advertiser is so to shape the habit expectancy of the individual, that when he walks through a department store or grocery market and sees the mountains of merchandise, his habit patterns lead him intuitively to the products advertised. . . . TV is, in fact, a *sales*, rather than just an advertising medium.[25]

The somewhat tacit assumption that is operative here is not simply that TV programming is "brought to you by" one sponsor or another but that TV is a particularly effective medium used by companies to sell products to viewers and, ultimately, to shape the habits of consumers. This line of reasoning has been especially influential among those who have attempted to engage the medium of television from a theological perspective. The only problem is that this viewpoint fundamentally misunderstands the economic transaction that is taking place, for commercial broadcasts are not principally about advertisers selling products to audiences. Instead, television networks are selling audiences to advertisers.

Networks collect information on audience shares, time-shifted viewing, and overnight ratings for one simple purpose: to deliver audiences to the advertiser. With these data in hand, networks are able to establish their pricing for a program's ad space, which is based upon not only how many viewers will be tuning in at any given time but, even more specifically, the kind of viewers who will be watching the show. Somewhat famously, the cost of an ad during *Thirtysomething* was more than the same ad space during *Murder, She Wrote* (which had nearly twice the total viewership) in part because of advertisers' perceptions regarding which audience had more money to spend on the products they were selling. Ultimately, the end result of these speculative marketing strategies is corporations purchasing airtime from networks, paying increasingly hefty sums for the largest of audiences with the most expendable incomes. There is a reason that networks charge upwards of $4 million for a thirty-second ad during the Super Bowl.[26] They are selling one of the most highly valued commodities in the contemporary world: the eyeballs of consumers.

With the recent proliferation of subscription, pay-per-view, and online streaming services, the economic model for television production, distribution, and consumption is indeed changing and will continue to change, but the end game remains relatively stable. That is, television is a commercial business in which distributors are seeking to make a profit on the programs they offer up for consumption. Some have even argued that, at least in the United States, new technologies like television and its immediate forerunners actually helped create the world's first consumer economy.[27] Birthed in the context of this emerging consumer economy, American television (as opposed to its British counterpart) developed as a distinctly commercial enterprise and even gave rise to the current form of free-market capitalism that exists in the United States. This is not to offer any sort of judgment on TV's commercial constitution or to somehow suggest that it is inherently "bad" or "wrong." Rather, it is simply to point out that when it comes to our ability to understand theologically what audiences are consuming, it is essential that we recognize that television is a product designed to "give people what the majority seem to want and what makes the most profit."[28] And while a number of other forces (political, ideological, aesthetic) are also involved in determining which programming ultimately reaches our TV sets, computer monitors, and mobile devices, the "bottom line" remains an ever-present reality that is continually (and often silently) shaping the entire enterprise.

Ritual

Although those who have followed in Carnell's wake share his misunderstanding regarding the actual product that TV sells (i.e., viewers), they have benefited from his insights concerning the habitual dimensions of commercial television consumption. "Habit-forming," however, is not ideal language, in part because of its negative connotations. It may be more helpful to speak of television as a medium that organizes, orients, and patterns the viewer's daily life. In other words, television capacitates (or "habituates") us through ritual. It is a portal through which we engage in various kinds of deeply formative practices. These practices are structured in part by the economics of the TV industry, but the questions we want to raise are not merely concerned with the ways in which television contributes to our patterns of consumption. We are also concerned with exploring how these rituals might capacitate viewers to be, for example, more empathetic, more networked, and even more sensitized to "otherness." In this regard, our posture toward television's influence is decidedly more generous and even sympathetic than other critical frameworks might allow. To be sure, television shapes our spending habits, but as it touches on the whole of our daily lives, its influence is much broader and more varied than simply affecting how we consume.

Because it has always existed as a centerpiece of the home and now also exists as a technological extension of that space, TV rituals primarily structure our everyday, domestic lives. In doing so, the "power" of TV to shape daily life is clearly evident, but its "meaning" often remains elusive, if not downright obscure. What exactly does a television program "mean" when it blares in the background of a family meal or serves as white noise while someone works on household chores? Does this meaning change if the same program captures a viewer's imagination to such a degree that she organizes and hosts a weekly viewing party that is followed by passionate discussion? In each of these cases, TV is surely functioning in both powerful and meaningful ways, but the danger for a theologian or any other cultural critic is to confuse or conflate the two, failing to distinguish between what television programs mean and how they mean.

Among critics who identify with the Christian tradition, it is often the case that the primary (if not only) concern when it comes to TV's formative influence has been the *effects* of TV on the audience more so than the ways in which people actually *use* and *enjoy* the medium.[29] However, by approaching TV as a portal for our ritual lives, we hope to challenge this effects-based focus and shift to an understanding of TV as the ritual enactment of our core cultural myths. By "myths" we mean not "fiction" but rather the stories that cultures tell that offer a way of seeing and understanding the world. Myths reveal the deep structures that orient and give meaning to the lived realities of those embedded in a particular culture. Rituals allow communities to enact their myths. By doing so, they serve as both "mirrors" and "models." That is, participants enact what is believed to be true about the world and also demonstrate what could or should be true about the world.

Television rituals function in much the same way, even when changes in TV technology reconfigure them. Early television rituals were oriented around live broadcasts. Prior to the 1940s, when television became firmly ensconced in American homes, most broadcasts communicated live events such as the 1939

World's Fair. Viewers would gather around a television set to see what they otherwise would not be able to see. "Tele-vision" thus provided exactly what its name suggested: a distant vision. But these live TV broadcasts also served as a shared experience for communities that were otherwise geographically dislocated. Television technology thus extended the town center so that localized communities were able to participate in the ritual life of a much broader and more diverse "community" by convening in front of a television.

This ritual pattern has remained relatively stable throughout TV history. The chief example is perhaps the Super Bowl, which is not only the most watched telecast every year, but even collects viewers who have no real interest in the actual sporting event itself. In fact, interest in the advertisements often exceeds interest in the game. The overtly commercial appeal of the Super Bowl only highlights the fact that television is always operating on multiple levels at once. It has opened up a ritual space within our contemporary culture, but it is a form of life that traffics in highly commodified narrative resources and is delivered through cutting-edge technology. The end result? Each and every year on Super Bowl Sunday, more than one hundred million Americans orient their lives around this televised event. It has become a shared cultural practice in which we embody and enact our deep-seated mythology. Along the way, it reveals a great deal about our collective hopes, our common values, and our often unspoken conceptions regarding human flourishing.

From the moment TV was first brought into the home, it fundamentally reimagined domestic space.[30] Over time, as technology became less expensive and programming more accessible, TV also effected a shift in the location of domestic rituals—from a common room with a single television set to multiple rooms in the home all equipped with custom-built media centers. Along with this reworking of household space came a change in viewing practices themselves. Indeed, with the explosion of personal media devices, it is now possible to consume television in the very same space as other viewers, but without the hassle of having to negotiate over which program to watch (e.g., *The Bachelorette* or *The Daily Show*?).

As we consider the broad, sweeping changes in TV viewing habits that were brought about by TV technology, it might be tempting to say that what was once a thoroughly communal activity has become an increasingly individual endeavor. But this would be to misread the situation. While emerging technologies and delivery systems certainly create the possibility for a viewer to consume television without regard for any other human being, this does not mean that all contemporary TV viewing takes place in isolation. In fact, in many cases, technology has actually created new opportunities for communal viewing, even if that "community" looks quite different from the way it once did.

As discussed above, broadcasts like the Super Bowl still consistently gather communities together at the same time and in the same physical place. However, in the age of social media, where cultural commentary is lurking around every digital corner, many fans are prone to watch live episodes of their favorite shows to avoid any "spoilers." For example, in chapter 3 we will consider in more depth the viewing habits of *Glee* fans (aka "Gleeks"). Within this community, it was not uncommon at all for avid viewers to engage in conversation via Twitter during live broadcasts of the program. In these instances, the location of the ritual is different and is decidedly mediated or "networked," but the communal impulse standing behind the ritual remains. Even binge-viewing on Netflix, made possible by the company's highly individualized and asynchronous delivery system, lends itself to a kind of interconnected practice. Almost in spite of the fact that Netflix delivers individualized playlists to the subscriber's profile, over half of those who admit to binge-watching do so in the company of others. So our physical, embodied presence in these rituals still matters; it just matters differently.

While television viewing habits can and often do assume far more private and individualistic forms, our main goal in calling out these particular examples is to more accurately describe the ways in which television serves as a portal through which contemporary persons engage in ritual behavior. Because TV is a part of our contemporary entertainment culture and is thus one of the principal commodities of the United States, these rituals certainly have a formative effect on our habits as consumers. Indeed, they quite literally inscribe certain patterns and postures into our bodies. And in the context of late capitalism, theology surely needs to explore these practices of consumption and the ultimate ends to which these practices point. A much more robust theology of consumption is called for, and this is something we will take up in later chapters.

But as we have shown, television shapes the ritual lives of viewers in other significant ways as well, so that even when these enacted myths are not directing persons toward explicitly commercial ends, they nevertheless embody and express our deepest desires. Such is the power of ritual. Indeed, the same can be said about TV more generally. As we have suggested throughout this chapter, television's cultural "power" is not the product of any single dimension but is rooted in its ability to draw upon multiple registers of meaning at once. As a technology, television serves as an extension of our bodies. As a narrative art form, TV programming makes sense of the disparate and incoherent events of our lives. As a commodity, television cultivates our desires. And as a ritual, TV shapes our habits and capacities. In short, television relates us to the world. Thus, we would do well not to reduce the concept of "TV" to any one of its various elements but to approach the medium in the broadest of senses. So pervasive is its influence that it structures our most basic understanding of our day-to-day experiences. It is truly a "metaphor we live by."[31]

Along with this symbolic conception of what TV "is" and how it functions, the four categories we have outlined reflect our particular interests and the unique questions we are raising. As we seek to engage television theologically and enter into a mutually enriching conversation with the medium, we must take seriously both the commercial aspect of television and the way it facilitates our embodied practices. So too must we develop critical tools for understanding television stories. At the same time, we cannot forget the ways in which TV technology determines how those stories are produced, distributed, and consumed. We will consider each of these elements in greater detail in the chapters that follow. But the goal in doing so is not to erect some conceptual scaffolding upon which a series of independent elements are suspended. Instead, our goal is coherence. No, better—wisdom. To be sure, we will proceed critically and at times analytically, but we must never lose sight of the larger, more integrated whole that is in fact the object of our study.

Because it impinges on so many aspects of our daily lives at once, television is nothing if not holistic. And it is only in our late-modern world that this would even come as a surprise to us. As Marshall McLuhan has observed, our technological society presses us to engage the world in fragmented and disintegrated ways. But actual human beings live mythically and integrally.[32] Drawing upon a deep well of cultural resources, they are constantly taking up the disparate pieces of their lived experiences and narrating them into a more coherent whole. Here then is our starting point—the fundamental awareness of the world that television narratives provide. And it is the goal of this book not only to explore this phenomenon critically but also to respond from our theological core.

Of course, engaging faithfully with our contemporary culture and the worlds of meaning it opens up requires a great deal of humility, a fierce commitment to listening, and even a willingness to enjoy and appreciate a diverse collection of cultural forms. This is no small task, but constructive theology never is. And it is to this task that we now turn.

2

becoming tv literate

formal analysis

This much we know: television is obsessed with coffee. In fact, TV is so in love with this caffeine-infused elixir that, in its absence, it is difficult to imagine how some of the most popular shows in recent history would have taken shape. Where would the gang from *Friends* hang out if Central Perk did not exist? More important, what would the characters even do if they had no coffee to drink? And how could the world of *Frasier* exist without Café Nervosa? Its predecessor, *Cheers*, was set in a bar. But in the successful spin-off, Niles and Frasier don't go to a pub to socialize. They drink lattes and eat biscotti in their favorite coffee shop. Likewise, the principal characters in *Seinfeld* meet at Monk's Restaurant in almost every episode. More often than not, Jerry, George, Elaine, and Kramer are busy drinking coffee as they talk about . . . well, nothing. Fifteen years after the *Seinfeld* finale, Jerry Seinfeld launched a new web series called *Comedians in Cars Getting Coffee*. If the title isn't clear enough, the show is about comedians who drive around in cars and drink coffee. It's almost as if Seinfeld created the whole production just so that he and his comedian pals could have an excuse to drink more coffee.

We of course say all of this with our tongues planted firmly in our cheeks (and with coffee mugs planted firmly in our hands). We fully realize that television is not only concerned with coffee and coffee drinking. But the coffee culture that TV depicts (and in some ways creates) provides us with a helpful image for our approach to television. That is, taking a cue from Niles and Frasier, we want to consider in this chapter how we might engage television much like a

David Hyde Pierce (left) and Kelsey Grammer (right) as Niles and Frasier in NBC's *Frasier*

connoisseur does coffee—by developing a critical vocabulary and an interpretive framework for understanding, evaluating, and even enjoying TV more fully. Or to put it in explicitly theological terms, we are interested in acquiring what the psalmist describes as "goodness of taste and understanding" (*tov taam vadaath*, Ps. 119:66 author's translation), a more robust awareness of the world that is rooted in both evaluation (goodness of taste) and critical insight (understanding).

Understanding and evaluating are both multifaceted endeavors. By developing a medium-specific vocabulary, we are able not only to describe TV with more precision but also to offer a deeper level of insight regarding what a program or series actually means. As a result, we foster our capacity to communicate the subtleties and nuances of TV both among passionate fans who already find it meaningful and to casual observers who are only marginally interested in its value or significance. In a similar vein, a greater awareness of how TV works provides us with the necessary resources for appreciating and enjoying television. Without a language to describe the distinctive elements of a particular show or a framework to consider its relationship to others, it is nearly impossible to distinguish between an excellent production and one that is simply lazy or uninspired. We may certainly intuit it at some level ("I know it when I see it"), but the more versatile and robust our critical toolbox is, the greater our ability to discern the good from the not-so-good and, thus, to appreciate excellent storytelling all the more.

The operative assumption in play here is that our capacity to understand and appreciate the power and meaning of a piece of art is directly related to the critical, analytical, and interpretive tools we have at our disposal. In other words, the more nuanced, descriptive, and contextual our language is, the more meaningful (and faithful) our interaction with television can become.[1] In an important sense, then, we seek to become like a coffee aficionado who is not only able to identify the particular region where a coffee bean is grown, harvested, and roasted but can also speak thoughtfully and articulately about the ways in which particular processing methods affect its taste (earthy! floral! mushroomy! delicate!) and describe the finished product in terms of the "brightness" of its aroma, the "complexity" of its flavor, and the "balance" of its finish when compared to other coffees.

Just as coffee lovers may occasionally do with their beverage of choice, it is certainly possible to treat television in a purely instrumental fashion—to simply consume it without regard for its aesthetic qualities or to pass judgment on it without any attempt to truly understand how and what it means. Truth be told, many viewers and critics interact with TV in just this way, falling somewhere along a spectrum that ranges between addiction or gluttony on the one hand (TV is my "fix") and reflexive disapproval on the other (TV is simply a "drug," so just say no!).

And just as people often drink coffee while doing something else (talking with friends, eating their breakfast, or digesting a meal), TV viewers are increasingly engaged in a number of activities simultaneously. In the early days, people watched TV while ironing, or eating dinner, or doing the laundry. Now, they are more likely to be texting, tweeting, or surfing the internet on their mobile devices.

In contrast to these extremes of addictive gluttony and mindless flippancy, this chapter develops a critical framework that will enhance our ability to understand, appreciate, and actively engage TV as art. That is, we aim to thoughtfully assess the formal elements of television and, perhaps more important, to do so without reading into it what is not actually there. By taking a show on its own aesthetic terms, we are able to more fully understand both how television works and what it says about the world. And beyond just how TV works, we might also discern something about how it works so well.[2]

If theologians—professional or amateur—are to be in any way successful in this endeavor, "they must learn something of the craft of viewing and reflecting; they must develop their critical skills."[3] But our goal is not only the development of critical skills. It is also to discipline our senses in such a way that we are more equipped to interpret and evaluate various kinds of television based not upon some external criteria but upon the aesthetic criteria given to us by the medium itself. Again, this requires us to assume a more humble posture toward TV—one that takes an episode or series or genre on its own terms rather than placing ourselves in a position of superiority over these televisual programs or practices.[4] Rather than traffic in the flippant or glib interpretations that result from reductive analyses, we seek a more robust understanding of this cultural form that is as nuanced and sensitive as it is critically competent and informed.

By moving toward this kind of understanding, we are not attempting to draw definitive conclusions regarding exactly what a show means. Nor are we trying to create unassailable criteria for what constitutes "quality" television. We will no doubt employ our critical and evaluative skills to make a case for why we believe certain shows are deeper, richer, or more rewarding than others, but our central focus is simply to provide a common vocabulary for dialogue and debate among a community of interpreters. In other words, it is an "invitation to dialogue rather than an attempt to impose a critical judgment onto others."[5]

This invitation to enter into dialogue with a broader interpretive community directs and shapes our critical tools, which are themselves the product of a communal, iterative process. They emerge, not from some primordial void, but as viewers (a) discover or construct meaning from their encounter with a television series, (b) examine why it "worked" for them on affective and aesthetic levels, and then (c) discuss this assessment with a broader community of TV viewers and TV makers. These communally negotiated assessments in turn form the criteria by which other television programs are understood and evaluated. Without these critical tools, our descriptions and analyses would be thin and underdeveloped at best and destructive at worst—a form of violence to the art form. But to truly understand not only how TV works but also how viewers invest themselves in the medium and what inspires them to make it a meaningful part of their lives, our criticism must take place in conversation with others.[6]

Or to put all of this differently, we can talk all day long about the darkness of a particular roast, the boldness of an exciting flavor, or the effervescence of a surprising mouthfeel, but in the absence of an interpretive community to help us see beyond our limited perspective, we run the risk of expending a great deal of energy and a wealth of resources developing an appreciation for coffee, only to discover that we have been drinking tea all along.

In order to avoid this bleak, tea-drinking fate (sorry, tea lovers), we turn now to the various ways in which the structure, sights, and sounds of television—its formal elements—contribute to its power and meaning.

Structure

Every storytelling medium has some kind of underlying structure. Even when a particular story is intentionally pressing the limits of that structure, it is still operating as a response to or a subversion of some recognized construct. When they work well, televisual stories seem to simply reflect "the way things are" rather than allow viewers to see what they really are—artificial constructions of reality. This is not to suggest that TV programs should or even could picture the world as it is, for that is not their purpose or aim. As Aristotle noted long ago, storytelling is about *poiesis*—a purposeful bringing-into-being of a world of form that has an integrity all its own.[7] So the question of how a television program is structured is really a question about the organization that takes place "behind the scenes"—the ways in which TV narratives are constructed and arranged in order to bring the world it depicts into being. For our purposes, it will be helpful to analyze TV structure in three related ways: **narrative flow**, **narrative complexity**, and **narrative world**.

Narrative Flow

Part of the reason that we prefer the language of "trace" rather than "text" is because TV shows are at once individual, self-contained objects and, at the very same time, minuscule droplets that blend into a vast stream of twenty-four-hour, wall-to-wall programming. In this way TV is similar to light. Light exists as both a wave and a particle. Only when it is observed does light behave as either a particle or a wave. Television is much the same. It is structured around various "particles" that serve as the essential building blocks of the medium, but it is also organized as part of a much larger "flow" of commercial programming. So when we consider the way television is structured in terms of narrative flow, it is important to keep in mind not only the discrete units we are analyzing but also each unit's location in the programming that precedes and follows it.[8]

Every TV program exists along a narrative spectrum that moves from the individual segment all the way to the multinational corporation (see figure 2.1).

Figure 2.1 Television's Narrative Flow

The **segment**, which is the smallest unit, is a "relatively self-contained scene [rarely exceeding five minutes in length] which conveys an incident, a mood or a particular meaning."[9] Take for example the show *New Girl*, which debuted on Fox in 2011. The 2014 Thanksgiving episode (creatively titled "Thanksgiving IV") opens with a brief teaser segment that features the character Schmidt attempting to persuade his roommates that they should observe what he calls "Bangs-giving." Each participant is to bring a handpicked guest to their Thanksgiving dinner who will make an ideal sex partner for one of the other roommates. The segment lasts barely ninety seconds, but its meaning is as concise as it is clear: inconsequential sex is a key to these characters' flourishing. It then cuts to the *New Girl* inter-title sequence (approximately seven seconds long), which then flows directly into the first commercial break.

We will return to this notion again in the next chapter when we consider the ways in which commercial breaks inform the process of writing TV stories. But when it comes to issues of structure, the presence or absence of planned commercial interruptions significantly affects how we understand the narrative flow of a particular television program. Shows that are originally produced and delivered by premium providers like HBO (e.g., *Boardwalk Empire*) or online streaming services like Netflix (e.g., *Orange Is the New Black*) still feature discrete units that need to be analyzed accordingly, but these segments are the product of the episode's narrative structure more so than its need to break for commercials. So while they do bear some similarities, it is helpful to think through the ways in which different kinds of segmentation shape our understanding of particular TV narratives in different ways.

For example, as a program designed for network television, the opening segment (or **teaser**) in *New Girl* works to frame the entire **episode** efficiently and effectively, which is the second level along the narrative continuum. It not only presents us with the particular subject matter that the episode will contain, but it also conveys the playful mood through which this content will be addressed and establishes one of the primary themes that the series continually explores from one episode to the next. So the entire episode can be understood in terms of how it unpacks the material contained in this opening segment. The reverse is also true; the teaser embodies the core concern of the episode.

But this opening segment does more than encapsulate the meaning of the individual episode in which it is located. It also gives expression to the series as a whole. From segment to segment, episode to episode, and season to season, *New Girl* is a show about a diverse group of thirtysomething misfits who function as a kind of proxy family for one another. In certain respects, they epitomize life in the late-modern world. Disconnected from their biological families and seemingly without any roots in another community or tradition, they walk alongside one another as they struggle to forge a sense of direction, purpose, and wholeness in their lives. In many cases, this shared quest for meaning leads them from one intimate relationship to another. But equally as often, they discover that their connection with one another offers a depth of intimacy that goes unmatched by their frequent sexual liaisons. If considered in isolation, this opening segment would seem to suggest that the Thanksgiving holiday is simply a prop (both for the characters and the audience). And on some level it is exactly that. Yet when seen in light of the larger narrative flow of the series, it becomes clear that while otherwise unmoored from any organized tradition, these characters are actually appropriating and remaking a set of cultural practices in order to give their various endeavors a semblance of meaning.

And here—at the **season** and **series** level—is where the discrete segments of *New Girl* begin to blend into a larger stream of broadcasting. "Thanksgiving IV" was the eleventh episode of the series' fourth season. However we might understand the overarching narrative of *New Girl* as a self-contained show, the series was originally sandwiched between *Glee* and *The Mindy Project*, which means that it both contributed to and drew an audience from these other programs. Not surprisingly, both *Glee* and *The Mindy Project* explore similar thematic terrain as *New Girl* does, and as a consequence they all have overlapping audiences. When these shows are understood to be working together as a part of a prime-time lineup, we begin to see the ways in which a network (in this case Fox Broadcasting Company) is intentionally organizing shows (and commercials!) over the course of an evening and distributing them throughout the week. In other words, the **network** becomes the unseen narrator for these individual stories, offering audiences a particular framework for making sense of the various shows they watch.

There is more to the story though. The Fox network is a subsidiary of 21st Century Fox, a global mass-media conglomerate headed by Rupert Murdoch. From its ownership of additional TV networks such as Fox News and other media outlets such as the *Wall Street Journal* and HarperCollins Publishers, corporations like 21st Century Fox are in the business of shaping large-scale narratives and profiting from their public consumption. To understand the power and meaning of TV then is to understand something of how multinational corporations structure cultural narratives.

It would therefore be perfectly reasonable to consider *New Girl* in terms of how the opening segment of "Thanksgiving IV" frames the individual episode and perhaps even the entire series. But in addition to this, we might also unpack the power and meaning of the show by considering how it contributes to the larger narrative provided by 21st Century Fox regarding nontraditional families, ritual practices, and intimate relationships. How does *New Girl* address these themes in ways that either align with or diverge from *Glee* and *The*

Mindy Project? How do the products advertised between segments underwrite or undercut this narrative? Does the meaning of an individual episode change if it airs immediately following the Super Bowl (as a *New Girl* episode did in 2013) instead of on a Tuesday night in March? In what ways does our viewing of *New Girl* shape our awareness of other media "traces," and how does our interaction with these other media inform our understanding of the power and meaning of *New Girl*?

The point here is not to suggest that we must first possess a comprehensive knowledge of all the inner workings of broadcast media before we can understand the power and meaning of a single episode or series. It is rather to highlight the fact that TV does not exist in a vacuum, and part of analyzing the structure of television is to raise questions concerning the location of a discrete unit as it blends into a larger flow of mediated narratives. Depending upon the parameters that the program itself establishes, it may be appropriate to focus more on an individual unit. At other times, we may need to draw from the larger media landscape in order to make sense of a particular program or series. But we draw these distinctions for purely analytical purposes. The reality is never so straightforward. Discrete segments are always blurring into a larger flow of broadcasting so that, just as it is with light, it is not until we try to observe the structure of TV that it behaves in one way or another.

Narrative Complexity

One of the hallmarks of TV storytelling involves its potential for developing narrative complexity. By and large, this complexity is a function of episodic serialization, which means that the structure of TV stories is more closely related to that of radio stories than perhaps any other medium. It is also true that serialized storytelling goes as far back as Charles Dickens, who is believed to be one of the first authors to publish serialized fiction. In general, this complexity moves in one of two directions—either **centripetally** or **centrifugally**. That is, the narrative spirals "inward" upon itself (centripetally) or "outward" toward the broader world in which it is set (centrifugally). As with flow, serial complexity exists on a continuum between these two poles. However, by identifying the basic direction in which a show's narrative is moving, we are granted insight into the unique ways that serialization both functions dramatically and contributes to televisual meaning (see figure 2.2).

Figure 2.2 Narrative Complexity

The much-acclaimed *Breaking Bad* offers a wonderful example of centripetal serialization.[10] Taken as an entire series, the show charts the downward spiral of Walter White—a man who knowingly chooses to "break bad" and, by doing so, to watch his own life and the lives of others in his community collapse in on themselves. Numerous other characters are involved in Walt's demise, of course, notably Jesse Pinkman, who serves as his partner in crime and dramatic foil. And over the course of five seasons, the plot even forces Walt and Jesse to leave Albuquerque, New Mexico, where the story is set. But at every turn, the series returns to an exploration of something inside the character of Walt. "Instead of subsequent seasons spinning outward from the core characters and setting, the show layers itself inward, creating deeper layers of Walt's psychological makeup."[11] By focusing on the inner psyche of a person who gives himself over to his unbridled lust for power and control, the narrative is a cautionary tale about this one man. The larger world around Walt becomes almost irrelevant. He could be selling meth or coffee. He could be a drug dealer in New Mexico or a stockbroker in New York. It doesn't really matter. What matters is that each episode gives us a glimpse into this character's inner turmoil and, by extension, that which churns in all of us regarding our attempts to find meaning in relation to our toil. So if there is any "universality" that we can speak of here, it is rooted in how particular the story is.

On the other end of the spectrum is a show like *The Wire*, which, in contrast to *Breaking Bad*, bears the markings of centrifugal serialization. It too is a show "about" drugs, but it ultimately "reveals itself to be more interested in using crime as a window into the larger urban condition of twenty-first century America."[12] Whereas Walt is responsible for the choices he makes and is thus also responsible for the havoc he wreaks in his community, the characters in *The Wire* have virtually no ability to affect the larger machinations of the systems and institutions that make the rules of the story-world. If *Breaking Bad* reminds us of the horror that lies within us all, *The Wire* reminds us that, in the larger scheme of things, one's agency doesn't really make a difference.

Both of these modes of complexity (centripetal and centrifugal) are related to broad, sweeping narrative trajectories that cannot be entirely contained in any single episode (although individual episodes will still generally lean in one direction or another). And the best TV programs are often able to leverage the power of both kinds of complexity at one point or another. However, in addition to centripetal and centrifugal serialization, we can also unpack a show's meaning in terms of how it encourages audiences to interact and participate with its content on an episode-to-episode basis—that is, how **drillable** the program is.[13] A helpful way to picture the relationship between serial complexity and drillable complexity is to set the two spectrums along intersecting lines.

Figure 2.3 Narrative Complexity: Direction and Drillability

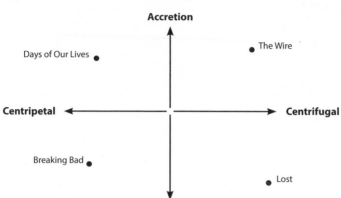

By plotting out where a narrative falls in relation to these distinct modes of storytelling, we are able to gain a bit of clarity regarding both what and how various shows mean (see figure 2.3).

For example, programs can be drillable either through **density** or **accretion**. *Lost* is a prime example of dense storytelling because each of its episodes contains a "depth" that encourages viewers to "dig deeper," to probe beneath the surface and discover additional levels of meaning that are rarely evident during the initial viewing. One of the more overt ways that the creators of *Lost* generate this kind of narrative depth is by placing "Easter eggs" throughout the show. This kind of depth often aligns well with a more centrifugal trajectory because it assumes that the audience is an active participant in the show's meaning, which not only broadens the outward movement of the narrative but also calls into question the agency of the characters in the show. If the characters in *The Wire* seem to be helpless in the face of powerful institutions, the characters in *Lost* are in dire straits, for in addition to dealing with the mysteries of the island and the Dharma Initiative, they are also navigating a world governed by the all-seeing, all-knowing, ever-present audience.

Another kind of drillable complexity emerges through accretion. That is, rather than creating layers of depth in each episode, this kind of complexity comes through volume and duration. Almost any of the long-running daytime soap operas demonstrates the ways in which a show's narrative becomes complex as its meaning accrues over time. On the level of the individual episode, it becomes difficult to say much of anything helpful or insightful regarding the characters, the story-world in which they live, or the ways that the narrative speaks to our own stories. It is rather in the daily, ritual-like interaction with the show that viewers are able to construct some semblance of meaning in and through its increasingly complicated (and at times convoluted) narrative.

The goal here is not to force any program into an artificial framework, if for no other reason than there will always be shows that turn out to be exceptions to the rules. The goal is rather to describe the ways in which different kinds of complexity make unique contributions to the power and meaning of television stories, thus allowing us to understand these serialized narratives with a greater level of depth and insight. So shows that lean toward centrifugal storytelling (like *The Wire* and *Lost*) tend to have no clear narrative center. They are about what happens to characters and institutions as they spread out. It is not simply that the story-world expands but that "its richness is found in the complex web of interconnectivity forged across the social system."[14] The focus is primarily on establishing a credible story-world (even if it is fantastic as it is in *Lost*). In contrast, centripetal shows (like *Breaking Bad* and daytime soaps) tend to have more cohesive narrative centers that are driven by the thickness of backstories and the development of character depth. The focus here is not so much on the plausibility of the story-world as on whether the characters *feel* true, which allows these shows to explore issues of identity, community, and moral responsibility.

Similarly, shows that generate a sense of drillability based upon accretion (like soaps and *The Wire*) require a commitment to a larger and ever-expanding narrative world. Because meaning accrues over time, we can only understand the parts in light of the whole. What is more, the enjoyment most viewers derive from these shows becomes a ritual kind of pleasure, which means that it draws from a realm beyond the narrative world—our mundane lives. However, shows that are drillable because of their depth (like *Lost* and *Breaking Bad*) tend to invite analyses that focus on the intimate details of each episode. Every segment of the program, while still part of a larger whole, bears a meaning all its own.

Narrative World

We have already made reference to the "story-world" of television, but we have yet to say exactly what this means. Regardless of the medium (television, film, novel, radio, or play), all stories operate on more than one narrative level. The **diegetic** level is the self-contained world that the characters inhabit. The **extra-diegetic** level refers to the world of the narrator, whether that narrator is an actual agent in the story (like the voice-over in a film) or an implied narrator (such as the author of a novel who writes from an omniscient, third-person point of view). The **non-diegetic** sphere is the space where the audience sees, hears, reads, or otherwise encounters the story.

The boundaries between these various diegetic levels are not entirely solid, but it is still uncommon for a story to transgress them (music/sound being a notable exception to this rule). Rarely do characters interact with an implied narrator, and even less often do characters break the "fourth wall" and directly address the audience. These diegetic boundaries have become such a conventional element of televisual narratives that when characters do break the fourth wall (e.g., in *Family Guy*, *Malcolm in the Middle*, and *Saved by the Bell*), it is all the more significant and at times even unsettling (e.g., *House of Cards*). So when we analyze a program's meaning according to how its narrative world is structured, our focus is primarily on the diegetic and extra-diegetic levels, although, as we will discuss in chapter 4, these stories are always bumping up against and alluding to the non-diegetic level in order to generate meaning.

Borrowing as they do from previous forms of serialized fiction (e.g., periodicals and radio), TV narratives are both like and unlike other stories. In ways that are similar to literature, televisual stories can be understood in terms of **character**, **plot**, **atmosphere**, and **point of view**.[15] Some stories are mostly concerned with characters and how they interact with one another and society at large. These stories address the question of human need and potential, thereby offering us paradigms for what it means to be human. Others are more plot driven and are therefore meaningful in relation to how they move us through time. They are about the process by which we move from point A to point B. Stories that emphasize atmosphere are grappling with the unalterable givens in life—death, systemic injustices, and "otherness." They raise the question of boundaries, of what is possible, and what limits human beings. Finally, stories are told from a particular point of view, which is often expressed through various narration techniques, both overt and implied. By identifying which of these elements a story emphasizes, we are provided a point of entry for understanding more fully its power and meaning.

However, given their generally episodic and serialized structure, TV stories handle these narrative elements in unique ways. For example, **binary oppositions** make up the underlying narrative structure of many programs. Sitcoms especially leverage oppositions such as "masculine/feminine, work/domesticity, rationality/emotionalism, intolerance/tolerance" as a way of setting up narrative tensions that can be diffused in less than thirty minutes.[16] A show like *The Big Bang Theory* is a character-driven program to be sure, but its characters function less like paradigms for humanity and more like caricatures—clearly identifiable extremes that are set over against other extremes. The character of Sheldon is not "realistic" in the sense that real-life theoretical physicists working at Cal Tech are just like him (at least not entirely like him). He would be unable to hold down a job anywhere, much less at a high-caliber research university.

Sheldon only has to "feel" true in the sense that his character is fully realized in ways that are appropriate for his particular environment, which happens to be filled with other characters that are his polar opposite. The same goes for Penny, Leonard, Raj, Amy, and Bernadette.

In televisual stories, then, there is an intimate relationship between characters and their space. They "find each other, so that the discovery of location is inseparable from the investigation of psychology: the performers look to their environment to realize their characters."[17] It is for this reason that, when taken at face value, certain television plots—especially on sitcoms—can seem somewhat flimsy or contrived. It's because they are. But it isn't about the action taking place so much as it is about characters occupying a particular space from one moment to the next.

Sheldon and his binary opposite, Penny, often engage in a cycle of conflict resolution over Sheldon's "spot" on the sofa. Sheldon is a self-important know-it-all who is as neurotic and controlling as he is condescending, but who desperately needs friends who can endure his idiosyncrasies. Penny is an out-of-work actress who gets by on her good looks but who desperately longs for friends who will acknowledge her substance and value. As they navigate this particular space within the diegetic world, we are given insight into who these characters are and what they are all about. Their interaction is not driven by any kind of plot or atmosphere per se, because there is more to the action than simply advancing the plot. Instead, these repeated couch-related incidents suggest that the plot is not irrelevant but can be drawn into anything—even seemingly insignificant conflicts over seating assignments. In this way, the story-worlds of TV narratives have a tendency to move away from the stories we see in the cinema. Whereas film stories often involve the revelation that what appears to be ordinary is actually extraordinary, televisual stories are concerned with the significance of the mundane—as the mundane. Ordinariness is not necessarily extraordinary in the story-world of television, but it doesn't need to be because the world TV gives us is one in which everyday life, by the very fact that it is ordinary and mundane, is shot through with significance. "Ordinary things," as G. K. Chesterton once said, "are more valuable than extraordinary things; nay, they are more extraordinary."[18]

Sights

To state the obvious, "vision" is an integral part of the word "television." Interestingly, the question of what audiences actually see when they watch television and how these sights inform our engagement with TV is often overlooked.

This is especially true for those interested in the theological significance of TV. In many cases, whether approaching the medium from a media studies perspective, a cultural theory perspective, or a religious studies perspective, the primary focus tends to be on the narrative elements of the program or series. The unfolding of the plot or the development of characters from one season to the next, the general atmosphere the show establishes, or the point of view of the showrunner or auteur—these are often the central concerns of most analyses. And this makes sense to some degree. We too have taken care to think through questions of narrative structure. However, by definition, television is a visual medium, so any engagement with it must account for the various ways in which TV images contribute not only to the meaning of an individual program but also to our vision of the broader world in which we live. In order to understand more fully the various sights of TV, we want to focus here on television cameras, mise-en-scène, and editing.

Camera(s)

One of the reasons that television technology was originally so compelling was its potential for broadcasting live events—in time, moment by moment. Indeed, as is the case with sporting events, political theater, and civic rituals like Macy's Thanksgiving Day Parade or the Rose Parade on New Year's Day, this capacity remains one of television's central contributions to the broader media landscape. Capturing live events is no small task though. It requires the use of multiple cameras positioned at various angles in the hopes that no significant aspect of the event goes unseen or unnoticed. For events that are broadcast through Federal Communication Commission (FCC)–controlled channels, it also demands that producers establish mechanisms for censoring potentially offensive content that is captured unexpectedly (exhibit A: Janet Jackson and Justin Timberlake's Super Bowl XXXVIII halftime show). Given the potential for FCC fines and the amount of money that corporations put on the line to sponsor these events, a lack of execution in this regard can prove quite costly. So when it comes to live programming, the event itself is the driving force behind certain camera setups and the visuals they ultimately capture and broadcast.

However, when it comes to programs that are not created for live broadcast, the reverse is often true. In these instances, the camera(s) dictates both the images we see and how those images mean what they mean. Significantly, it did not take long for the established conventions of capturing live events to shape the way TV fictions were produced. One of the primary results of this influence was the standard practice of using a **multi-camera setup** for sitcoms. Much as with a live event, more than one camera was required to ensure that no element of the singular performance was missed. As a result, many of the first sitcoms were constructed almost like stage plays, in part because many of the assumptions regarding the recording and broadcasting of live events carried over to the production of these narratives. Following these standardized conventions, numerous sitcoms throughout TV history have assumed a similar shape—a live performance, delivered to a live studio audience, taking place on sets modeled after a **proscenium theater**.[19] And while many contemporary sitcoms have shifted away from the multi-camera scheme, the stylistic elements of the "traditional" sitcom continue to shape TV narratives in significant ways.

This history of the development of TV sitcoms may be interesting in its own right, but what matters here is the way in which an understanding of stylistic choices about cameras grants us insight into the power and meaning of a television program. *The Honeymooners*, for example, was one of the first sitcoms created for broadcast television. It featured (and in important respects, established) all the elements associated with "traditional" sitcoms—three cameras, a live (and laughing!) studio audience, and a static set. The result was a show that was meaningful primarily in relation to the ways that the characters inhabited a particular space—moment by moment. This space just happened to be a tiny apartment in a blue-collar area of Brooklyn. It functioned as a dining room, a living room, and a kitchen. In other words, it was the epitome of domesticity. But when this otherwise mundane space is captured by a multi-camera setup designed to stress the "liveness" of the event or performance, what emerges is actually something rather un/eventful. And by "un/eventful" we do not mean unimportant or boring. Rather, it simply means that the cameras place the audience in a position whereby it is seeing (and continually monitoring) a series of slices in time—moments that contain the eventful and uneventful together in the same space. The net effect is that we see the quotidian not as lifeless drudgery but as something teeming with movement and energy. So one way of reading *The Honeymooners* in terms of what the cameras allow us to see is to suggest that its use of cameras blurs the boundaries between what is and is not "eventful," what is and is not filled with "life." And such is life really, if we're being honest. Married life is no honeymoon. But no honeymoon could hold a candle to a life lived daily with the one we love.

Compare the images given to us by *The Honeymooners'* multi-camera scheme to the images we see in the more recent sitcom *Parks and Recreation*, which makes use of a single camera and a **mockumentary** aesthetic. Because there is no "live" performance to capture, no "live" audience for whom to perform, and thus no "fourth wall" to cross, only a single camera is used. The end result is that what we see does not resemble anything close to a static proscenium stage, for it isn't a performance; it's a production. This does not mean that single-camera productions are unaware or unconcerned with their audience. In fact, because it is a mockumentary, the characters of *Parks and Recreation* often look directly into the camera, explicitly acknowledging their awareness of a viewing audience. So rather than exhibiting a disregard for the audience, single-camera programs like *Parks and Recreation* position the audience differently than three-camera programs do. What we see and how we see it changes the way we relate to the narrative—and also how we relate to other members of the viewing audience. Are we in the presence of others, witnessing a public performance about the travails of marriage? Or have we been given intimate access to the behind-the-scenes workings of local government?

A much different example of a character directly addressing the audience using a single-camera scheme is seen in *House of Cards*. Starring Kevin Spacey as Francis Underwood and Robin Wright as his wife, Claire Underwood, *House of Cards* intentionally plays with the boundaries of the medium. The show can be categorized as a drama, and for the most part it abides by the realist aesthetic of its genre. But at significant moments in the narrative, Frank Underwood turns toward the camera and speaks directly to the viewer. By breaking the fourth wall and the diegetic boundary, the character Frank not only acknowledges the presence of an audience but makes it complicit in his various machinations.[20] Once again, the camera positions the audience in a particular way by what it does and does not allow viewers to see.

Whether we are considering *House of Cards*, *Parks and Recreation*, or *The Honeymooners*, the critical question we must ask is not simply what these camera choices mean from one program to the next but how they function to produce meaning. While every example we identify is going to bear its own unique markings given the demands of the particular story it is telling, it would seem that, in various ways, TV narratives are prone to create worlds with porous boundaries.[21] There is always something or someone outside the camera's view—even if it is just us, the audience. In other words, when it comes to the images given to us by a show's camera(s), there is always more than meets the eye.

Mise-en-scène

Mise-en-scène is a somewhat broad concept that assumes a more technical meaning depending upon the context in which it is used. It literally means "placing on stage" and is most often used to describe the visual elements of theatrical or cinematic productions. When applied to television, it really has to do with anything that appears before the camera. From the set design to the lighting to the costuming to the representation of space, mise-en-scène analysis is concerned with how a story is told visually.

Composition is one element of the mise-en-scène that concerns the intentional placement and arrangement of visual elements within the camera's frame. In many respects, the composition of televisual images is bound up with other conventions of the medium, such as camera choices, set design, and even corporate sponsorships. For example, the possibilities for framing a three-wall set are relatively few, which means that the composition of many multi-camera programs remains somewhat "flat" and lacks a sense of depth. In fact, it is for this reason that many sets, like the well-known Central Perk on *Friends*, are built as optical illusions. The background is physically smaller than the foreground so that, when captured by a camera that will only ever move along the x-axis, the otherwise flattened image appears to possess some manner of depth.

Some insist that this lack of visual depth is one of television's aesthetic "limitations."[22] Terms such as "zero-degree style" are used to describe a *lack* of visual style that simply comes with the territory of depicting live performances. But this negative judgment of TV's mise-en-scène is overstated for two reasons. The first is that, much as in live theater, the conventions of a multiple-camera setup and a proscenium stage create the very structure for television narratives to become meaningful in the way that they do. One such meaning is related to the sense of community that these programs generate. For viewers at home, a rebroadcast studio audience is not the same thing as living, breathing human beings watching a program together, but the visual cues of a "flattened" stage are nevertheless indicators of a communal orientation. They not only create a sense of a public spectacle, but they also urge the viewer to include (or at least maintain an awareness of) others in their own viewing. This communal impulse is especially pronounced when the mise-en-scène contains sets that function as spaces for communities to gather—coffee shops (*Friends*), bars (*Cheers*), apartments (*The Big Bang Theory*), and living rooms (*The King of Queens*). There is a certain kind of intimacy that emerges when, time and again, characters inhabit spaces marked by a "zero-degree" style. Even the way chairs and tables are arranged points toward a kind of common experience. Sets are generally arranged in a semicircle so that characters are facing the audience, and, as a result, the audience becomes an active part of the meal or drink or coffee break.

The second reason that mise-en-scène analysis points toward the possibilities of TV visuals rather than their limitations is related to the diversity of forms that TV actually takes. The mise-en-scène of *Scandal*, for example, is a far cry from what we see in *Friends*. Rather than a central stage, *Scandal* features numerous different sets and makes use of a single camera that is able to invade the space of the set and the characters. It too is interested in intimacy, but of a different kind. Rather than generating a sense of intimacy that leads toward community, *Scandal* employs visual imagery to depict a kind of intimacy that is both fractured and fracturing—the kind of intimacy that, as the title would suggest, is scandalous.

Like *House of Cards*, *Scandal* is set in Washington, DC, so the mise-en-scène grants the viewer access to the politicking, seductions, and power plays that take place behind closed doors. Unlike *House of Cards*, the visual elements in *Scandal* do not function as a device for involving the viewer in the seedy schemes of its characters. Instead, they function to highlight the dissonance and hypocrisy of selling one's soul to gain the world. In almost every instance where a group gathers to conspire, the camera passes through objects that are blurred by their proximity to the lens. The result is that the faces and bodies of characters are continuously moving in and out of a state of fissure. The objects placed in the frame create both a mirroring effect and a splintering effect. As an audience, we may never know who these people truly are, whether a pale reflection of a former self or a completely fabricated persona. But what we do know comes through the mise-en-scène. That is, their attempts to shape the world according to their own will to power have fractured them in irrevocable ways.

Editing

Analyses focused on cameras and mise-en-scène are concerned with the various visual elements that are included in a particular TV program. **Editing**, however, is primarily about what is excluded—what is cut. In his prescient analysis of contemporary culture, *The Rise of the Image, the Fall of the Word*, Mitchell Stephens suggests that we are transitioning from a culture dominated by printed words to one that is dominated (and thus shaped) by moving images.[23] Stephens claims that it is not simply the increased availability of images that has caused this shift but rather our ability to edit these images in new ways—a capacity brought about through digital technology. Writing in 1998, he slightly overstates the potential for fast-cut moving images (the "MTV aesthetic"), but the core of his argument remains: television produces meaning not so much through the display of static, singular images but as it places images into a dynamic relationship with one another.

Because images are able to convey certain types of content in an incredibly condensed and efficient manner, they traffic in both information and impressions. In other words, according to Stephens, the power and meaning of moving images has less to do with the content of the visuals than with the way those visuals make us feel.[24] Editing thus leverages the fact that we feel far more quickly than we think, and we think far more emotionally than we are willing to admit. Some are suspicious of moving images for exactly this reason, especially within the Protestant theological tradition. We will return again to a consideration of theology and emotions, but for now we simply want to consider how editing works to make us feel in certain ways and how those emotions contribute to the power and meaning of the televisual stories we see.

Think for a moment about the **opening credits** to the US version of *The Office*. Just as it does in other productions, this title sequence serves a rather basic function by introducing us to the principal cast. But this fifteen-second **montage** does something else as well. Through a series of audiovisual edits, it establishes and reinforces the basic tone of the show—how we should feel about what we are seeing. Music plays a key role in the montage, but we are bracketing music's contribution for the time being as we will consider it more fully below. In terms of how the visuals are edited, however, the sequence begins with multiple fast-cuts between generic images of Scranton, Pennsylvania, in the winter: a government building, a traffic-congested road, a welcome sign. None of the images lasts longer than a second. Yet by editing the establishing sequence in this way, we are not only introduced to the setting of the narrative but are effectively "welcomed," so to speak, into small-town USA. Because these images depict the actual city of Scranton, Pennsylvania, we are also led to believe that what we are about to see is taking place in the "real world." Or at least it could.

Following this brief lead-in, the segment jumps from one member of the cast to the next. In every case, we witness the characters in their office environment. As each subsequent image passes before us, it becomes clear that these people are engaged in the most mundane and rote activities. They are sitting at their desks, talking on the phones to customers, shredding documents, staring blankly at computer screens. In other words, they are going about the same mind-numbing tasks that have been endured by anyone who has ever worked in a similar sea of cubicles. And for those who have, it is not difficult to feel with (i.e., to empathize with) the characters as they perform this drudgery. As image after image accrues, so too does our visceral response to this mechanized view of life and labor. Even for viewers who have never had the pleasure of experiencing office life, this same sense of monotony and automation looms over the images. And it is this basic tone that serves as the backdrop for the entire series—a particular mood established by the editing that plays itself out in different ways from episode to episode and season to season.

Contrast this with the way that the opening credits are edited for the UK version of *The Office*. The music is different, yes. But the images are also significantly different. The cuts occur at a much slower pace, and rather than depicting any people at all (characters or otherwise), they simply feature shots of the city of Slough. The "feel" of this montage is therefore decidedly different. Its pace is certainly slower, but with its numerous images of office buildings, parking structures, and mass transit, it is also much more institutional in its orientation and far less personal. In part a reflection of cultural differences between the United States and the United Kingdom, the sense evoked by this editing is something more like humdrum dreariness than industrialized automation per se. The employees of the two fictionalized paper companies are still all cogs in a machine, but these are qualitatively different kinds of machines. One demands robotic efficiency (the United States); the other, dutiful submission (the United Kingdom).

In both cases, however, the editing draws the audience into an emotional engagement with the details of mundane office life. Viewers are given the chance to feel out everyday realities such as copiers and voice mails and interoffice politics as they touch on the larger meaning of life in the world. In this way, televisual editing is very much about the poetics of the everyday. That is, it concerns the affective awareness of the world that we construct based upon our lived experiences. And whether the setting is Scranton or Slough, a thoughtful consideration of how TV images are edited allows us both to unpack the meaning of TV narratives and to understand more fully their power to shape our emotional engagement with the world.

Sounds

Television is more than a script. It is also more than a series of moving images broadcast over great distances. Television is an *audio*visual medium, and to treat it as anything less is to fundamentally misunderstand it. In this respect, it demonstrates its closest resemblance to the cinema. And much like this distant cousin, even though TV is acknowledged as being audiovisual through and through, the meaning-making function of TV sound often goes unnoticed. Indeed, it would be possible to fill an entire book on the topic of the theological significance of TV sound.[25] However, given our focus on the medium as a whole, our consideration of the sounds of TV must be brief and, admittedly, incomplete. More work will need to be done in this area, but the first step we can take is to organize our assessment of sound into three categories: music, dialogue, and sound effects.

Music

When tethered to moving images, music can be analyzed along a few different trajectories, each of which concerns the ways in which music functions in relation to televisual narratives. The **contextual** function involves music's role in the context of a particular TV show and its ability to draw meaning from the viewer's broader musical-cultural context. **Affective** musical codes provide us with interpretive access to that which is unseen—namely, a show's tone or mood, the inner workings of a character's psychology, and the audience's empathic bond with the narrative. Finally, we can analyze musical meaning in TV according to what might be called the **musical other**. Music is often rooted in the diegetic world established by the narrative. However, music also has the unique capacity to detach itself from the narrative world and "speak" from a location beyond the narrative. At times, this location is the non-diegetic sphere inhabited by the audience. But at other times, it is another location altogether.[26]

To return for a moment to our example of the opening credits for *The Office*, consider the ways in which the music contributes to the segment in terms of its context. In one sense, the music serves as a buffer of sorts that helps viewers transition from the world outside the narrative into the diegesis itself, from one meaning-filled context to the next. But once the audience is relocated inside the confines of the narrative world, the music actively shapes the formal makeup of this world. The entire opening montage is actually edited to the music and not the other way around. As a result, music lends to the sequence a "beat" that it doesn't otherwise possess—a seemingly natural beginning, middle, and end. This ability to shape the audience's perception of time and pacing is one of music's key contributions.

But the music in this sequence works on affective levels too. As we noted, the images are edited in a way that highlights the perfunctory nature of office life. But the music is, by comparison, incredibly cheerful—bubbly even. It is relatively up-tempo, features a 4/4 time signature, and is notably in a major key. Thus, it offers us interpretive insight that runs counter to the images we see. Yes, the office may be dreary and altogether ordinary. But there is joy to be found in this ordinariness. We might even say that the music points to something that is not found in these images—something that will only be revealed at a much later point in the narrative. That is, the music intuits what is later confirmed by the flowering of Jim and Pam's relationship. Even in the midst of these dehumanizing conditions, love remains a real possibility.

Music thus becomes something that, at times, seems to operate outside the confines of the narrative world, offering us hints of a reality that is "already but not yet," while also setting the pace by which the narrative moves. It is still a key part of the characters' world (and of ours), but it has become something "other" as well. It has the capacity to come to the foreground and say, "Listen to me, for I am significant." But we pay attention because, in fact, it is significant, even though we may be unable to articulate why. Music's ability to function as a difficult-to-define "other" is perhaps the most innately theological of its contributions, so we would do well to incorporate it into any of our critical analyses of TV narratives.

Dialogue

It would be tempting to treat TV dialogue as if it were nothing more than the words in a script, as if the whole of its meaning could be reduced to some kind of linguistic content. To be sure, our analysis of dialogue must consider its actual content, but it must also account for the fact that, once these words are spoken, their meaning changes. In the context of a television program, dialogue is heard, not read. It is a sound before it is anything else. And as sound, dialogue tends to function more along the lines of music and sound effects than the written word. Like music, it helps us "feel" the beat of TV images. And like sound effects, it contributes to the construction of the narrative's physical space. Dialogue not only has a rhythm, but it is voiced from a three-dimensional body and recorded in a three-dimensional space. Although the technology that reproduces this dialogue in our homes or on our computer monitors exists independently of that space, the words we hear retain the imprint of the physical location in which they were originally voiced. So to understand how TV dialogue works on a concrete level, we must understand something of the intimate relationship between what words mean and how they mean—between the sounds they make and the content they convey.

Aaron Sorkin knows something about the relationship that exists between the form and content of dialogue. He should. He puts copious amounts of it into his characters' mouths. Sorkin is known for writing dense and rapid-fire dialogue; his résumé includes series such as *Sports Night*, *Studio 60 on the Sunset Strip*, and *The West Wing*. Each of these shows features Sorkin's signature style of dialogue, but his comments about writing the script for *The Newsroom* offer helpful insight into the auditory dimensions of dialogue and how the sounds of these words contribute to their power and meaning. Significantly, he thinks of dialogue in musical terms: "A song in a musical works best when a character has to sing—when words won't do the trick anymore. The same idea applies to a long speech in a play or a movie or on television. You want to force the character out of a conversational pattern."[27]

This musical conception of dialogue is epitomized in the opening sequence to *The Newsroom*, in which journalist Will McAvoy (Jeff Daniels) responds to a question about America being the greatest country while he serves as a panelist at a local college. In order to gain a sense for the musicality of the scene, it is worth quoting both Sorkin and his references to the show's dialogue at length:

The fact-dump that's coming . . . serves several purposes. It backs up [MacAvoy's] argument, it reveals him to be exceptional (what normal person has these stats at their fingertips?), but mostly it's musical. This is the allegro.

> And you—sorority girl—yeah—just in case you accidentally wander into a voting booth one day, there are some things you should know, and one of them is that there is absolutely no evidence to support the statement that we're the greatest country in the world. We're seventh in literacy, twenty-seventh in math, twenty-second in science, forty-ninth in life expectancy, 178th in infant mortality, third in median household income, number four in labor force, and number four in exports. We lead the world in only three categories: number of incarcerated citizens per capita, number of adults who believe angels are real, and defense spending, where we spend more than the next twenty-six countries combined, twenty-five of whom are allies. None of this is the fault of a 20-year-old college student, but you, nonetheless, are without a doubt, a member of the WORST-period-GENERATION-period-EVER-period.

Now we slow down and get a glimpse into his pain. The oratorical technique is called "floating opposites"—we did, we didn't, we did, we didn't. . . . But rhythmically you don't want this to be too on the money. You're not just testing the human ear anymore; you want people to hear what he's saying.

> We sure used to be. We stood up for what was right! We fought for moral reasons, we passed and struck down laws for moral reasons. We waged wars on poverty, not poor people. We sacrificed, we cared about our neighbors, we put our money where our mouths were, and we never beat our chest. . . . The first step in solving any problem is recognizing there is one—America is not the greatest country in the world anymore.

To resolve a melody, you have to end on either the tonic or the dominant. (Try humming "Mary Had a Little Lamb" right now, but leave off "snow." You'll feel like you need to sneeze.) So Will ends where he started. Then, just to acknowledge that he just sang an aria—which is unusual in the course of a normal conversation—he turns to the moderator who'd been needling him and casually asks . . . Enough?[28]

Whether one is particularly fond of Sorkin's style or not is beside the point here. Rather, it is his intentionality that is striking, and it underscores the musicality of his approach to writing dialogue. At first, McAvoy's speech is a verbal onslaught—a barrage of sounds more than the communication of digestible content. Overwhelming statistics are spewed forth at a rapid pace. If not violent, it surely is visceral. But all this "testing of the human ear" is for the sake of clearing a path so that the audience can actually hear what follows—the content of his words. Here, form and content are bound up with each other in such a way that they cannot be separated. As a result, our ability to understand what this dialogue "means" begins and ends with a recognition that the power of these words is inextricably connected to their content, and vice versa.

Sound Effects

Seeing or hearing TV is not an either/or proposition; we see/hear it. Although we have been distinguishing between the structure, sights, and sounds of TV narratives for the sake of analysis, in concrete terms, audiences experience television as a unified whole. In a parallel move, we have separated sound effects from music and dialogue for purely analytical reasons. In actual fact, though, the functions of each element in TV's soundscape overlap and in some cases even merge.

Television music, for example, can and does function as music, dialogue, and sound effect all at once, especially when the music is a lyrical pop song. Hour-long dramas like *Grey's Anatomy* and *The O.C.* frequently call upon music to function in these roles simultaneously. In fact, it has become somewhat standardized practice for shows in this genre to feature preexisting popular songs as non-diegetic underscoring in the climactic or concluding scenes of an episode. In these instances, the music imbues the images with an emotional depth (or schmaltziness) that they would otherwise lack. The music contributes so significantly to the dramatic shape of the narrative that even the briefest of allusions to a particular song is enough to send it (and the songwriter) to the top of the *Billboard* charts.

Because it is lyrical, this music also has the capacity to function as dialogue or voice-over narration. During the second season of *Grey's Anatomy*, the episode titled "Losing My Religion" (also the title of a popular song by R.E.M.) depicted the young medical intern Izzie Stevens (Katherine Heigl) lying in a hospital bed clutching the recently deceased patient with whom she had fallen in love. Snow Patrol's "Chasing Cars" moves to the foreground with the lyrics "If I lay here. If I just lay here. Would you lie with me and just forget the world?" These words would be a bit on the nose if they were simply dialogue. Even as music, it is somewhat heavy-handed, but that is exactly the point. In one fell swoop, the music grants us insight into the inner workings of the characters' psychological state, invites the audience to feel along with them, establishes the mood and pacing of the climactic moment, and comments plaintively on the images we are watching. In other words, the sounds we hear shift the drama into the realm of the melodramatic.

Much like music and dialogue, sound effects are also able to lend the story-world a sense of pacing and even "comment" on the scene. However, sound effects have as their principal function the creation of an **authentic narrative space**. The laugh track that is used in multi-camera sitcoms is perhaps one of the most overt examples of the ways in which sound effects are able to flesh out narrative space. The origins of this sound dynamic predate television and its use of a live studio audience. Some suggest that the performance of audible laughter in the context of a comedy production can be traced back to nineteenth-century minstrel shows, which in turn influenced both radio and TV broadcasts.[29] Following these exhibition practices, the sound of the audience's laughter was a central part of the earliest television comedies, and it became a fixture of the medium when TV productions were increasingly shot on film rather than being broadcasts of live performances.[30] By including laughter as part of the sound design, recorded programs were able to maintain a sense of the "liveness" and the "presence" of the studio audience. That is, the laugh track re-created the aural dimensions of a live event, thereby granting the television show an authenticity it otherwise lacked. As Jacob Smith notes, the sound of audience laughter served as an "expression of authentic, embodied presence."[31]

A number of comedy writers, critics, and industry insiders were highly critical of TV's frequent use of recorded laughter. This particular sound effect was thought to be overly demanding in the way it clearly identifies for viewers when and where to laugh. However, blanket critiques of the laugh track underestimate the radically social nature of laughter. They also could not account for the incredible success of shows like *I Love Lucy*, which paved the way for other programs to include a prerecorded laugh track. Fewer and fewer sitcoms are produced today with any reference to a live studio audience. Yet even in this emerging televisual landscape, shows that do feature a laugh track (like *Two and a Half Men*) are some of the highest-rated programs—sitcom or otherwise.

None of this is to suggest that shows with a laugh track are somehow better or more humorous than those without one. It is rather to underscore the ways that an awareness of sound effects can enhance our understanding of what and how different programs mean. Numerous dramas, sitcoms, and reality TV shows do not have any prerecorded laughter. This does not mean that these shows are not authentically communal or care nothing for the embodied presence of a collective viewing audience. It simply means they must create a sense of this broader community through different means. Conversely, when a laugh track is called upon to make up for a script that simply is not funny, it can work counter to its intended purpose. Ultimately, then, if sound effects are about creating authentic space, and laughter is a fundamentally social reality, then the questions we must ask of a show's sound effects are not simply whether they are appropriate but if they move the audience toward authentic, embodied, and communal forms of meaning-making.

With these critical questions in mind, we now turn from our analysis of the structures, sights, and sounds of television and consider the process by which all these elements are chosen, organized, and put into place—that is, the artists and artistry behind the creation of television.

3

becoming tv literate

process and practice

Art and life have always had a habit of imitating each other. But in the contemporary world, it's more of a collision—one that blurs the boundaries between the "real" and the "reproduced." In July 2013, Cory Monteith, the actor who played Finn Hudson on *Glee*, died of a drug overdose. In response, the producers of the show chose to write his character out of the series—by having Finn Hudson die too. "The Quarterback" episode offers no dramatization or narrative details regarding the circumstances of Finn's death. Rather, it provides a meditation on the tragedy and a memorializing of his life through a number of staged pop-music covers—*Glee*'s hallmark. Lea Michele, the actress who played Finn's love interest, Rachel, brings the episode to its climax by performing a rendition of "Make You Feel My Love." The production itself is understated. A lone piano accompanies Rachel's restrained vocals. The camera shifts from close-ups of her tear-streaked face to various shots of the remaining glee club members processing all that has transpired. The mood is somber and reflective, exactly what one might expect from an episode of this nature.

But this episode was doing something more than simply wrapping up loose narrative ends. In the first place, Lea Michele was not simply playing the part of Finn's girlfriend but was involved in an off-screen romance with Monteith. Along with the entire cast and crew, she was actually mourning the loss of a friend, a colleague, and a significant other in and through her performance. No matter how polished or produced the music or how sincere the writing, this episode embodied and enacted the real grief of those who knew and loved the actor Cory Monteith. It at least appears to have been an honest attempt by the creators of the show to provide viewers and the cast a moment of catharsis that would honor Monteith without, in the words of one character in the episode, "making a self-serving spectacle of our own sadness."[1]

Glee's merging of the real and the reproduced, the remembered and the re-mixed, underscores the reality that television is never self-contained. In the case of "The Quarterback" episode, it matters that real human beings were mourning the loss of another human being by producing a televised tribute on a series that has as its principal conceit a group of beautiful outcasts performing remixed "mash-ups" of popular songs. In this odd space, "authenticity" is held out as a real possibility, but it assumes the form of the derivative and the recycled.

It also matters that the ratings for the Monteith tribute were nearly double that of the average episode of *Glee*—a decidedly commercial reality that only complicates our understanding of the episode. A question that will forever hover over the series is whether the producers exploited the suffering of the cast and crew for economic gain, or whether this was an appropriate tribute to a deceased cast member. Because of Monteith's celebrity status, casual viewers tuned in, but hard-core fans of the show, known as "Gleeks," responded over-whelmingly. On Twitter alone, hundreds of thousands of Gleeks live-tweeted during the broadcast of the memorial episode, posting prayers, voicing laments, and uploading video mash-ups of their own. To use common parlance, the hashtag #RememberingCory was trending.

Regardless of whether one considers a fictionalized memorial to be a fit-ting or appropriate way to respond to the tragic death of a young person, it is impossible to understand the full depth of this particular episode's cultural significance without taking into consideration both how it was produced and how it was put to use by audiences—that is, the *process* that shaped its creation and the *practice(s)* by which it was consumed. Thus, to develop a more compre-hensive understanding of how a TV show like *Glee* is (or is not) a meaningful experience, we must explore the connection that an episode or a series has both to its creators and to its audience. The "meaning" of a program is never some static entity that simply needs to be uncovered and then plucked out of its televisual container. Rather, meaning emerges from the dynamic interaction that takes place between the author (process), the show itself (trace), and the audience (practice).[2]

Put differently, a fundamental connection exists between the way a TV show is received and its specific formal features. Likewise, standing behind any TV program is some kind of shaping force—an author or, more commonly, a collection of authors whose work informs our interpretation and analysis. In fact, an entire web of relationships exists both "behind" and "in front" of a TV program that creates the very conditions for meaning to emerge. It is a dynamic, relational space that works in tandem with an audience's basic awareness of life and its understanding of the world. So while it is true that, in the previous chapter, we focused on the structure, sights, and sounds of television in order to engage the medium on its own terms and allow it to "speak" first, our examination cannot stop there without minimizing the true object of our analysis: the entire world of meaning that television opens up. In this chapter, then, we consider a number of ways in which the process of creating television and the practice of consuming television offer critical insights into TV's power and meaning.

Process

Just as the painter chooses to work within a particular frame and with the materials available to him or her, TV writers have their own set of rules—some that define how the stories are told, and others that contribute to how the stories are made, and still others that determine which stories ultimately find their way into our homes and onto our mobile devices. Thus, in order to understand more fully televisual storytelling, it is necessary to look at the process of story-making—that is, how TV shows are actually put together and the rules by which they are defined. And as we expand upon a few "television-writing specific" terms, it will become increasingly clear how much the method of actually creating television contributes to its power and meaning.

The Writers' Room

The **writers' room** is a communal place (note where the apostrophe is located: it's not a room for one writer; it's a room filled with several of them). It's the room in which television writers—as a group—spend most of their time. More commonly referred to simply as "the room" (as it will be from this point on), this is where ideas are "pitched," stories are "broken," notes are given, and "punch-up" is done. Each of these words and phrases show that this space has a language and an ethos all its own.

It is significant to understand that the making of television—especially the writing of scripts—is a communal effort. While many people's idea of a screenwriter is that of a solitary figure hunched over his or her computer in a private office (or, more commonly, a coffee shop), television stories are created by a group, led by one supervisor (called the "**showrunner**," usually having the on-screen title of executive producer). In other words, everyone contributes to the final product.

The Dick Van Dyke Show or, as a more recent example, *30 Rock* are good examples of how this works. Both shows depict comedy writers spending a lot of time not actually writing comedy, but working together as they are about to write, or having just written. Eventually, they get to work, but a great deal of their time is spent sharing their lives, talking about what they did over the weekend or joking about things that have nothing to do with the script they are writing. When they do finally get to work, they hone their ideas down and start making actual suggestions (TV writers call that "**pitching**"), and those pitches are accepted or rejected by the showrunner (another term for this is "head writer"). Dick Van Dyke's character was the showrunner on his show, and Tina Fey's character had that same job on hers. In most rooms, there is a writer's assistant (with the not-very-creative title of "writer's assistant") at the table typing just about everything that is said as the showrunner eventually decides what goes into the script. Some shows actually make audio recordings of the goings-on to make sure nothing is missed.

The TV show that demonstrates the making of television the best is actually a medical show: *House M.D.* Dr. House and those who work for him spend a lot

CBS/Photofest © CBS

On the set of CBS's *The Dick Van Dyke Show*, from left to right, Dick Van Dyke, Richard Deacon, and Carl Reiner

of time in a conference room, at a table, writing on a whiteboard. They all come up with ideas, diagnoses, and suggestions—"What about this?" or "Maybe it could be that." House—think of him as the showrunner—then decides which of the ideas he likes best and directs his staff to go down certain roads, consider certain options, and make specific decisions. And then, as the diagnosis become clear, he focuses the team on only the most significant nuances of the case.

A writers' room works similarly. "What ifs" and "How abouts" are considered all day long—and sometimes late into the night. Even after a script is written, the room will work to make it better. (Notice that "the room" not only refers to the place where the work is done but also to the collective of people doing the work.) Many shows will have the actors read through the script, out loud, in the presence of the writers, who will then spend time rewriting or (in the case of comedies) trying to make the script funnier. Certain shows will then do rehearsal performances for the writers (called "run-throughs"), after which even more rewriting will be done.

It is fair for consumers of television to wonder, with all that rewriting, why every episode of television isn't significantly better, funnier, more compelling, or nearly perfect. The answer is a somewhat boring "because there was a deadline." Episodes have to be delivered by a certain date (or, in the case of shows filmed in front of an audience, cameras are going to roll at a certain time), and the goal is to get the script as good as it can be by the time it needs to be done. So no matter how many writers are in that room, it has to be finished, eventually, regardless of whether it's good.

That TV writing is so communal says something about the stories that emerge. No matter how diverse the various room members are, the script needs to seem as if it was written by one person. It's a little bit like an orchestra: all the instruments are supposed to work together in a complementary way. And in that sense, the showrunner could be thought of as the conductor, trying to bring all the voices into harmony. But that one voice starts out as something of a cacophony before becoming the words in the script and the scenes on the screens.

Pitching the Story

"Pitching" is just a fancy word for "suggesting" (though writers tend to "pitch" with a bit more fervor than the average person "suggests"). By one definition, nearly everything a writer says in the room could be considered a pitch; the rest could be charitably defined as either "pointing out a problem" or the much more important "ordering lunch."

Story ideas, scene locations, character choices, dialogue, jokes, emotional development—all of these begin as a pitch, often preceded by the aforementioned

"How abouts" or "What ifs." In fact, sometimes dialogue is just shouted out, often in the style, accent, and voice of the character (a process that is naturally more comedic if the writers are pitching for shows with distinctive voice characters like *The Simpsons* or *Family Guy*).

Usually, the room agrees on which ideas are best. There's a collective nod, or laugh, or "yes!" when a good idea is pitched. But it's the showrunner who makes the actual decision. Rooms function as a sort of "dictatorial democracy" that way. The showrunner decides which story pitches get turned into episodes and which dialogue pitches make it into the script.

There are other players involved here as well—specifically, the studio and the network. As the funder and buyer of the product, they technically—and, in the case of the network, literally—have final say about what goes on the air or online, which means that what we see on television is ultimately under their control. Scripted television largely represents what broadcasters decide to broadcast. We will return to this topic in more detail in the chapter on TV ethics, but this is one of the reasons why the concentration of media ownership is so problematic. Writers take ideas for TV series to studios and networks (or, rather, to people at studios and networks), and those people decide whether those shows are put on the air. Just as curators decide what goes into museums, and publishers decide which books are published, network executives are the ones who decide what audiences will see.

These executives are generally looking for some sort of "hook" from a series rather than just a solid "premise." There has to be something extra in order to get people to pay attention. And the decision to put a show on the air or not can depend on numerous variables. They might turn down a show because they have other shows similar to it, or they can't get the perfect actor or actress for the lead role. Or they might feel the subject matter is something an audience might not be interested in or is too controversial to air.

So when writers pitch a pilot idea to an executive, they are also expected to describe where the series is headed. Some writers start their pitch by talking about the characters or their relationships. Others might focus on the setting or the premise. Hardly ever is a series pitched by talking about the first scene of the first episode. It's less about the beginning, middle, and end of episode 1 than it is about the overall themes and style of the series as a whole. A collection of sample episode ideas is almost always included, and season-long arcs are often suggested. All of this happens over the course of about ten to fifteen minutes, which then generally leads into a time of questions and ideas from the executive. "How will this series last for 100 episodes?" is one question that nearly always has to be answered in a series pitch. "Where do you see this series in seven years?" is another. That writers generally need to know the end of the story before they have even written the beginning puts a certain amount of strain and pressure on a pitch. It also forces a kind of artificial structure on the story that may not align with the writers' original intentions. But such are the demands of series television.

At the end of the day, what is important to note is that while TV shows are always written communally, screenwriters are not the only active parties involved in authoring a script. That is, they are not the only writers in the writers' room. And the head writer—the showrunner—does not always have the final say on how the narrative takes shape. In an important sense, then, the ultimate head writer is the network executive.

Breaking the Story

Once the basic elements of the show are agreed upon, the process of **breaking the story** can begin. Overworked writers like to point out that the word "breaking" is used to describe "coming up with" a story because it is such hard work. And it can be a difficult task. Breaking a story is deciding not just what is going to happen but also how it's going to happen. And it's the how that is the most complicated and takes the longest time to work out. At the end of a story-breaking session (or two, three, or more story-breaking sessions), the room will have generally decided what scenes are going to happen, where they will take place, who is going to be in them, what is going to be revealed, and what the attitudes of the characters are going to be—as well as (in some cases) specific dialogue that is going to be said or jokes that are going to be a part of the scene.[3]

After the kernel of an idea is pitched, the possibilities of a story with that core idea are discussed, and if it seems to be a decent avenue for an episode to explore, scenes will start to take shape: "We could do an interesting scene where such and such happens" or "Maybe the character changes her mind halfway through the episode." These ideas are sketched out (the way Dr. House and his team would jot down ideas), and eventually a full story starts to emerge.

Many nonwriters are surprised to learn that stories aren't always "broken" in order—that is, the first scene often isn't the first scene that is pitched, followed by the second, and the rest, through to the last. The nature of story-breaking often leads to writers coming up with ideas for scenes that happen at the end of the story or in the middle. And then those scenes create the need for earlier (or later) scenes to set up or fill out the episode. It's a bit like putting together a jigsaw puzzle that doesn't have a picture on it, and the best parts of the drawing are filled in as the pieces are assembled.

Beating Out the Story

Most writers' rooms use a whiteboard on which story and scene ideas are written (usually with barely legible handwriting). So in the process of breaking a story, once a scene is agreed upon, it'll eventually get put "on the board," placed according to where the room thinks it will appear in the episode—perhaps it's late in the story, or perhaps it's the perfect idea for the midpoint. Special attention is given to the opening scenes, the final scene, and the **act break scenes**—those scenes that come right before commercials on broadcast television (though even cable and streamed shows look for important things to happen at certain intervals). And, of course, the story that is being told has to fit into the time constraints of the medium: about twenty-two minutes for a half-hour sitcom; about forty-four minutes for an hour-long drama. Certain stories never make it past the board because there is "not enough story to tell" or, in some cases, "too much" to fit into the limited time frame.

Cable and streamed shows have a different amount of freedom in their storytelling length. Many hour-long shows are now truly an hour long—sixty full minutes, and sometimes a few minutes more. The freedom of not having to break for commercials and not squeeze everything into forty-four minutes allows for a different depth of storytelling and character development (although, as we will discuss further below, the presence of commercials is still enshrined in the DNA of TV shows, even when the commercials aren't there).

Once the order of scenes has been decided—this process is often referred to as "**beating out the story**," since it generally involves sketching out only the basic story points—the room will go back through the episode and discuss each story beat in depth. A **story beat** is not always a full scene; sometimes it's just a moment of revelation within a longer scene: "they find the body" is a standard story beat in a murder investigation show. But the actual scene might involve other story beats as well: "They question a suspect," and/or "The two detectives argue about how they are going to solve the case." So if "beating out the story" could be looked at as drawing the outline of the picture, it's this next step that paints in all of the colors. Snippets of dialogue might emerge in this process, and when breaking stories for comedies, jokes inevitably are pitched. Sometimes—if a joke or comedic beat is good enough—an entire scene will be structured around it for comedic effect.

A famous scene in the "Chuckles Bites the Dust" episode of *The Mary Tyler Moore Show*—where the ultra-serious Mary finally breaks into laughter at the most inappropriate moment during Chuckles the Clown's eulogy—probably developed in this nonlinear way. Once it was pitched and agreed upon that Mary (who, throughout the episode, is offended by the jokes her coworkers are telling about their coworker, who was killed by a rogue elephant during a parade . . . while the doomed Chuckles was dressed as a peanut) was going to break out in laughter during the eulogy, the scene had to be structured around that incident: she needed to be extra somber in the moments preceding it. And if she was going to be extra somber, a writer might have suggested that the other characters should be telling more jokes right there in the funeral home—so that Mary could take offense. Then, when the eulogist solemnly starts listing off some of Chuckles's characters (Aunt Yoo-Hoo and Mr. Fee-Fi-Fo are just a couple of them; the room probably pitched dozens of others that never made it to the air), Mary herself starts to chuckle—while the rest of the characters look stricken by her inappropriate outbreak. The scene ends when, after the eulogist encourages Mary to "laugh for Chuckles," Mary bursts into tears. Huge, blubbering, Mary Richards tears.

So the beat, and the entire episode, played quite linearly: this happens, then this happens, then this happens. But it was more than likely built—or "broken"—the way most scenes and stories in television are: from the inside out. We know we want this funeral scene near the end of the episode, the writers said, but what comes before that? And is there anything that has to happen after? Each of these decisions makes subsequent demands on the rest of the story.

The Beat Sheet

Once a story is broken, the writer (or writers) assigned to that episode writes a "**beat sheet**"—usually two to four pages that lay out the story (which has already been broken in the room, but a beat sheet will be slightly more coherent, and definitely more legible). Then the story is discussed a bit more before a longer outline is written—anywhere from eight to twenty pages, depending on the show. This will include many more story details, lines of dialogue (or sometimes complete exchanges) and, if it's a comedy, jokes. This outline is then discussed, and often changes are made again. Even after a first draft is written (which follows after the outline), the story beats need to be changed: it's not until a script is written that certain story problems become evident. And sometimes after the second or third draft, issues will emerge that necessitate a trip back to the room to restructure or completely re-break an episode. Writers will often view run-throughs of the episode and then return to the room to improve, shorten, or punch-up a script, which brings up one of the more significant dimensions of the TV creation process.

It could accurately be said about sitcom writing that every joke is "the winner of a contest," and that fact greatly affects the quality (or lack thereof) of what jokes make it onto the screen. Frequently, writers will sit around trying to fix a joke, and within a five-minute period dozens of jokes might be pitched. The one that goes in the script is generally the one that makes the writers laugh the most (although some that make them laugh even harder might get rejected because the writers know the joke will never pass muster with the standards and practices executive—more commonly known as "the network censor"). But notice how this format doesn't necessarily reward the best-structured joke, or the most meaningful, or the one that might resonate with any deeper truth. If the room laughs, the joke wins the contest, and it goes into the script.

It is an imperfect way to create art, and the tinkering doesn't stop there. During filming, lines might be changed, and even after an episode is filmed, additional dialogue might be dubbed in, or a scene might be moved in editing to a different place than it was in the order of the script, giving the story an entirely different focus or emphasizing the point of view of a specific character.

"Writing is rewriting," or at least that's how the aphorism goes. It could just as easily be said that "story breaking is re-breaking," or "television making is re-making," as scenes and dialogue get moved around, added, subtracted, and adjusted all the way through to the end.

Because this process is both conversational and ever evolving, a single voice can exert a tremendous amount of influence on the final script. While some might be pitching character choices based on the unrestrained life that was sung about in the theme song for *Dawson's Creek* ("I don't want to wait for my life to be over / I want to know right now the way it feels"), others might be pitching something altogether different. This is not to say that these counter-voices will always be heard, but just as one lone juror among those "twelve angry men" was able to convince his fellow adjudicators of the innocence of a not-guilty defendant, the mere presence of a differing point of view can often lead to rather unexpected outcomes.

This reference to the twelve angry jurors is of course meant to bring to mind "Fonzie for the Defense," an episode of *Happy Days* where Fonzie manages to convince Mr. Cunningham and other members of the jury that a motorcycle-riding defendant on trial is not guilty. That there exists a stage play and famous movie starring Henry Fonda with the same plot is certainly true, but this is a book about TV, so on these pages, Mr. Fonzarelli's coolness trumps Mr. Fonda's.

An episode of *My Name Is Earl* serves as a helpful example of how the direction and tone of an entire television series can change based on what might have been first presented as a "What if?" And in this case, the dialogue that made it to the screen actually includes those two words.

My Name Is Earl is about a guy named Earl who wins a great deal of money in the lottery and decides that he needs to change his life as a way of "paying back karma." So he puts together a list of all the bad things he has done to people and sets out to right those wrongs. He returns things he had stolen and tries to fulfill promises that he had broken. One of those promises was to his two sons, whom he told he would take to an amusement park years before but never did. When he finally takes them in the episode, they learn that the amusement park is no longer in operation. Earl is upset that he can't do for his kids what he told them he would do and wonders how he can ever make the situation right.

"What if we just forgive you?" asks one of his sons, and Earl seems confused by the concept. Earl's sons go on to say that they don't need their dad to make anything up to them. Earl has already said he was sorry for what he had not done in the past; his sons are ready to forgive him and consider the entire incident behind them.

Now, short of interviewing the writers on the show, it's hard to know for sure how this story came about. But this story beat ("Why don't we just forgive you?") was a radical pitch for a show that was about a man who, week after week, was quite literally seeking atonement through his own efforts and initiative. He was trying to set things right in the world through his own agency. And somebody in the writers' room—it might have been the showrunner, or it might have been a voice at the other end of the table—had to suggest, "What if his sons forgive him?" Taken to the extreme, this pitch could have put an end to the series. If everyone with whom Earl tried to make amends said, "What if I just forgive you?" Earl would have nothing to do, and episodes would have been about three minutes long. But this idea, wherever it came from, marks a decided shift in the episode and the series—a shift toward something that we might even call "grace." And all because somebody pitched, "What if . . . ?"

The Script and the Episode

Once the room has pitched enough ideas so that the story is broken, and the showrunner has approved all the ideas, and the beat sheets and outlines have been reworked—that, finally, is when the TV writer becomes an actual TV writer. A script is written in a format that might look odd to the casual observer: margins are set to seemingly arbitrary places; scene headings follow strict rules; lines denoting action and camera angles have to be written in a certain way. (The first page of the introduction to this book is formatted in a way similar to TV and film scripts, setting apart action and focusing the reader on certain images and angles.) Numerous books and various computer programs have been written to serve the needs of both the struggling writer and established professionals, because to Hollywood scriptwriters, "format matters." And that formatting inevitably contributes to what is eventually presented on-screen.

Script pages are formatted so that one page of script equals approximately one minute of screen time. So a script for an hour-long drama will be about fifty pages, and a half-hour comedy will be about twenty-five. Multi-camera sitcoms—the kind recorded in front of a live studio audience—have their own formatting, but they still try to get close to a certain number of pages in order to predict how long the episode will be after it's filmed. This page count inevitably affects how the story is told (and how it was broken). Hour-long dramas are told in anywhere from four to seven acts; half-hours are usually either three acts or two. A short "teaser" might set up the story in the first pages (preceding act 1), and a "tag" might be added on to the end (following the final act of the show). Even during the "breaking the story" phase, page count often enters into the discussion: "This scene should be less than a page" might be the directive once a story beat is decided on. "This act needs another scene" might be said if a certain portion of the script feels light or simply needs more time in order to make it to the next commercial.

These commercials affect the story structure in numerous ways (even on shows that don't have commercials). Before the show is edited—when the story is still just a kernel of an idea—writers are already asking, "What are the act breaks?" which is another way of asking, "What will be the thing that happens before we go to a commercial?" Once that is decided, another question is asked: "Do we have enough story to last until the act break?" Sometimes, artificial delays will be added to the story so that the act break comes at the proper time.

For the many acts of an hour-long show, the placement of those commercials affects the storytelling just as much. Things have to happen—there need to be story twists or emotionally significant moments—every few minutes, usually followed by a fade-out or blackout that leads into a commercial. These moments are designed to get viewers to "stay tuned" (or at least fast forward) to see what's going to happen: Will the hero get out of danger? Will the sick patient survive? Will two lovers reconcile after their big fight? They are mini cliff-hangers, designed almost like the crescendos and decrescendos of a symphony. But they also create an artificial sense of reality. Why can't these mini cliff-hangers happen every one minute, or every thirty-five minutes, or not at all? What would happen if a story was told with a six-minute first act, and a six-minute second act, but then a third act that lasted only a minute, and a fourth act that extended more than fifteen minutes? More important, what if the subject of the story demanded that the story should be told that way?

The hidden rules of television storytelling and the commerciality that comes with it suggest that such a story simply would not be told. Or if it were to be told, it would be told differently, in a way that fit with these artificial constructs. All because TV watchers have become accustomed to those once-every-few-minutes breaks, with important things happening at appointed times. Even shows that don't have commercial breaks are unconsciously following this decades-old structure.

In actual fact, the key moments in our lives don't happen according to a schedule, but the format of television dictates that they must—not just moment by moment, but in the final moment of an episode, as well. A fight between two characters on a sitcom almost always has to be resolved by the end of the episode so that the series can return to its basic concept. (A sitcom called *Friends Always Arguing and Never Getting Along* would not have been nearly as successful as the one that was called *Friends*.) On a show with police officers and detectives, the criminal generally gets caught (otherwise *Law and Order* would have been *Breaking the Law and Not Being Punished for the Disorder*). And even on shows with story lines that continue week to week (*24* is a good example), every episode presents a certain level of completion—a beginning, a middle, and an end that resolve something, at least a little bit.

Of course, life is not this way at all. Arguments that happen one day still affect the relationship the next day, and often into the next weeks, months, or years. Criminals get away with crimes, potential lovers who are supposed to be together never get together, and many of our stories remain incomplete and unresolved. Nevertheless, it would seem that viewers of television have to some degree internalized the expectations established by these twenty-two- and forty-four-minute storytelling formats. In turn, their viewing habits dictate the continued production of TV stories that fit into these neat and tidy packages.

For example, criminal cases that get wrapped up before the top of the hour don't represent the mechanics of the legal system. But this expectation about crimes has crept into the judicial system, where—during jury selection—it has become commonplace for lawyers and judges to remind prospective jurists that real life isn't like the TV show *CSI*. Not every case, the judge has to remind those in the courtroom, is solved by finding a strand of hair or matching the DNA found on a doorknob. And in Los Angeles, where nearly every jury pool includes someone who works in the entertainment industry, it's inevitably asked of prospective jurors who have worked in television what kind of shows they have worked on. Having a résumé that includes a large amount of police or detective shows is enough to get someone excused from a criminal case.

The expectation that "everything will be okay by the time the show ends"—or by the time the season or series ends—affects not only the way the audience understands the stories told on TV but also our ability to unpack the power and meaning of these stories. How many viewers have been engrossed in a show and then looked at a clock near the TV (or the "time remaining" bar on their computer screen) and wondered, "How are they going to wrap all of this up within the next few minutes?" Television creators both depend upon and leverage these expectations to tell stories that are not only dramatic but also compelling. Indeed, the process of creating TV is always connected to the practice of TV watching, for at the end of the day, regardless of how well crafted a story might be, an audience that doesn't return for another episode means, in the eyes of its creators, that the show is nothing more than an interesting failure.

Practice

A greater awareness of the process by which TV is made not only enriches our understanding of a particular TV program but also sheds light on the intentional nature of television creation. Borrowing from the language of cultural studies, we might say that, in and through the creative process, TV producers "encode" certain meanings into their programs—whether consciously or unconsciously.[4] But as audiences "decode" these cultural products, they too become actively involved in an ongoing process of meaning-making. As a result, popular cultural artifacts like TV become sites for the negotiation of meaning.[5] While consumers can and do decode cultural products according to the "dominant" or intended interpretation given by the author(s) (if there is one), they are just as likely to "read against the grain" and engage TV in negotiated, or oppositional, ways.[6] To be sure, it is important to maintain an awareness of how TV creators intend their programs to be understood if we are to come to a robust interpretation of how audiences actually make sense of them. It is for this very reason that the first half of this chapter focused on the TV-making process. Nevertheless, these interpretive insights will only ever be partial if we fail to consider what audiences bring into this system of meaning-making.

Of course, it is one thing to ask how audiences contribute to the meaning of a particular TV program when they interpret (i.e., decode) its various signs and symbols. It is quite another thing to ask how TV becomes a meaningful part of our daily lives. The former question, although an important one, is somewhat tidy and self-contained. It operates best in the realm of semiotics, which is primarily concerned with television's internal system of signification and how viewers "interpret" those signs. The latter, however, merges with the messy world of daily life, the "meaning" of which is often difficult to capture or conceptualize. It connects more readily with a "lived-religion" approach to culture, which is concerned with how religion is actually practiced and experienced in and through our day-to-day engagement with various media.[7] This focus on lived religion allows us to recognize the ways in which viewers do more than simply "interpret" TV (although they are certainly engaged in interpretive work). Instead, they develop certain kinds of relationships with television, which means that the meaning of any given episode or series is directly connected to the various ways in which people consciously (or unconsciously) interact with and ultimately make use of that program.

Our interests in this second half of the chapter are primarily ethnographic or "audience focused," which reflects a similar shift in emphasis within the broader religion and popular culture conversation and, indeed, in various academic disciplines within the humanities and the arts. Clive Marsh and Vaughan Roberts have suggested that any work done in the realm of religion and popular culture takes place in the context of three major conceptual shifts: from mass culture to popular culture, from a transmission view to a ritual view of communication, and from production to reception.[8] Because we are operating very much within the contemporary context that Marsh and Roberts identify, we are concerned with the content that TV communicates and the system of encoding and decoding within which TV operates. But we are equally concerned with the many ways that real human beings understand and articulate the role that television plays in their daily attempts to forge a meaningful life—with the ways they consume and ritualize the medium both as individuals and as a community.

If only things were so simple. The truth of the matter is that any attempt to understand how viewers are receiving TV content and putting it to use is shaped by the preexisting interpretive models that we employ (sometimes unknowingly) regarding the relationship between media and audiences. The two interpretive frameworks that are most commonly used in the fields of communication theory and media studies are what Janet Staiger calls "reinforcement" and "power relations" models.[9] Reinforcement models assume that media reinforce ideologies through hidden means. Power relations models assume that media such as TV have the upper hand over the audience. From this perspective, television overpowers viewers, lulling them into a state of complacency and ultimately causing them to believe that the status quo is simply "the way things are." In other words, TV is designed to perpetuate the ideologies of those in power by overwhelming the critical faculties of an otherwise passive audience. And to top it all off, it convinces viewers that all of this is simply "what the people want."

Interestingly, this conception of the media's hypnotic power is rather common among those interested in the cultural significance of television, whether they are approaching TV with specifically religious concerns or not.[10] And while reinforcement and power relations models do offer us a helpful reminder that all late-modern life is bound up within political and economic structures of power, they tend to overlook and even disregard the incredibly active, conscious, and even deliberate ways in which consumers use media for their own purposes. What is more, these models are unable to account for one of the major shifts that has taken place within our contemporary convergence culture—namely, the collapsing of the boundaries between consumers and producers.[11] So what is needed here is a model that pictures the relationship between media and audiences not as the transmission of mass-produced content from all-powerful producers to passive consumers but as an interactive process in which engaged consumers consciously make use of media in particular ways and even participate at times in its cocreation.

Put differently, the contemporary practice of TV viewing is no longer shaped by the logics of broadcasting but by the logics of grassroots participation. Thus, our theoretical models need to undergo a similar shift, setting aside the paradigm of network broadcasting in favor of a paradigm that accounts for a world of Netflix narrowcasting. To demonstrate how an approach of this kind might enhance our ability to understand both what and how television means in the contemporary context, let us briefly consider some of the ways in which Gleeks, the highly involved fans of *Glee*, participated in a network that received, decoded, and then repurposed their favorite show.

Discovering Our Inner Gleek

Before it is anything else, *Glee* is a performance. A self-referential, expertly practiced, highly produced performance, but a performance nonetheless. Significantly, though, what sets *Glee* apart from multi-camera sitcoms or live-broadcast sporting events is that no actual performance ever takes place. Even though the entire show hinges upon a series of what appear to be live stage productions, there is no stage and no live audience. The actors provide their own vocals, but the music, the singing, the dancing—all of it is captured separately and then reconstructed in postproduction. In other words, the performances on *Glee* don't actually exist. They are not "real" in any objective sense but are far closer to what Jean Baudrillard calls the "hyper-real"—pure simulacra.[12] Nearly every musical number is a "new" arrangement of preexisting popular music, and this approach informs the entire production. Everything is reproduced, recycled, and remixed. Or to use a phrase commonly referenced on the show itself, the performances on *Glee* are "mash-ups."

It is in this hyper-real space that audiences encounter and interact with *Glee*, participating in its (re)construction and thus engaging in a collaborative form of meaning-making. At the height of the show's popularity, Gleeks were a highly active fan base, creating robust digital networks organized around a shared passion for *Glee*. Indeed, we could consider any number of digital platforms as examples of these networked communities (Facebook, fan websites, blogs, etc.). However, we want to focus in particular on Twitter, highlighting a few of the themes that emerge when we consider how fans are consciously incorporating *Glee* into the broader, meaning-filled landscape of their daily lives.

Augmenting the Performance

The first theme concerns the live viewing groups that Gleeks coordinated through Twitter. Rather than gathering together in a physical location, numerous Gleeks watched the original broadcasts of *Glee* and interacted with one another by live-tweeting during the show. The conversations ranged from commentary on the episode to completely unrelated topics that were of interest to the group—much like an actual conversation that takes place with those who watch television in a shared geographical location. In a post-broadcast world that allows viewers to record and then watch programming at any time, this phenomenon seems to run counter to the direction that most media consumption is headed (although, in an effort to avoid spoilers, other groups of fans have started to adopt similar practices). In spite of the other viewing options at their disposal, Gleeks were consciously choosing to make *Glee* the centerpiece of a routinized gathering that, while entirely mediated, functioned as a communal form of meaning-making. In this viewing practice, "being with" others becomes an integral part of the show's significance.

Some have noted how this participatory practice is an extension of the performances on *Glee* rather than an extension of its storytelling per se.[13] In some respects, this is exactly what was taking place. The dialogue that started on Twitter during the original broadcast spun off into larger conversations throughout the remainder of the week. In some cases, Gleeks simply tweeted links to YouTube or Vimeo that featured the performances they particularly enjoyed, a practice that Fox made possible by releasing official videos of the musical numbers. On Twitter, these links are often accompanied by 140-characters-or-less commentary. For example, live-tweeting during the season 5 finale, @JustACraig noted, "Blaine singing 'All Of Me' just made my night #GleeSeasonFinale."[14] At other times, Gleeks like @BShakeitUp posted screenshots of key moments in the episode, created memes and GIFs by repurposing originally broadcast content, and even provided simple commentary such as "This will never not be funny #glee #GleeSeasonFinale @msleamichele @chriscolfer."[15] In these instances, the original televisual "event" was relived and reexperienced in and through these other forms of media, which, in turn, routinely reinforced the audience's participation in subsequent broadcasts.

It is important to note that the musical set pieces are what served as the primary content that fueled these conversations. In this way, Gleeks were indeed extending the show's performance. However, something else was taking place here as well. As we have already noted, the performances in *Glee* are all hyper-real. There is no original—no non-digital referent standing behind the production. Yet Gleeks insisted on incorporating this hyper-reality into their lives in a way that allowed them to interact with a vast network of other fans in real time. In doing so, they were not simply extending the performance but augmenting it. They were injecting a sense of "live-ness" or "living-ness" into a production that was otherwise pure simulacra. Multi-camera sitcoms have long attempted to convey this sense of "alive-ness" to viewers by recording live stage productions in front of live studio audiences. But with *Glee*, the inverse is true. Everything about the show itself is simulated. Everything, that is, except the audience. They are the ones who are active, alive, inspired, and present in real time. We might even say that, because they are leveraging digital technology, they are "hyper-present." At least for Gleeks, then, the power and meaning of *Glee* could not be reduced merely to the content of an episode or season. Rather, *Glee* became a meaningful part of their daily lives in and through the routine practice of being digitally "present" with other living, breathing human beings.

Decoding as Meaningful Work

Glee tells the story of a group of outsiders at McKinley High School who, like many young adults, are struggling to construct their identities and discover their lives' purpose in an increasingly complex cultural context. But it is also about belonging, or perhaps more accurately, not belonging. The narrative engages a wide range of issues (teen pregnancy, substance abuse, bullying, race relations, and disability, among others), but if the show has an ideological bent, it would best be described as "radical inclusivity." High school is pictured as a world of social stratification, a world where winners and losers are clearly (and violently) demarcated, a world where only the fittest survive. As high school survivors ourselves, this sounds about right. The glee club, however, serves as an oasis from this Darwinian nightmare (most of the time). It is the place where the outcasts, the pariahs, and the "others" not only find acceptance and community but also find themselves.

As a result, *Glee* constructs a narrative world in which the greatest offense is the refusal or inability to accept difference. Nearly every point of tension within the story line can be traced back to a system or individual that simply cannot abide those who would dare challenge the status quo. Likewise, nearly every redemptive moment in the show turns on a person or group finally admitting their narrow-mindedness and assuming a more tolerant posture toward difference, even if begrudgingly.

Glee imagines a world of radical inclusion, which plays itself out in numerous ways. But most of the critical attention given to the show has focused on its depiction of the LGBTQ community in particular. Interestingly, fans and media critics on both sides of the political aisle have suggested that *Glee* has an "agenda" in this regard, even though the writers, producers, and cast deny such an agenda.[16] These differing perspectives underscore the reality that a show's creators do not ultimately control what or how television means. Whatever "meaning" the creators of *Glee* intended to encode (whether that meaning was agenda-driven or not), audiences are decoding it and making use of it in ways that suit their purposes, even if those purposes run counter to the intentions of the authors.

For example, Gleeks demonstrated their wide-ranging interpretations of the show when @GLAAD took to Twitter to celebrate the engagement of *Glee* characters Kurt and Blaine: "#Glee's Kurt and Blaine take a big step in their relationship [SPOILERS] . . . #gleepremiere @gleeonfox #lgbt."[17] As is typically the case, the Twitter conversation centered on (and linked to a YouTube post of) a particular musical segment where Blaine proposes to Kurt with a rendition of the Beatles' "All You Need Is Love." Some simply retweeted or "favorited" @GLAAD's original tweet as a way of expressing their support of the engagement. Others, like @klainky, voiced their approval by responding to the post directly with words of affirmation: "@glaad HOLLA."[18] Still others were more critical, raising concerns that were rooted in the narrative itself. @RevDebra noted the young age of the characters: "@glaad @GLEEonFOX But aren't they 18 and 20 years old?? I hope it's a long engagement."[19] @onthaedge487 was more concerned with the relational dynamics between Blaine and Kurt: "@glaad @GLEEonFOX Um, please don't tell me you support this emotionally abusive relationship? It's a bad representation of LBGTQ. #RIPKurt."[20]

The point here is twofold. First, audiences were evaluating, spreading, and in some cases even repurposing *Glee* in and through the mediated practice of live-tweeting. Second, they were doing it in ways that did not always align with the intentions of the show's creators. For many Gleeks, *Glee* functioned as a springboard for engaging in much-needed conversations about the plight of LGBTQ persons and the many ways they are (mis)understood or (mis)treated in the contemporary world. And at least as it concerns *Glee*, this dialogue was taking place irrespective of the (stated) agenda of the show's creators.

Given the prevalence of LGBTQ characters on *Glee* and the many plot points that feature them wrestling with their sexual identities, it is difficult to conclude that the writers and cast have no larger hopes for their depiction of LGBTQ young people, even if those hopes do not amount to a full-fledged "agenda." But the fact that the show's creators deny any broader agenda should at least cause us to pause. The "encoding" process should inform our analyses and interpretations. Nevertheless, audiences also have a say regarding both what and how a TV program means, and sometimes this meaning takes on a life of its own. Most often, the cultural "life" of a show emerges when audiences consume broadcast content and then share their analyses and interpretations with others in their network. Sometimes, as is the case with Gleeks, this involves the creation of media content like memes, GIFs, or remixes. But even when the only "product" they create is the critical and interpretive dialogue that surrounds the show, audiences are engaging in important and meaningful work by evaluating and spreading their interpretations of media content.[21] In doing so, they are not only contributing to the production of beliefs, values, and concepts that constitute a particular culture, but they are also forming and being formed by the interpretive community of which they are a part.[22]

Ritualizing Emotions

The final theme we want to address is related to the interaction between ritual and emotions. As Henry Jenkins has rightly suggested, in the emerging world of "affective economics," media content is not simply intellectual property; it is "emotional capital."[23] What this means is that groups of TV viewers like Gleeks are not simply engaged in water-cooler chatter (although this is part of what they are doing). Rather, they are identifying, joining, and then developing what we might call affective alliances—communities of feelings. These small-scale social groupings function as digital "tribes," which people join or create based upon a set of common practices rather than on the basis of race, religion, or class. Significantly, these tribal affiliations are not rooted in an ethical framework per se but are based almost entirely upon the emotional needs of the individual and the group. Indeed, they are about "passional logic. . . . Neo-tribes are sensual rather than moral. They are based on shared pleasures and doing what feels good."[24]

When it comes to the practice of watching TV, serialization acts as one of the driving forces behind the development of this "passional logic." As we have noted, Gleeks enjoyed interacting over Twitter with other members of their tribe during live broadcasts, but it is the serialized nature of *Glee* that encouraged viewers to routinely and repeatedly engage in this dialogue in the time that passed between episodes. Because season finales mark the lengthiest of intermissions, the responses to these episodes offer a prime example of how serialization invites a distinctly emotional (and even nostalgic) mode of reflection among fans. For example, @saskia_pita noted, "It makes me cry #GleeSeasonFinale"; @asma_jamel asked, "#GleeSeasonFinale OMG the feels :'(can you hear me crying?"; and

Fox Network/Photofest © Fox Network

Lea Michele as Rachel in the series finale of Fox's *Glee*

@Golden__Poppy reflected on the "many emotions when Rachel looks to the sky at the end of the final episode . . . #Glee @GLEEonFOX #GleeSeasonFinale."[25] It is especially interesting to note how Gleeks pressed the limitations of a medium like Twitter when they were expressing deeply felt emotions, drawing upon emoticons and other visual cues rather than limiting themselves to the text of their tweets. Regardless, though, what prompted these tweets was a season finale that followed the conventions of serialized fiction—unresolved, unfinished, and "to be determined." It was this pronounced ellipsis that fueled the ongoing interactions that took place between the season finale and the premier of the next season a full seven months later.[26]

Because Gleeks were structuring and orienting their lives around the ebb and flow of *Glee* broadcasts, the nature of their interactions assumed a distinctly ritual shape. In certain respects, these fans were even engaged in a type of devotion—to the show itself, to their emotional experience, and to the tribe known as Gleeks. Nowhere are these ritual and devotional dimensions seen more clearly than in the ways in which fans responded to Cory Monteith's death. The individual tweets with the #RememberingCory hashtag are simply too numerous to examine in detail here, but taken as a whole, they serve as a fitting example of not just what television can mean in the contemporary world but how it can mean.

The #RememberingCory hashtag was more than a convenient filter for those wanting to offer a tribute to a beloved actor. It functioned as a form of public lament. The untimely death of a young person is always traumatic, and traumatic experiences like these damage the basic fabric that connects people to one another and provides them with a sense of community. Gathering together with one's tribe in the wake of collective trauma is very basically how humans begin to reconnect, reintegrate, and even heal.[27] And while it was undeniably mediated and thus markedly different from gatherings that take place in physical locations, the #RememberingCory hashtag nevertheless functioned as a primary location for a community to grieve and to express its deep-seated emotions. In this way it was not unlike other ritualized forms of mourning, which is rather telling, for it is only in a televisual world that a show about a high school glee club is able to extend beyond the confines of any singular episode or season and shape the broader world in which we live.

A Theology of Reception

If in fact contemporary culture no longer operates according to the logics of broadcasting and instead operates according to the logics of participatory practices, we need to do more than simply develop a collection of critical tools. We need to construct a theology of reception that might actually address this shift. As we have made clear in the last few chapters, critical tools are an important part of the task. They grant us much-needed insight into TV's formal trace, the process of its creation, and the practices of its consumption. But our critical analyses of television need to be located within a larger theological framework. It is not enough simply to note that TV audiences are engaged in deeply emotional forms of meaning-making, or that they are seeking to be "present" with members of their digital community, or that their routinized collaborations with TV creators are functioning as a form of devotional practice. Each of these themes raises innately theological questions that are in need of further exploration.

In his book *Real Presences*, George Steiner sketches out what a theological exploration of this sort might look like.[28] Speaking about aesthetic experiences generally, he suggests that modern persons need to develop an ethics of reception—one rooted in a posture of hospitality. The first step in fostering our receptive capacity is to listen closely to the work of art. The second is to develop an understanding of the grammar of the artwork—a capacity not just to hear but to hear well. We have attempted to take these first two steps by developing a common vocabulary and a set of critical tools that will enable us to listen closely and well to what TV is saying.

But Steiner points to a third step that is equally important, and it sets the stage for the remainder of this book. The final step in developing a theology of reception is semantic. That is, we must be able to recognize the passage from the "means" of an artwork to its "meaning." To a certain degree, we are able to reach some kind of common ground regarding the formal "means" of an artwork—the unique "language" each medium employs. However, because it is innately contextual, "meaning" will always be a mystery to us on some level. We cannot know everything about the context of the other, so a fundamental humility is the prerequisite for any kind of "understanding." This is not to suggest that intelligibility is impossible; we can know something about what television means and how it means for those who watch it. However, we move forward recognizing that, because meaning is a dialogical reality, it entails a risk—a fundamental act of trust. So as we attempt to locate our understanding of TV within a larger theological framework, we are not seeking to place ourselves above this cultural artifact. Rather, our aim is to be hospitable. To use Steiner's words, we are taking the necessary risk of honoring the freedom of the other. And it is to the freedom of the televisual other that we now turn.

4

the *telos* of tv

It could be said that the last step of a journey determines the destination of the first. And while this might read a bit like a proverb or some other piece of pop wisdom, it's not a statement that's trying to be profound. It's actually saying something quite simple, and it strikes at the heart of the present chapter: "You never know where you're going until you get there." If this sounds like it might have been the lyric to a pop song, that's because it was, in 1946.[1]

Narrative storytelling demonstrates well what those songwriters knew in the mid-1940s: it's hard to determine the meaning of a story until that story is over. Until the end, any attempt to discern its purpose or point of view is going to be incomplete at best or at least somewhat premature. Take any murder mystery as an example—either in book or movie form. If a story is a "whodunit," up until that "who" is disclosed (and, sometimes even more important, why they "dunit"), the meaning of the story remains as much a mystery as the who, what, when, where, and why of the crime. Is it a story about revenge? Jealousy? Mental illness? The randomness of life and death? The answer to these questions depends on which of the suspects is the culprit and his or her motivation for committing the crime.

A classic example is the movie *The Sixth Sense*, which presents itself as a story about a young boy who sees dead people—and *why* he sees them seems to be one of the movie's driving questions. But then it's revealed that the psychologist who is trying to help the boy determine the reason for his visions is himself dead, and viewers suddenly realize that the movie is about something completely different. It's about the psychologist "moving on" from this life, and his journey toward closure regarding his relationship with the wife he left behind. Anyone trying to unpack the movie's meaning before that key revelation would be in the same category as the playgoer who slips out of *Romeo and Juliet* early after deciding that the play is nothing more than a sweet slice-of-life story about two teenagers experiencing puppy love. Point being, it's probably best to keep watching until "The End."

The stories on TV are much the same. *Seinfeld* was well known as being "a show about nothing." The show's cocreator (Larry David, who created the show with Jerry Seinfeld) made it clear that one of the dictums of each episode was "No hugging; no learning."[2] Episode after episode purposefully added up to nothing. Things happened, but nobody changed. The characters were famously self-centered and rarely achieved any level of success (and if they did, it was short-lived). Any sort of "meaning" was in the eye of the beholder, and the makers of the show might have shuddered had they learned that anyone was looking for meaning at all.

But then the final episode aired. In it, the four main characters are arrested and put on trial based on a "duty to rescue" law. They witness an overweight man being carjacked, and instead of helping him, they make fun of him. While on trial, a parade of witnesses (mostly characters from previous episodes) comes forth to testify about Jerry, George, Kramer, and Elaine's previous acts of selfishness. The judge sentences the Seinfeld gang to a year in prison for "criminal indifference," and the final scene is the four of them in a jail cell, conversing about the same things they talked about in episode number 1.

They did not hug, and the characters did not learn a thing. But does that mean that the series **finale**, like the show itself, meant nothing? Far from it. In an important sense, this finale reframed all 178 episodes that came before it. Whether it was the writers' intention or not, it allowed viewers to reexamine the entire series as a kind of morality tale: "The people who behave the way these characters behaved deserve to be punished" (because that's what eventually happened to them). When rewatching episodes, whether in syndication or streaming, it is simply a fact of these fictional lives that—whatever success their selfish behavior led to in any given episode—in the end, they were penalized for thinking only about themselves. But this construal of the series didn't even become a possibility until the very last moment of that very last show.[3]

It's important to note, however, that not all series get the chance to have a series finale like *Seinfeld* did. They all have a final *episode*, of course, but sometimes the final episode is just that—it's the final episode *produced* and *aired*. At the time of production, the writers might not have even known that it would be the last one. The fate of many shows is not determined until after all the episodes of a season are produced, and whether that season is the first, second, or eighth, some shows are not renewed or canceled until weeks or even months after the entire season airs. For a heavily **serialized** show that's canceled without the chance to produce a proper finale, this kind of **stoppage** can leave the characters in a constant state of limbo.[4]

A prime example of this phenomenon is the sitcom *Soap*, which aired from 1977 through 1981. As the name implies, it was positioned as a kind of soap opera, albeit in comedic and overly absurd ways (e.g., one of the characters was a ventriloquist dummy, and another believed he could make himself invisible by snapping his fingers).[5] It was serialized, with continuing stories from episode to episode and cliff-hangers at the end of each season—including the season finale of season 4, which had the matriarch of one of the families, Jessica Tate, standing in front of a firing squad. During the final seconds of the show, the words, "Ready, aim, fire!" are heard, and then shots ring out. The last image is of Jessica herself, reacting as if being hit by the bullets.

A number of other stories remained unresolved at the end of that episode, too, but there was no resolution to come. The show was canceled, leaving fans of the show—and anyone wanting to understand the show's ultimate take on these characters and their lives—in limbo.

The fact is that *most* shows end their TV lives with the same kind of non-completion as *Soap* (though not always with as much of a cliff-hanger) because most series get canceled after their first season. Some shows air for only a few episodes before being taken off of the air. Many of these shows' creators might have had grand plans for future seasons—revelations that might have completely changed viewers' understanding of what they saw in season 1—but they never had an opportunity to realize them. Even shows that last two or three seasons rarely get the chance to produce what could be considered a proper "series ender," which in many cases leaves the writers' intentions for those shows forever unknown.

Likewise, for any current series that is still in production, much remains unknown, based on the simple fact that there is still more and different information to come. One can critically engage the narrative *up to this point*, but beyond that, we must proceed with the recognition that any of the yet-to-air episodes might completely alter the basic assumptions upon which the story-world once operated, the way the big revelation in *The Sixth Sense* (Bruce Willis's character is dead!) suddenly changed the entire movie.

All this is to say, trying to unpack the power and meaning of a TV series in the middle of its run is a little bit like trying to solve a mathematical equation with only a portion of the information. You can make some progress, but you'll never be certain about the "is equal to" part until the last of the data are revealed. We will return (in our own "series finale" chapter, actually) to consider how we might think of each episode on a case-by-case basis—as having a coherence and integrity all its own. But in this chapter we want to consider more fully the ways in which a show's *telos* (both the actual end of the series and the imagined "end" toward which all narratives move) actively shapes our understanding of its individual parts.

The Ellipsis: "And They Lived Happily Ever After" (or Not)

Fairy tales that end with the words "And they lived happily ever after" establish their own (some would say extremely skewed) view of an "all will be well" future. The sleeping beauty and the handsome prince may or may not even be compatible, but according to the fancy scrawl at the end of the film, their lives ever after are happy. Same with that little mermaid and *her* prince, who didn't even hear the young woman speak before he kissed her. Many a premarital counselor would suggest that their relationship is headed for stormy seas, but—nope. According to the story, they end up happily ever after too. However we are to understand their journey to the altar, it is mostly overshadowed by the "happily" that follows it all.

Many TV series (especially comedies) end on a similarly optimistic note. The characters whom we've come to know continue on in life with few cares and hardly any troubles. Life goes on as it had in the previous seasons, just with a little less conflict and fewer of those pesky commercial breaks.[6] *Cheers* serves as a good example. Life at the bar ended not much different from where it began—with Sam serving drinks, Norm on his bar stool, and Carla taking orders and handing out insults. The final line of the series? "We're closed." But it was implied that the bar would open back up the next day (just not with the cameras and the live studio audience there, and without Frasier Crane, who moved on to a spin-off of his own).[7]

Similarly, *That '70s Show* stayed true to its name up to and including the final seconds of the show. It was December 31, 1979—New Year's Eve. The characters had all reassembled in the Formans' house, ready to greet the new decade. But their countdown of the last seconds of the seventies—three, two, one—never hit zero. It was as if to suggest that the residents of Point Place would be in the seventies forever (which they are, of course, in reruns and on other forms of video). But nothing about the ending significantly changed our understanding of the series as a whole. If anything, it extended the narrative into a kind of eternity, thus affirming our expectations that Eric and Donna, who had been the central relationship of the series for most of the show's life, would not only end up together but also stay together always and forever.

From left to right, Ashton Kutcher, Topher Grace, Wilmer Valderrama, and Danny Masterson in Fox's *That '70s Show*

This idea that "they end up together" is common to many series that have some sort of romantic relationship at their center. Giving the audience what it wants (that is, knowing that the characters that the viewers *wanted* to be together actually do end up that way) is not only satisfying storytelling but good business as well. Because shows are watched and rewatched years after a series goes off the air, it is far more satisfying for viewers to know that they were watching the early stages of a relationship that lasted, rather than one that never came to be.

A far-from-normal variation of this "and they lived happily ever after" ending occurred when *Mad About You* aired its finale after five seasons on the air. The final episode flashed forward more than twenty years into the future and featured the (by-then) grown daughter of the couple featured on the show, who was producing an autobiographical film about how she became the woman that she was. It was revealed that the couple—Paul and Jamie—had separated, and their daughter (the filmmaker) had grown up to be somewhat bitter and more than a little bit neurotic.[8] In the end, Paul and Jamie are brought back together—and the series actually ends with their daughter saying that her parents "lived happily ever after"—but the tone of the series had already been changed. To learn that these two characters who had been "mad about you, baby" (as the theme song declared) had decided to go their separate ways—regardless of the fact that they eventually got back together, and, more so, that the daughter

the *telos* of tv ———— 91

they raised had grown into a damaged, angry, and neurotic adult—recast the entire series. *Mad About You* suddenly looked different—much different. This is not to say that the episodes and the series can no longer be enjoyed as late-1990s domestic slices of TV life, but it's hard not to see the show, at least a little bit, as "scenes from a failing marriage." And when the daughter is born in season 5, it's difficult not to feel sorry for the little girl, knowing what kind of life she has to come.

Whether *Mad About You*'s ending negatively affected the series' life in syndication or contributed to the interest (or lack thereof) of future generations of viewers is hard to judge. But this example brings up one of the new realities of television viewing in the age of streaming and binge-watching. By the time many (it might be more than "many" and indeed is probably "most") viewers start watching a series, it may no longer be in production. Its ending might have been produced and aired years, or even decades, before. And unless one has a "spoiler alert" filter on the entire internet, it's hard to keep from knowing the ultimate fate of the passengers on Oceanic Flight 815, or what happened to Walter White, or who Bob Newhart woke up in bed with during the last scene of *Newhart*. (All three of those endings will be discussed later in this chapter, so for those who insist on being surprised, read no further.)

How much this kind of "knowledge about the future" affects a viewer's understanding of a show—especially as one experiences it in order, episode by episode—would be difficult to measure. But (to reference that 1940s pop song again) when we actually *do* know where we're going (or, in this case, how a television series is going to end), it is nearly impossible not to let that destination/ending affect or inform our perception of what we see along the way.

Sometimes, this knowledge of the future can be a good thing. Knowing that the couple will actually get together in the end can make their "will they or won't they?" escapades that much more fun to watch. Or knowing that a character who struggles to become a better person throughout the series actually *does* become a better person can make watching that person's series-long struggle even more rewarding.

Andy Sipowicz was one of those struggling characters. In the pilot of *NYPD Blue*, he was presented as a foul-mouthed (and especially cruel to one woman) alcoholic who made horrible life choices but somehow managed to be a good cop. The show received a lot of attention when it premiered in 1993 because of the harsh language and partial nudity, and a few ABC affiliates refused to air it in their markets.[9] But the show's cocreator, David Milch, frequently described the series as being about "the redemption of (Andy) Sipowicz,"[10] and each episode can be seen as a step toward that redemption. Andy became a little bit kinder, and (at various times) a little more sober—and then slid back into his old ways before climbing back out again. The woman to whom he was especially mean in the opening moments of the pilot eventually became his wife, and he strove to be a better person partly out of his love for her. When she died, he endeavored to become a better father in order to carry on her legacy. And by the time the series ended, Andy (though he still had his rough edges) had become demonstrably a better man than the person he was at the start. Just as Milch said, it really was a story of redemption—one that echoes a larger story of redemption that pervades much of the Western cultural imagination.

One of the final images in the last episode of *NYPD Blue* is of Andy, now promoted to captain, in the very office where he had had so much conflict with his previous captains. It was as if to say, "Look how far he's come. Andy deserves this office, this title, this respect." And he would carry this respect into the show's eternal life after life, otherwise known as syndication.

Re-imaginings: Things Might Not Have Been What They Seemed

Certain shows are completely redefined by their last moments—sometimes their very last seconds. One show that stands out in this category is *St. Elsewhere*. The critically acclaimed series aired in the mid-1980s for six seasons, earning thirteen Emmy Awards along the way. But it never attracted a lot of viewers, and almost always seemed on the brink of cancellation. In fact, the writers were so certain that they would not be returning after five seasons that the final image of the last episode of that year is a wrecking ball swinging toward St. Eligius (the hospital where the series took place). If the show was going down, it seemed that they were going to take the hospital with it. But the series returned for one more season and, after some creative "stop the demolition!" storytelling in the season 6 premiere, continued until its finale on May 25, 1988. Story lines were wrapped up, a major character died, and others moved on to greater things. The fat lady sang (quite literally; she was one of the patients being treated there), and the series seemed ready to fade to black.

Except that there was one more scene. As one of the series' main characters (Dr. Westphall) stared out his office window at the falling snow, the image shook a bit, then cut to an apartment that had never been seen before. "Dr. Westphall" came through the door, dressed not as a doctor but as a construction worker. An older colleague he had worked with greeted him, and the younger referred to the elder as "Pop," which was odd, since in the series they were not related. The construction-worker-whom-the-audience-thought-was-a-doctor told of finishing off "the twenty-second story" (a bit of a wink to the audience; most network series produce twenty-two episodes a year) and then asked about his fourteen-year-old son, who was sitting on the floor, looking as if he was lost in his own world. The boy was someone the audience knew: he was Tommy, the autistic child of St. Eligius's Dr. Westphall. Tommy's dad lamented to his own father that he didn't understand "this autism thing." He talked about how Tommy just sat there all day, lost in his thoughts, "staring at that toy." And then he added: "What's he thinking about?" As Tommy's dad tells his son to get ready for dinner, the autistic boy places the toy he's been holding—a snow globe—on the fireplace mantle, and the camera zooms in to show . . . a replica of St. Eligius.

In those few moments, and in the closing seconds of *St. Elsewhere*, viewers realized that the entire series had been this one boy's elaborate fantasy—nothing but stories he had made up. Prior to this moment, the show had already firmly established itself as a series that was willing to engage complex moral and even religious themes. So the episodes leading up to the finale stand on their own. But according to the final episode, nothing that had happened on the show had actually happened; it was all part of Tommy Westphall's imagination.

Hard-core television aficionados will suggest that there is even more to the ending of that story. Because several *St. Elsewhere* characters appeared on other shows (including *Cheers*, *Homicide: Life on the Street*, and *The White Shadow*) and references were made regarding connections between characters on *St. Elsewhere* and characters on other shows (a patient who had recurred on *The Bob Newhart Show* came in for treatment, and one of *St. Elsewhere*'s doctors revealed that he had worked with B. J. Hunnicutt, a character on *M*A*S*H*), some fans even developed "The Tommy Westphall Universe," an elaborate theory that details the interconnectedness of all the shows that Tommy might have imagined—including many series that are still on the air. Those who keep track of such things claim that this universe has grown to include more than four hundred shows.[11]

Another series that took place in the mind of one of its characters was *Roseanne*, but this too wasn't revealed until the last moment of the last episode. *Roseanne* aired for nine seasons starting in 1988, and was one of the top five most watched series on TV for its first six years on the air. The show presented the life of a blue-collar family, with the "domestic goddess" mother at the center of it all. But its ninth season started with a show-changing revelation: Roseanne won the lottery—$108 million. After a series of adventures, Roseanne and her family settled into a life without their previous financial woes. It was as if all of her dreams had come true.

Only it sort of *was* a dream. Or, at least, it was all made up. And not just the final season—the entire nine years. In the series' final scene, Roseanne (the character) is revealed to have written all the stories that made up *Roseanne* (the series) in the form of a book about her life. She changed various details (she switched up her daughters and sons-in-law, saying that she thought the couples she had showed us for years matched up better that way, and her husband had died of a heart attack), but she still lived in a house similar to the one seen on TV. It was a pretty stunning rug-pull, and in a series that was hailed for its realistic portrayal of a lower-class family, it was odd to learn that nothing had been realistic after all.[12]

How I Met Your Mother not only wasn't a figment of one of the characters' imagination; it was presented as an all-of-this-really-happened "oral history." The series was set up as a story being told in the future by a father (Ted) to his two children, and one of the riddles of the show's life span was, "Who is the mother?" As the episodes progressed in the early days, it was not clear if one of the female characters on the show was the mother, or if any of the women that the storytelling dad dated might turn out to be "the one"—though it was clear to regular viewers that Ted was probably in love with Robin, one of the women who was a regular on the show. At the end of the second-to-last season, the mother was finally introduced, but it wasn't until the end of the series finale that it was revealed she had actually died a few years after the children's births. The kids to whom the story was being narrated then tell their dad that he obviously was in love with Robin, and should go and be with her. He seeks her out, and, well, it's suggested that the two of them will probably live happily ever after. But the ultimate answer to the show's premise was answered. Ted *had* been telling his children the nine-season-long story of how he met their mother, albeit with a number of twists and turns and misleads, and it wasn't until the final chapter of his "story" that the answer to the mystery (and the meaning of what he had been talking about) was revealed.[13]

One more show with a series-altering final scene that should be mentioned (in a much lighter context) is *Newhart*. The final episode of that series had innkeeper Dick Loudon (played by Bob Newhart) being the only holdout when a Japanese firm attempts to tear down the inn that he ran and also buy the rest of the town, in order to build a resort. All the other characters take a very generous financial buyout and head off—millionaires, all—to live wonderful lives. But Dick and his wife stay. Years later, the regulars return to see how Dick is doing. "Pretty much the same" is the implication, and he's as annoyed as he ever was by the people with whom he used to interact.

The series could have ended there—all the characters living "ever after" in various stages of happiness or not-so-much. But then Dick is struck in the head by a golf ball and wakes up in bed with . . . Emily Hartley (played by Suzanne Pleshette). They're in the bedroom of Newhart's *previous* show, *The Bob Newhart*

Show, and it's revealed that the entirety of *Newhart* had been a dream of Bob Hartley's—the main character on *The Bob Newhart Show*.

It would be hard to argue that this finale fundamentally altered our understanding of either of the two shows, but it points out the reality that even fictional TV can present itself as even *more* fictional with these last-episode reality benders. In many ways, it's a reflection of the postmodern nominalism that has crept into pop-cultural life. Reality only becomes "real" when we give it a name. If one's head hurts as a result, well, perhaps Dr. Bob Hartley—a psychiatrist, after all—can help us sort it all out.

Open-Ended: If You Don't Know, We're Not Going to Tell You

Of all the shows that have significant finales, few are more worthy of discussion than *Lost*. Books and essays have been written about the themes, science, and philosophy of the show, including *The Gospel according to "Lost,"* which was published before the final episode aired. Little more will be added to the debate about *Lost's* meaning here, but it is valuable to look at what the finale tried to do, and how it did it, with the goal of better understanding the power and meaning of other shows.

After four seasons on the air, it was announced that *Lost* was going to air its season finale—nearly two years later. This was to give the writers a chance to know the "end point" of the series and tell the next two seasons of stories accordingly.[14] The show had created a number of mysteries and seemed in no hurry to answer the additional questions that arose each week. As the series headed toward its final episodes, more than a few scenes ended with characters saying some version of, "I'll tell you what you want to know . . . later," and by the time the finale aired on May 23, 2010, fans were ready to have the curtains pulled back and the secrets revealed.

What viewers saw is still open to interpretation, but the penultimate scene had Jack and most of the characters from his doomed flight meeting in a church. There was talk of death and moving on, and a bright light was thrown in for good measure. And then Jack was back on the island, and the final image of the series (before the end credits, which showed the plane wreckage on the island) bookended the opening image of the series: the first shot of *Lost* was Jack opening his eye; the last showed him closing it.

The characters may have been dead the whole time, or might have died more recently, or never been dead at all. And of the planeload of questions that had been brought up during the series' run—What did those numbers mean? Who built the statues? How did that monster get so smoky?—few were definitively answered. In one sense, the writers seemed to be saying that those answers didn't matter. *Lost's* themes of redemption, reinvention, and reconciliation had already been established. Its meaning was present in the DNA of every episode, and its ending—which could have reframed our understanding of the show's previous episodes in any number of directions—landed in a similar way as the Oceanic flight that brought the characters to the island: not at all perfect, but in a way few passengers will forget.[15]

Another show that might have created more questions than it answered in its last moments was *The Sopranos*. That show—which centered on mob boss Tony Soprano, who struggled to balance life as a violent criminal with that of a family man (with the help of his psychiatrist)—started out as a show about a "mobster in therapy having problems with his mother."[16] It eventually became both an intricate family drama and a bit of a how-to about being in the Mafia. Tony killed people and cheated on his wife (often both of those things happened in the same episode), and, though he struggled with the morality of it all, he rarely considered changing his ways. But throughout the series there always existed the possibility that he was either going to give up the mob life or be caught and punished for his actions. Either ending would have made a moral statement about what it meant to be a Soprano. But the actual finale was not so clear.

The last episode of *The Sopranos* felt like business as usual. Various mob dealings had left various characters dead or wanting to kill others, but Tony still has his wife and kids, and the Soprano family decides to meet at a diner for dinner. While looking over the menu, Tony glances toward the door whenever the bell over it rings signifying that someone is coming in or going out. It's hard to tell if the mob boss is hoping to see someone he wants to see or fearing he might see someone he doesn't. During all of this, Journey's "Don't Stop Believing" plays on the jukebox—because Tony picked out that song.

A suspicious-looking man crosses behind Tony into the restroom; some onion rings are delivered to the table; the bell over the door rings, Tony looks up—and the screen cuts to black. Ten seconds of nothing; total silence. It was so abrupt that many viewers thought their cable had gone out. And then the final credits rolled. The series was over, and it was open to interpretation whether Tony Soprano lived, died, got what he deserved, or enjoyed the rest of those onion rings.

What actually happened—if it could ever be determined what actually happened—would go a long way toward informing how we understand the series as a whole. If Tony was shot by that suspicious-looking man (or any of Tony's numerous enemies), then the series might be a morality tale. Each of the episodes preceding the finale could be rewatched knowing that ultimate outcome. There would have been a sense of "moral satisfaction" that Tony's life of immorality led to his receiving such punishment. But if his life went on, we would be forced to draw a different conclusion. From this view, the primary theme of *The Sopranos* might be "bad people are going to keep doing bad things." Or maybe it's "those who hurt others have to constantly watch the door to see who's coming in to take them down." Or maybe it was just meant as a twisted love story between an avuncular, murderous Italian American and, as Steve Perry described her in the song, "a small town girl living in a lonely world."

David Chase, the show's creator and writer of the final episode, doesn't seem too interested in clearing things up: "Whether Tony Soprano is alive or dead is not the point. To continue to search for this answer is fruitless. The final scene of *The Sopranos* raises a spiritual question that has no right or wrong answer."[17] We want to echo Chase's words and underscore the spiritual note on which the series ended. It seems that there is an inherently spiritual element to open-ended narratives. They are mysterious in part because they present us with countless possibilities. They point us beyond the confines of the story, suggesting that, in the final analysis, what ought to ultimately concern us is not whether Tony finished those onion rings.

Comeuppance: And Justice(?) for All

Walter White of *Breaking Bad* will always be one of TV's most memorable characters. A high school chemistry teacher diagnosed with cancer, he finds a way to supplement his income (so that he can leave his family financially secure) by making meth. The series kept Walt's moral choices front and center, and he variously succeeded and failed in his meth-making endeavors while trying to balance his life as a family man and a drug maker. He was the definition of the antihero. Audiences rooted for him, even though they knew he was doing bad—even evil—things. In the final episode, when Walter is shot and killed while freeing his drug-dealing partner from a rival drug gang, it seemed as if Walter got exactly what he deserved.

After the finale aired, the show's creator, Vince Gilligan, told *Entertainment Weekly*, "Walt is never going to redeem himself. He's just too far down the road to damnation. But at least he takes a few steps along that path."[18] In the same interview, Gilligan points out that Walt does achieve what he set out in the pilot to do—provide for his family. That is, he leaves them "just a ton of money."[19]

As we mentioned earlier on "process" (chap. 3), these comments need to be taken into account when critically engaging the show. It's important to understand what goes through a writer's mind when he or she is developing a series.

One of the most important questions is, "What does the main character want?" (The question is equally important for writers of films, books, plays—any sort of fiction—and needs to be answered for other characters, as well.) In the case of Walter White, it was set up in episode 1 that he just wanted to take care of his family. But as an underpaid teacher, he did not feel he was able to do so. So he got a second job—in this case, making illegal drugs. As the series progressed, he became more than just a drug manufacturer; he became a drug dealer. This led Walter into increasingly fraught moral compromises, but the entire series could still be related back to his initial "want": to take care of his family. It was a virtuous desire at its core, but it led to questions of, "How far will this one man go to do what he set out to do?" Walt is thus presented as an everyman, and his decisions seem to be challenges and warnings to us all: "What would you, the viewer, do? How far would *you* go?"

Vince Gilligan's statement after the finale aired sheds light on how we might make sense of the larger scope of the series. That the show's creator felt that Walter was "never going to redeem himself" and was "too far down the road to damnation" meant that the final moments of the series were, if not preordained, then at least contained by Gilligan's artistic vision. It is certainly fair for the show's creator to believe that the character he created was never going to change his ways, but it nevertheless marks out the limits of how we might understand the narrative. Gilligan's comments also suggest that Walter was never going to redeem *himself*, as if Walter was the only one who had the power to do so. To close off that possibility meant that Walter's fate had already been sealed. He died, unredeemed, by himself or anyone else.

During that same interview with *Entertainment Weekly*, Gilligan revealed that other endings were considered. One possibility was that Walter survived, but his whole family was destroyed. Another had Walter killed by his partner.[20] Significantly, none involved Walter changing his ways.

Dexter dealt with similarly complex issues as *Breaking Bad*. *Dexter* was about a serial killer who kills serial killers. Though he was a murderer himself, Dexter actually lived by a strict moral code: he killed only people who (he determined) "deserved" to be killed, and he had appointed himself both judge and jury—a sort of "determinator." Dexter showed little mercy to his victims. In fact, he caused many of them to suffer—a lot. That he was doing "justice" seemed to allow him the freedom to not even consider mercy as an option, and his role as executioner created the kind of conflicts and moral questions that fueled the series for eight seasons.

The last of those episodes was not well received. In the final moments of the finale, Dexter—who had killed too many people to count over the years—is seen driving his boat into a hurricane, and a few days later, another character reads about his death. But then Dexter is seen alive, somewhere in the woods of the northwest. He seems to be living his life, carefree, as a bearded lumberjack who has put his serial-killing days behind him (though the ending does not specifically address that point). In the end, Dexter didn't suffer at all, aside from the extreme emotional losses he had endured throughout the series; various characters that he loved had died. He kept his own life, and according to the series, he's out there living free among the trees. He literally got away with murder(s)—many of them—and, unlike Walter White and *perhaps* Tony Soprano, Dexter didn't pay the consequences that many thought he should have paid.

It could have been very different. Clyde Phillips, who served as the showrunner for the first four years of the show, told *E! Online* how he would have ended the show: with Dexter on an executioner's table, receiving a lethal injection.[21] Yet a writer on the show's final season revealed an interesting detail: the network that aired the show would not let them kill off Dexter. "Showtime was very clear about that," the writer revealed. "They just said, 'Just to be clear, he's going to live.'"[22] How much might our understanding of this series have changed if the network hadn't made that demand? Perhaps Dexter's fate would have been the same as it eventually turned out to be, but the comments from this writer show how the process of making TV—what the network wants, which writers are in charge, and who is in the room—gives shape not only to how the story is told but also to its ultimate "end."

In contrast to Dexter, one character who *did* suffer for his wrongdoings was *Boardwalk Empire*'s Nucky Thompson. Nucky was a Prohibition-era gangster who ruled Atlantic City. Like Tony Soprano, he murdered people when he felt he had to and also tried to balance these activities with some semblance of a family life. He makes his basic approach to life clear while committing one particularly personal killing: he tells the victim, his former protégé, "I'm not seeking forgiveness."[23] At various times after that in the series, although still not seeking to justify his actions or seek forgiveness, Nucky does seem to question his life choices as he becomes more isolated from the people he loves.

Boardwalk Empire's finale reveals the series to have been one of those aforementioned morality tales, somewhat Shakespearean in its scope. In the last scene, Nucky is killed by the son of the former protégé whom he had himself killed (and the killer was also the grandson of a woman Nucky had led into a life of prostitution). It was as if the things Nucky had done in the past had come back to haunt him—repaying evil with more evil. There was no mercy involved, but it certainly felt like justice.

In light of the *Boardwalk Empire* finale, it would seem that Nucky got what he deserved, even though it is presented as a tragedy. There is a karma-like feel to the way the series comes to a close. The last image—as Nucky lies dying on the boardwalk that he had come to rule—recalls his days as a child. Previously in the episode, Nucky had told another character about the dangers of always wanting more. Nucky talked of his childhood days working as a porter at a boardwalk hotel: "The first time I got a nickel tip, I thought the world is great. . . . But a dime would be better. And then I wanted a quarter."[24] As the episode concludes, the dying Nucky reaches out with his last ounce of strength while the young Nucky dives for coins that tourists have tossed into the sea. He grabs a nickel, and the series ends.

This poignant memory in no way justifies the gangster's later-in-life evil deeds, but it calls for a level of understanding and empathy regarding the man that Nucky eventually became. It urges us to re-view the entire series from a different point of view.

The Afterlife: The End . . . Just Kidding!

Twin Peaks premiered on April 8, 1990, and its last episode aired a little more than a year later. Only thirty episodes were produced, yet it is consistently regarded as one of the best TV shows of all time—and one of the most enigmatic. The series was based around a mystery ("Who killed Laura Palmer?") and hinted that the answer might involve supernatural forces. The final scene of the last episode of season 2, which featured one of the main characters seemingly possessed by the spirit of another, left fans intrigued but perplexed. After this **wrap-up** to the season, producers announced that there would not be a third season, which meant that all the questions that the series had created—and, in a broader sense, the meaning of the entire series—were left frustratingly unanswered.[25]

Surprisingly, though, one month after the series was canceled, a *Twin Peaks* movie was announced. *Fire Walk with Me* appeared in theaters less than a year later, featuring many of the same characters as the television series. But it was more of a prequel than a sequel (the story involved the investigation of a murder that was related to that of Laura Palmer and also examined the last seven days of Laura's life) and only shed small slivers of light on the questions left hanging at the end of the series. Like the series itself, the fate of the main characters would remain forever unknown.

But wait, there's more. In the fall of 2014, Showtime announced that a new season of *Twin Peaks* would be airing in 2016. The show's original creators (Mark Frost and David Lynch) had agreed to write and produce the episodes, which will take place twenty-five years after the original series. Whether this third-season **resurrection**[26] of *Twin Peaks* answers lingering questions or makes anything about its narrative clearer remains to be seen, but the life of *Twin Peaks'* story-world—as a canceled series, then a movie, then a series again—highlights the complications of trying to unpack the power and meaning of a television series before the last part of the story has been told, because sometimes that last part might not even be written until years later. And even after it is told, there might still be more to the story.[27]

No one would argue that the quality of the 1960s sitcom *Gilligan's Island* was in any way equal to *Twin Peaks*, but the show about the passengers on the SS *Minnow* similarly showed how there's TV life after cancellation—and also shows how that "series afterlife" can affect or alter the meaning of a series.

Gilligan's Island premiered in 1964 and followed the lives of "seven stranded castaways" who were shipwrecked on a desert island (not at all like the island of *Lost*; there were no smoke monsters or mysterious "others" here, although there were the occasional Russian cosmonauts and Beatles-like rock bands). Nearly each episode presented what seemed to be an exercise in futility: the castaways looked like they might get rescued, but something would go wrong (it was usually Gilligan's fault) and they remained stranded. Their struggle was almost Sisyphean. No matter what they did, they ended up right back where they started. And when the series **concluded** in 1967, they were no closer to being rescued than when they were first shipwrecked.[28]

The show became quite successful in syndication, airing more than once a day in some cities. This further reinforced the idea that Gilligan and the rest were perpetually stuck on, and trying to get off, their desert island. So any construal of the show would have to take into account the castaways' fruitless attempts to leave the island on which they had built their seven-person society.

But there were more adventures to come. In 1978, the TV movie *Rescue from Gilligan's Island* depicted exactly what its title suggests. So their journey had not been fruitless, except that, at the end of *that* movie, they became stranded once again—on the same island. They were rescued once again at the beginning of 1979's *The Castaways on Gilligan's Island* (they turned the island into a resort in that movie) and experienced even more island life in 1981's *The Harlem Globetrotters on Gilligan's Island*.[29]

Of course, these films don't entirely undo all that came before them, but they do create a different experience for those watching reruns of the show who know that the castaways were eventually rescued rather than being left wondering if they remained on that island forever.

Carrie Bradshaw and her friends lived on a different island—Manhattan—and shared their stories on *Sex and the City*. The show was both praised and criticized for its portrayal of four women who seemed to delight in talking openly and explicitly about their sexual encounters (when they weren't talking about their new shoes). None of the women wanted to be defined by the men they were with, and none of them was in any hurry to settle down. The series seemed to promote female independence (whether sexual, economic, or relational), and its final episode did little to change the fact that many of its ninety-four episodes could easily be described as advertisements for this kind of approach to life and the world.

The series finale aired in 2004, but it was followed by a feature film in 2008 and another in 2010. In the first movie, all four women are practicing monogamy. Two are married and one is about to be, with the fourth in a committed relationship (though she breaks it off near the end of the movie). In the second film, three of the women are still married, and—though not quite experiencing wedded bliss—seem to have found satisfaction with only one man apiece.

Whether the writer of the movies meant to or not, the most recent "episodes" of the series (whether the 2010 film serves as the series "finale" is yet to be determined, as there might be more movies to come) cast a new light on the six years of episodes that came before it. These women who had expressed very little interest in settling down had mostly settled down and—their life choices speaking volumes—seemed to be saying that they preferred life with one sexual partner to the lives they had once lived with many. It was a long (and MA-rated) journey to get there, but could it be that the entire series was a journey toward understanding and promoting the value of marriage? That a life of promiscuity is ultimately unsatisfying, no matter how many shoes you collect along the way? It is doubtful that large numbers of viewers will sit through the entire series simply because they know that *Sex and the City* makes a strong case for marriage, but that's the aisle down which the women eventually walk. And if the early episodes in the series are any indication, it's safe to say that Carrie and her friends also had no idea where they were going until they got there.

And what about other shows that weren't over until they were over—and *still* might not be over? *Arrested Development* was canceled in 2006 but got an additional season eight years later, although it was unclear after the initial **cessation** whether the series would ever be resurrected.[30] *Firefly* lasted only one season, but a feature film was produced two years after that. And the characters in *Boy Meets World* returned in the series *Girl Meets World*, continuing their story nearly fifteen years after their TV lives had seemingly ended. In other words, a series' final episode may or may not actually be final. There might always be more scenes to come.

Of course, no discussion about the possibility of seemingly-gone-forever shows would be complete without mentioning the character of John Munch. As played by Richard Belzer, Detective Munch was a regular character for the entire 122-episode run of *Homicide: Life on the Street* and also appeared in the series-ending TV movie, *Homicide: The Movie* in 2000. But during that time he also appeared as the same character in crossover episodes of *Law and Order*, an episode of *The X-Files*, and an episode of the short-lived *The Beat*. After *Homicide* ended, the character continued to appear—on shows ranging from *Arrested Development* to *The Wire*, and (most notably) *Law and Order: SVU*, where the character that had begun on *Homicide: Life on the Street* continued for another fifteen seasons. It's impossible to say if we've seen the last of John Munch, which means we can't fully close the book on the show in which he first appeared. It is doubtful that his journey will end with him staring into a snow globe or waking up in bed with Suzanne Pleshette. Nevertheless, his story has a life . . . after life.

Goodbye, Farewell, and Amen

The above categorization of finales is not meant to be in any way complete. How can it be, with so many different kinds of shows that have aired throughout the history of television? One could easily list subcategories for the ones listed. Some shows veer from "they lived happily ever after" to "they moved on to different and/or better things." *The Mary Tyler Moore Show* ended with all the coworkers being fired (except for anchor Ted Baxter), but each of the characters remained optimistic about his or her future, with a few implied "even greener pastures" for them on the horizon.[31] The last episode of *Friday Night Lights* had Tim and Tami Taylor (he had been the high school football coach around which the show revolved; she the school guidance counselor) moving to a new city, where she starts a prestigious new job and he takes over a struggling high school football team. And the final episode of *Smallville* shows the no-longer-a-teen Clark Kent living in Metropolis, ready to embrace his role as Superman.

Both *Smallville* and *Bates Motel* are in a different sort of category altogether, along with *Gotham* and the early 1990s series *The Young Indiana Jones Chronicles*. Those shows all fall into a category that might be called "prequel television." The audience knows how the story is going to end—Norman is going to murder Marion Crane in the shower; Indiana Jones is going to grow up and find the ark of the covenant. But just because the ending is known doesn't mean audiences aren't ready and willing to take the journey that gets them there. For these kinds of shows, it's the "getting them there" that partly sustains the audience's interest, sometimes for years. *Smallville*, for example, ran for ten seasons.

Even the way in which the TV industry approaches series finales serves to underscore the ongoing, episodic nature of television storytelling. During the height of TV's broadcast era, series finales for highly rated shows like *M*A*S*H* functioned as ready-made cultural events. Over 100 million viewers tuned in to say good-bye to Hawkeye, Major Houlihan, and Klinger.[32] The title of the episode—"Goodbye, Farewell, and Amen"—even invoked a theological referent.[33]

But the *M*A*S*H* finale was not driven by some climactic moment of crisis within the arc of the story. It portrayed a climactic *event*—the end of the Korean War—and there were various moments of closure for some of the relationships, but this series finale very clearly presented a point at which these stories were no longer going to be told. The members of the 4077th were not going to be in the cross fire forever. The war was over; they were going home.

A twist on that phrase—"They're still at home, but the war goes on"—could easily describe the ending of *Everybody Loves Raymond* (which was on the air for nine years, compared to *M*A*S*H*'s eleven). The *Raymond* finale gave viewers no indication that Ray Barone's family had suddenly resolved their dysfunctions. If anything, years after the pilot episode, they were the same group of people dealing with the same series of problems. Instead of bringing a sense of finality to this family's story, the finale simply celebrated their awkward yet endearing journey and marked the moment when the audience would no longer

Principal cast members of CBS's *Everybody Loves Raymond* on the set at the series finale

be granted access to the show's narrative world.[34] This "curtain call" allowed viewers one last opportunity to commiserate with the Barones and acknowledge that the story of this dysfunctional family would continue to be told not only in syndication and online streaming but also through the daily escapades of their own dysfunctional families.

Both the *M*A*S*H* and *Raymond* examples suggest that, at least for some shows, episodic storytelling can be more about the journey than the destination. Although "what happens" to characters and how they subsequently respond is important, the primary focus of certain kinds of TV storytelling is the process rather than the plot. Yet even when a TV series is highly "serialized" (e.g., *24*, *Breaking Bad*, *Grey's Anatomy*, *Game of Thrones*), the primary question that concerns both critics and everyday viewers is whether the finale actually offers a "satisfying" conclusion to the story. Part of the reason why people engage in spirited conversations about TV finales is related to the enjoyment they derive from negotiating meaning with a larger community of passionate viewers. But this dialogue is only made possible by the particular way in which TV stories are told. These conversations about whether a finale "worked" are not always (exclusively) about the plot or the ending but rather about whether the events in the final episode offer an appropriate conclusion to the entire journey—a way to say "farewell" to the characters whom viewers have come to know and love (for it's never actually "good-bye" when one can revisit a show again and again). And because television stories unfold over the course of many seasons, their power and meaning cannot be reduced to any single episode—including the last one, even though it can carry special significance. Rather, meaning accumulates over time. Thus, just as it is with life, it is difficult to bring a story to a close in a way that is fitting for all that preceded it, for our stories are always greater than the sum of their parts.

If TV's episodic form does more fully reflect our lived experiences in this way, then any attempt to engage television theologically must take into consideration the medium-specific ways in which television tells its stories. This is no easy task for contemporary Christian theology. To be sure, the recent emergence of "narrative theology" has brought about a much-needed critique of the arid and abstract theologies that took shape in the Western, post-Enlightenment context.[35] But this move toward a more narrative approach to theology allows little room for understanding stories that are fundamentally episodic in nature. There is of course a bit of irony here, for in an important sense the Christian story is inherently teleological. It has a clear and discernible end. Indeed, the prominence of this story in Western culture is partly the reason that contemporary TV writers and TV audiences continue to conceive of narrative "ends" in the way they do. However, the end to which the entire Christian narrative is being drawn is in fact the renewal of the original created order—that which God unequivocally called "very good" in the beginning (Gen. 1). So a paradox is embedded within the tradition itself regarding the intrinsic value (i.e., the goodness, truth, and/or beauty) of individual episodes that may or may not make any reference to the story's final consummation. Rather than favor either side of this paradox, arguing for creation's inherent goodness, on the one hand, or the eventual renewal of that creation, on the other, our goal throughout the remainder of the book is to construct a theology of television that holds them both in a fruitful tension.

The tendency within modern Christian theology, especially its Protestant expressions, has been to emphasize the end of the Christian story's narrative arc at the expense of its individual segments—which would be like watching Walter White's death over and over again without considering what happened during his life. Such an emphasis leads to a theology where humanity's immediate, on-the-ground experiences are found to be meaningful only in relation to a larger narrative trajectory (that is, leading to one's ultimate restoration). But this (over)emphasis on God's final saving work overlooks and even devalues significant segments of the tradition's own story, such as the wisdom found in Proverbs, Ecclesiastes, and Song of Solomon—unique episodes that are not concerned with bringing the larger narrative to any kind of climax or resolution. Those writings could be considered "stand-alone" episodes, the same term used for television episodes that don't serve to advance the overarching story of a series. But the Bible would be woefully incomplete without them. And in the same way that TV viewers tend to put so much (too much?) emphasis on how a series ends, theologians have often been guilty of reducing a years-long "episodic journey" (in other words, a human life lived day to day) down to the "series finale" (that is, the final state of God's redemptive project). As a consequence, Christian theology not only interprets its own story according to the ending that is to come but it also defines, understands, and limits the stories of others in much the same way.

Consider the following (made-up-for-this-purpose) series, and note how the ending affects everything that comes before it. Note, too, how an audience—especially a religious one—might respond to the series along the way, and how it might also react to its ending.

Imagine a television series about a character who personifies evil. He lies; he cheats; he kills. In addition to actually taking part in killings, he oversees an entire organization that kills under his command. And he's celebrated for every horrible act. He's racist, too, going after people not for what they have done but for who they are (or who they are not). He's a bit of a crime boss, seeking out those with whom he disagrees simply as a vendetta. And he's also a government official, using his position of power to do evil. He's worse than *House of Cards'* Frank Underwood, more murderous than *Dexter*, and more soulless than anyone on *The Sopranos* or *Boardwalk Empire*.

Now, imagine that this series goes on for years, adding up to more than a hundred episodes of hatred and violence and evil. And every year, Christian watchdog groups protest the series—for its violence, and (wait, did we mention this?) because the lead character is a religious figure. And not just a layman, but a leader in his church. He goes from houses of worship to the scenes of his crimes in the same episode. He praises God while killing fellow human beings.

And then the series finale happens, and throughout the episode he's doing more of the same, and maybe being extra evil, as if he's in a rush to finish what he started. And then in the last scene, he decides to take a trip, and his destination suggests a certain meaning for those who know the Story.

He's going to Damascus.

Perhaps the series ends there, or it continues for one more scene—on a road, where this character is blinded by a light, and he hears a voice calling his name.

Fade out.

End of series.

It is only in that final episode that viewers realize that this seasons-long episodic journey of sin and evil was a contemporary retelling of the life of Saul—everything that led up to his conversion. Suddenly, the series needs to be looked at in a completely different (pardon the pun) light. Those who protested the show would now be praising it. And those who had watched it would probably want to watch it again. They might even want to show it in their churches.

The point is that episodic storytelling has to be evaluated *both* in its entirety *and* according to its individual episodes. (An obvious parallel to that statement: "So does the Bible.") The life of King David does not end at his sin with Bathsheba, though an interesting TV series might. And an even more interesting series would *start* there. Likewise, it is only because of what happens on Easter Sunday that Good Friday is "Good" at all. Nevertheless, it is still vital that we learn to sit fully in the tension and seeming hopelessness and tragedy of Good Friday. The biblical witness contains numerous episodic stories about sinful men and women of God. These are the kind of people whose stories continue into another season. They are the kind of people who never knew where they were going until they got there, which might be a bit disconcerting for some readers. But as we all know, as long as Tommy Westphall is still staring into that snow globe, nobody's television story is complete.

5

a very brief history
of the church and tv

Like Sam and Diane (from *Cheers*), Ross and Rachel (from *Friends*), or Penny and Leonard (from *The Big Bang Theory*), television and the church have a history. Oh, and it's complicated. An on-again, off-again story that we did not start and most certainly will not bring to a close, it is nevertheless the one in which we presently find ourselves. And while we have to admit that the relationship between the church and TV is far less comedic than that of sitcom royalty (but no less melodramatic!), it is still important to understand how it has developed in order to locate our current exploration within a historical narrative and to remain conscious of (and self-critical about) the many ways in which the past both informs the present and shapes our future. With these two aims in mind, then, we want to consider in this chapter the various ways in which theologians, laypeople of faith, and the church as a whole have responded to and interacted with TV over the course of the medium's history. Much like a "clip-show" episode that features a montage of scenes from seasons past, this chapter takes a step back in order to provide a historical framework for the remainder of our discussion.

The story we want to tell begins with the advent of television technology, but its real origins lie in a far more distant past than the twentieth century. As early as the first century, the Christian community was already asking questions that concerned communication. By what means was the church to "go and make disciples of all the nations . . . teaching them to obey everything I have commanded you" (Matt. 28:19–20 NET)? It is for this reason that the biblical texts about the life, death, and resurrection of Jesus are known as "Gospels" (*euangelion*)—a word that originally denoted the "bearer of good tidings" who brought positive communications in the ancient world, and later simply meant the "good news" of the Jesus story, or even Jesus himself.[1] This story (or rather, collection of stories) was first communicated directly from person to person by word of mouth. But soon thereafter, the accounts of Jesus's life were organized and converted into written form, which allowed for the dissemination of these Gospel stories through indirect means as well.

In addition to the Gospel narratives, though, the teachings of the apostles also took on a form that was ideally suited for distribution along first-century communication channels. Paul in particular leveraged technological advancements such as the expansive Roman road system and media like the epistle to communicate with his growing network of individuals and churches. Biblical historian N. T. Wright has noted that the Pax Romana allowed Paul's gospel message to spread in unprecedented ways because the treachery of travel in the ancient world was essentially eliminated by the pervasive presence of the Roman army.[2] But Rome's extensive system of roads and sea routes gave rise to the possibility of transporting something other than just soldiers; it could carry information as well. It is thus no small wonder that the development and organization of reliable routes of travel also aided in the establishment of a regular postal system in the Roman world. Not only was travel a far more efficient and less dangerous endeavor than it had ever been before, but in terms of communication, nothing could beat the speed, ease, and low cost of sending a letter via courier along these same routes. In other words, to be a bit anachronistic, the Roman road system was the world's first information superhighway, and the church took full advantage of it for the sake of communicating its gospel story.

So from the church's very inception, an intimate relationship was established between the community of faith and the communication technologies of the day. And this relationship directly informs our consideration of the church and TV because, as we made clear in chapter 1, television is a communication technology before it is anything else. Some have even argued that it is possible to distinguish between the various Christian traditions and subdivisions in the United States (e.g., Roman Catholic, Protestant, mainline, and evangelical) according to the ways in which each of these religious communities has either avoided or made use of the medium of television.[3]

Our historical assessment takes as its point of departure this broader Christian tradition, but we focus the bulk of our attention on Protestant groups in the United States and, even more particularly, on evangelical Protestants. The reason for focusing on these particular groups has to do in part with the simple fact that space will not allow us to cover everything. Yet even if we could be comprehensive, the result would be a completely unmanageable pile of data, and it would ultimately work against our goal of comprehending the past in relationship to the present.[4]

Also, although we will certainly refer to numerous Christian traditions along the way, we decided to focus on Protestant evangelicals to recognize the unique historical connection that exists between the emergence of evangelicalism(s) in the United States and evangelicals' approach to mass communication in general.[5] As Michele Rosenthal has suggested, "The construction of evangelical identity . . . was closely related to evangelical negotiations with broadcast media—radio and then television."[6]

Historically speaking, then, evangelicals are an interesting group to focus on because they have often functioned as both ardent critics and champions of TV at one and the same time: "For sixty years, the most outspoken critics of American television have been Christian evangelicals. . . . American evangelicals have always been among the earliest adopters of new media, but their enthusiasm for innovative channels of communication has been limited to religious applications; their suspicion of mainstream media, particularly film and television, has been persistent and strong."[7]

Like a system of well-maintained roads that allowed for the delivery of letters to distant audiences, television became evangelicals' communications technology of choice for spreading the gospel message to the masses. And our telling of the story will suggest that, even while decrying a great deal of television programming, TV is now inextricably bound up with evangelical identity—for good and for ill.

Theological Approaches to TV

As we survey television's relatively brief history, we can observe a wide variety of theological responses to the medium. In the church's attempts to understand and/or influence television and televisual culture, the majority of these responses falls into one of five broad categories: avoidance, caution, dialogue, appropriation, and divine encounter. By organizing the history of theological responses in this way, we can identify some of the key differences and similarities that exist from one "type" to the next.

Robert Banks originally developed these categorizations, and Robert K. Johnston later expanded them in his book *Reel Spirituality*. Banks and Johnston are concerned primarily with film, but their typology actually helps us process the various ways in which the Christian church has responded to contemporary culture in general, whether it be television, literature, or any other cultural artifact. They plot these five types of theological responses along a continuum, noting that all five approaches have contemporary representatives (see figure 5.1).[8]

Figure 5.1 The Theologian/Critic's Posture

| Avoidance | Caution | Dialogue | Appropriation | Divine Encounter |

As with any typology, not everyone fits neatly within each category. Some theologians have adopted different perspectives over time, and others employ intentionally eclectic approaches. So these are artificial constructs that simply help us organize data. As such, they are more like motifs or themes than hardened types. However, what is most helpful for our consideration of TV is that Johnston graphs these approaches using a matrix to show "(1) whether a given theologian/critic begins his or her reflection with the [TV program] itself or with a theological position, and (2) whether a given response centers on the [show] more ethically or aesthetically" (see figure 5.2).[9] In other words, the starting point greatly affects both the direction and the destination of the journey.

Figure 5.2 The Theologian/Critic's Approach

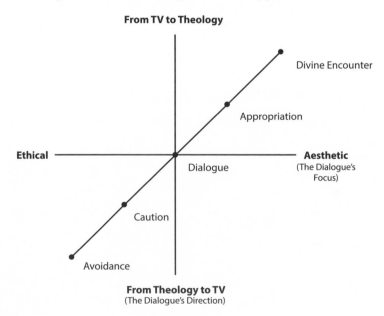

Depending upon the circumstances, each of these responses has its appropriate time and place. As we hope we have made clear by now, our approach toward the theology and TV dialogue begins with questions about the aesthetics of TV narratives, which somewhat naturally lends itself to a conversation that moves from TV to theology rather than the other way around. And while we favor this approach in general and therefore rarely advocate for complete avoidance of TV, we are not identifying these types in order to determine which ones are "better" or "worse." As will become clear in the chapter on ethics, lay and professional theologians can and should be cautious of certain TV content and TV viewing practices, even if that occasionally means encouraging Christians to embrace a posture of avoidance. Some kinds of television are simply not worth anyone's time and energy.

But as we survey the various approaches others have taken throughout history, we will continue to maintain that, for theology to remain actively engaged in dialogue with culture, we must allow TV to speak first by focusing on the aesthetic criteria it establishes in order to determine what the appropriate theological response should be. In many cases, questions of aesthetics lead to questions of ethics, but interestingly, the reverse is rarely true. We almost never get to a program's artistic merit when we begin with an assessment of its "morality" or "values." So the issue is not whether there is a place for avoidance in our theological engagement with TV. There certainly is. The question is rather how we understand the direction and focus of the dialogue. That is, what posture will we assume as we engage our televisual culture? Can we let television take the lead?

One significant difference between the historical development of the church's response to film and its response to television is that, when it comes to TV, these categories did not emerge chronologically. Indeed, all five approaches have existed since the advent of TV technology, at least in the US context. This can be explained in part by the fact that the church had already developed some basic theological responses to other forms of media such as film, so there were well-worn paths already in place by the time TV came along. Also, the time in which television was first introduced to the public (1930s and 1940s) coincided with a time of great upheaval and redefinition within US Protestantism. Television was therefore something more than just another form of electronic media to which the church had to respond; it became a site for the negotiation of Protestant identity in America. And this great diversity of thought regarding how American Christians ought to relate to culture is reflected in the equally variegated approaches that currently exist within US Protestant traditions.

There is more to the story though. The history of the church's interaction with TV is unique because it features two parallel but distinct modes of engagement with the medium (see figure 5.3).

Figure 5.3 The Theologian/Critic's Approach: Technology and Content

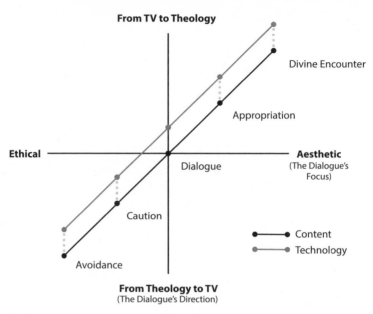

The first is concerned primarily with television *programming*—the content that is broadcast by mainstream media producers. The second is concerned with television *technology*—the instrument by which TV programming is delivered. In some cases, those who strongly advocate for an avoidance strategy regarding TV content are the very same people who consider TV technology to be an ideal medium for broadcasting a divine encounter—as long as the content aligns with certain theological norms. Similarly, those who believe that some TV programs have the potential to mediate a kind of divine encounter to the viewer are rather cautious about the ways in which TV technology shapes all its messages, religious or otherwise.

As it concerns the church's response to TV, the reality is that very little has changed over the past seventy years. To be sure, some individuals and groups have adopted different strategies and thus shifted categories over time, but even this fluidity serves to underscore the enduring nature of these five approaches. So in order to bring some clarity to our historical situation, we want to consider each of the five types along two distinct but overlapping trajectories—one that charts the church's response to TV technology and the other describing its response to TV content.

Avoidance

Avoiding TV Technology

Television broadcasting practices in the United States were originally based upon a model borrowed from radio.[10] Just as they were required to do with radio broadcasts, networks dedicated a certain percentage of airtime to religious programming in order to meet their "public service" obligations for FCC license renewal. As the self-designated representatives of America's majority faith, mainline Protestant groups such as the Broadcast and Film Commission (BFC) of the National Council of Churches formed a mutually beneficial partnership with TV networks in order to produce content that reinforced Protestant American culture. However, as the fates would have it, this endeavor just so happened to take place during a time when the hegemony of the Protestant church in the United States was increasingly being called into question. Especially during the years leading up to and immediately following World War II (i.e., the 1930s and 1940s), efforts to reform and shape cultural life according to mainline Protestant norms could no longer be maintained. Also, the uneasiness that mainline churchgoers felt toward commercial and popular forms of culture highlighted the reality that many within these denominations equated Protestant American culture with "high culture." Regardless of how well produced or theologically sophisticated television content was, it was seen as simply too lowbrow to do anything but stand in the way of the Protestant vision for American culture.

However, because the common assumption was that television would be highly effective at shaping public opinion, it was difficult to build a case for why the church should not be in the business of producing TV content. As one of the leading voices in the BFC put it, "I think we have to be in television simply because there is television."[11] At the time, it appeared that the only thing that could effectively counteract the degradation of culture brought about by commercial television was the broadcasting of equally high-minded content produced by the caretakers of modern society.

It was not long before a number of social-scientific studies began to suggest that television exerted far less influence over its audience than had originally been imagined. Suddenly, TV's greatest strength—its capacity to "evangelize" (i.e., to shape people into cultural Protestants)—was eliminated, which meant that it could no longer be seen as an effective tool for maintaining a culturally Christian America. Along with their broader concerns about commercial culture subverting the Christian ethos, this newfound awareness regarding TV's incapacities caused mainline Protestants to significantly withdraw from their engagement with TV. They were still interested in maintaining cultural prominence, but rather than doing so by producing TV content, they assumed the position of cultural critic, denouncing lowbrow productions and (somewhat begrudgingly) advocating for the kind of middlebrow culture we now find on PBS.[12]

In other words, from the perspective of groups like the BFC, the best advice they could give to the American public was simply to turn their TVs off. At its core, this admonition to avoid TV was directed toward the technology itself; it was only somewhat related to the particular programs that were seen as trivial or morally bankrupt. A similar kind of response can be identified in the works of numerous Christian critics over the ensuing decades. Although the specifics of their critiques bear the markings of the televisual culture of their time, the common reason for their strategy of avoidance was the belief that television technology communicated lies. Writing in the 1960s from the core of his Christian convictions, Jacques Ellul conceived of technological society (*La technique*) as concerned above all else with efficiency and utility. As such, it could not help turning human beings into machines.[13] For Ellul, it was mass media such as TV that formed the essential link between individuals and the inhumane demands of this technological society.

Following a trajectory similar to Ellul's, Malcolm Muggeridge was equally suspicious of television technology and warned against its inherent evils. In his book *Christ and the Media* (1977), Muggeridge suggested that the central problem with television was not that it consumed too much of the audience's time and attention (although he thought that it did) but that it fundamentally distorted reality. Television is a technology that traffics in illusions. If Jesus had lived in the modern world, imagines Muggeridge, his "fourth temptation" would have been the offer of a worldwide TV network.[14] Writing only a few years later, Virginia Stem Owens echoed the need to avoid such technological temptation on theological grounds when she published *The Total Image: Or Selling Jesus in the Modern Age*.[15]

All told, these critics represent one historical trajectory of theologically motivated responses to TV technology. It's not that they were indifferent to the kind of content that TV conveyed. Rather, their bigger concern was that the battle has already been lost the moment a viewer sits in front of the television screen. No matter the content, the overwhelming visual appeal of television has already been given the opportunity to work its magic, bombarding viewers with images that transform them into mindless "videots" incapable of discerning "what, when, and how much to watch."[16] And while there are presently very few theologians or critics who are calling for Christians to avoid communications technology altogether, these voices from the past still cast a significant shadow over the ways in which the church currently approaches TV technology.[17] It has become nearly impossible to completely avoid mediated technology in the twenty-first century. Nevertheless, this deep-rooted suspicion of technology's "power" still looms large.

Avoiding TV Content

The decision for some within the church to avoid television technology never really generated enough interest to make the nightly news. The same cannot be said of those who have adopted an avoidance strategy toward television content, in part because their approach has also involved compelling others to do the same—often loudly and publicly. In a kind of inversion of the mainline Protestant desire to shape public life according to Protestant norms, some evangelical Protestants have attempted to influence content producers to create television programming that aligns with their conservative evangelical values. This type of approach generally begins with a ready-made theological framework and focuses almost exclusively on questions of morality rather than aesthetics (see figure 5.2). But it also assumes that the church's primary public role is to bring culture into alignment with certain Christian norms. The result has been an active rather than passive form of avoidance, epitomized by the various boycotts Christian groups have organized around specific TV programs and the producers of that content.

Individual activists of this kind can be found during the early days of TV history, but it was not until the late 1970s, when evangelical leaders became uneasy bedfellows with conservative Republican politics, that avoiding TV content became an organized and concerted effort. As members of the newly designated "Moral Majority," some evangelical leaders approached televisual media as if it were one of the greatest contributors to the moral decline of American culture. Indeed, a handful of very public "battles" took place between evangelical leaders and the major networks over seemingly innocuous television shows. For example, Dan Quayle received overwhelming support from his evangelical constituency (and an equal amount of criticism from his detractors) when he accused Murphy Brown, a TV character, of "glamorizing" single motherhood and thus undermining the family values of conservative Christianity. Almost overnight, the front lines of the so-called culture wars landed right in the middle of the American living room.

Founded in 1977 by Donald Wildmon, the American Family Association (AFA) led the charge in organizing numerous boycotts of television sponsors.[18] In the 1980s, their ire was directed toward *Saturday Night Live*, while in the

1990s it was *NYPD Blue*, both of which, according to the AFA, demonstrated TV's propensity for depicting excessive acts of violence, profanity, and sexuality.[19] In 1998, leaders of the Southern Baptist Convention made a similar move by urging every Southern Baptist to avoid any media content produced by the Disney Company. Richard Land's book *Send a Message to Mickey* attempts to provide a rationale for this decision. According to Land, regardless of whether a particular program on ABC or ESPN (Disney-owned subsidiaries) contained questionable content itself, Christians were to boycott Disney as a whole because of its increasing promotion of "immoral ideologies such as homosexuality, infidelity, and adultery, which are biblically reprehensible and abhorrent to God and His plan for the world that He loves."[20] More recently, One Million Moms, a division of AFA, has called for boycotts of companies sponsoring shows like *Black Jesus*, *The New Normal*, *How to Get Away with Murder*, and *2 Broke Girls*. In almost every case, the sole criterion for justifying these boycotts is content, whether violent, sexual, or sacrilegious.

Formal boycotts are rather overt examples of an avoidance strategy. They represent but one of the ways in which the church has responded to television. Because a boycott hinges upon a small group creating the loudest possible clamor, this form of avoidance tends to grab the headlines. However, more often than not, evangelical Christians have historically avoided TV content by simply choosing not to watch programs that are believed to be "immoral," "offensive," or run counter to "family values."[21] In fact, numerous evangelical media outlets such as Focus on the Family's *Plugged-In* were created to help individuals, churches, and families make informed decisions about what TV content to avoid. And while this is a far more selective (and less vocal) kind of response than an organized boycott or a public denouncement, it nevertheless exemplifies a common theme that has run throughout the history of the church's engagement with TV, especially among those who self-identify as evangelicals. That is, much like their mainline counterparts, many within evangelical circles have routinely responded to television not through letter-writing campaigns or public demonstrations but by simply changing the channel.[22]

Caution

Caution and Technology

Perhaps because of the presence of television in the home, avoidance has proven the exception rather than the rule. A more common approach has been to engage televisual media with a moderate degree of caution. Although the five types we are using to classify the church's theological responses to TV give the impression that these categories are clearly distinct, the historical reality is far more complex and muddied. For instance, those who demonstrate a cautious approach at times have a tendency to lean toward a strategy of avoidance, but it is also true that some theologians and Christian critics who are cautious about TV are more open to a constructive dialogue. A historical perspective is helpful here because it allows us to see the ways in which, over time, the church has made some significant (although subtle) shifts in its approach, even among those whose primary response can still be categorized as "cautious."

In what is now a rather well-known and somewhat polarizing text, *Amusing Ourselves to Death: Public Discourse in the Age of Show Business*, Neil Postman offers a pointed critique of the culture created by television technology. Writing as a Christian but addressing citizens of democratic society as a whole, Postman exemplifies a cautious approach toward TV technology—one that appears at times to be suggesting avoidance. Following Marshall McLuhan, Postman suggests that "to maintain that technology is neutral, to make the assumption that technology is always a friend to culture is, at this late hour, stupidity plain and simple."[23] Postman's misgivings about TV technology are not so much about the trivial or frivolous content it communicates. For example, *The A-Team* and *Cheers* are, in his mind, nonthreatening. Rather, he is concerned with the ways in which that same technology co-opts serious public discourse and transforms it into "mere entertainment." Thus, *60 Minutes*, *Sesame Street*, and the local *Eyewitness News* are all threats to public health, for in the hands of TV technology, news, politics, science, commerce, and religion are packaged and sold simply for our amusement.[24]

It is hard to argue with certain elements of Postman's critique—especially as it concerns for-profit news media and how they contribute to the current state of political discourse in the United States. Writing in the mid-1980s, he rightly predicted what can happen when journalism and politics are measured purely in terms of their entertainment value. But Postman frames his concerns about TV technology so starkly that we are left with few options other than to avoid television entirely. He does point out that it would be "ludicrous" to assume the position of the straight Luddite given the centrality of television technology in American life and culture. But his argument for approaching television technology with caution concedes so much influence and power to television technology and the entertainment culture it mediates that it leaves viewers with little reason to be hopeful about its possibilities, much less take the risk of actually watching it. Postman himself admits that the only way Americans might gain some measure of control over the medium is to demystify and demythologize it, and this will take place only if schools begin to teach students how to put themselves at a critical distance from their information technology.

Of course, for Postman, this is to ask something of the school system that it is hardly capable of doing. Once again, his caution in theory seems to suggest avoidance in practice.

Caution and Content

If all of this sounds like bad news, that's because it is, at least for Postman. But the good news is that some things have changed in the thirty years since he first penned the words to his book. And one of the most significant changes concerns the way that the church demonstrates a cautious approach not only toward TV technology but also TV content. A contemporary of Postman's, William Fore, was equally concerned about the ill effects of TV technology on American culture and religion. Writing in the late 1980s, Fore suggested that television had usurped the role that traditional religion once played in society and thus shifted the center of American culture from religion to technology.[25] Much like Postman, he called for the church to be cautious in its approach to TV technology. Fore went one step further, however, and suggested that TV's core content was also antithetical to the Christian faith. According to Fore, TV narratives communicate myths that tell us what the world is like, how it works, and what it means. Because these myths operate with a worldview in which consumption is inherently good, and material acquisition leads to happiness, they function in diametric opposition to Christianity. Thus, in Fore's mind, Christians should develop critical attitudes toward television viewing because the very act of engaging TV critically allows them to be something that TV does not encourage: active participants rather than passive receivers. This critical engagement encourages viewers to watch, discuss, and evaluate TV, but equally as often, it leads them to "just plain leave it alone."[26] As such, Fore exemplifies a cautious approach but, like Postman, one that is inclined toward avoidance.

In more recent years, a number of church leaders and Christian critics have embraced Postman's and Fore's cautious attitudes toward TV, but their tendency has been to lean away from rather than toward avoidance. Jeff Wright, president of Urban Ministries Inc. (a leading publisher of resources targeted toward African American churches), developed a book-length study to help congregants consider their TV consumption from a Christian perspective.[27] In *God's Vision or Television*, Wright is cautious about television primarily because of its questionable moral content (e.g., he lists the Super Bowl, *Sex and the City*, and *Friends* as exemplars of TV's moral bankruptcy), but also because it communicates the message that money is the chief aim of human life. Even with his reservations, though, Wright created and published these church resources not to preach avoidance of TV but to involve churchgoers in a form of engaged criticism. So his is a cautious approach that nevertheless seeks engagement rather than complete withdrawal.

Robert Woods and Paul Patton offer an interesting parallel to Wright. Analyzing TV from a media studies perspective, they explicitly connect their approach to the prophetic tradition of the Hebrew Bible.[28] Borrowing from the work of Abraham Heschel and Walter Brueggemann, Woods and Patton seek to offer a "prophetic critique" of the "dominant consciousness" embodied by televisual media. Put differently, they urge the Christian community not to avoid TV per se but to constructively critique the ethos of North American culture through its engagement with TV, which, according to them, is defined by consumerism.

This approach is not entirely unlike Postman's or Fore's, especially in its criticism of consumerism. But one of the historical shifts Woods and Patton represent is the recognition that the church's response to TV must involve an awareness of both content and technology. As a result, their form of caution lends itself more toward the dialogue side of the continuum than the avoidance side. To be sure, they remain fundamentally suspicious of TV's inherent "values"—its elevation of personality over propositions (e.g., televangelists like Joel Osteen and T. D. Jakes), its disconnection from a larger historical context (e.g., *Little House on the Prairie*; *Dr. Quinn, Medicine Woman*; and *Mad Men*), and its propensity to tell stories that "lead nowhere" (e.g., *All in the Family* and *Seinfeld*).[29] However, they are also able to affirm those instances when TV content runs counter to its technological "biases"—when its stories wrestle honestly with the complexity of human life (e.g., *The Shield*, *The Closer*, and *Desperate Housewives*), confront ultimate human problems (e.g., *M*A*S*H*), and invoke ties between humanity's past and present (e.g., *Holocaust* and *Band of Brothers*).[30] Much like Wright, Woods and Patton still proceed with caution regarding TV's ideological work (especially when it goes unnoticed), but their response is different from their predecessors' in that they are willing to be "cautiously optimistic."

Dialogue

Dialogue and Technology

We noted earlier that, distinct from the ways in which the church developed its response to movies over time, the various approaches we are discussing here have all existed in some form since the advent of TV technology. So the historical shifts that have taken place generally represent the movement of individuals from one category to the next or a slight change in posture among those in a given category (e.g., from "cautious pessimism" to "cautious optimism").

One possible explanation for this phenomenon involves the variety of starting points that are used by lay and professional theologians in their critical engagement with television. Various groups within the church have different concerns regarding the production, distribution, and reception of TV, so they each begin with a different set of critical questions. These guiding questions establish both the limits and the possibilities of our engagement. And while this critical dialogue can begin anywhere along the continuum (i.e., anywhere from avoidance to divine encounter [figure 2.1]), we have been suggesting that the Christian community must first be willing to take TV on its own terms before it "theologizes" about television—to listen before it speaks.

It is interesting to note here that throughout the medium's short history, many of those who have approached the relationship between the church and TV as a "dialogue" have generally done so for deeply theological reasons. For example, adapting some of Marshall McLuhan's work, Walter Ong has suggested that, much like the transition from oral culture to literate culture that was brought about by the printing press, televisual technology has transformed the contemporary imagination.[31] For Ong, electronic media such as TV have returned to prominence the aural nature of communication that was once prevalent in oral culture, but without displacing the visual.[32] As a result, the contemporary consciousness is a fundamentally audiovisual sensibility, one in which we neither just see, nor simply hear, but do something altogether different: we now see/hear and hear/see the world in which we live. In other words, along with all our theorizing about the images we see and our analyzing of the words we read, we are always already feeling/sensing/intuiting the sounds we hear.

Significantly, Ong frames TV technology (and all communication technologies for that matter) in explicitly theological terms. He points to the spoken word as the primary point of reference for understanding the Word of God as a revelatory word. Just as TV is meaningful because it encounters the viewer as something more than a collection of disparate images or static text on a screen, so too God speaks in a form that humans can experience. To contemporary persons whose basic awareness of the world is structured by an audiovisual landscape, God speaks. The Word is not a written text; it is a living utterance, a bringing forth of sound. It is a sensory experience that can only be communicated in physical, embodied ways. Thus, in Ong's view, God discloses Godself by inviting us into a dialogue that engages our audiovisual imagination, a conversation that is not closed and static but open and dynamic.[33]

From this perspective, television is more than simply a technology that shapes the contemporary imagination; it also mediates the Word of God to us through pictures and sounds. As such, according to Ong, both lay and professional theologians ought to engage in dialogue with this medium not only because it has the capacity to help us understand more about the contemporary imagination but also because it has the potential for telling us something about who this Word is that chooses to speak. And our engagement is fundamentally dialogical because it begins with audio-viewers granting epistemological priority to the multisensory experience of hear-seeing TV. That is, whether conversing with a word or the Word, an approach of this kind lets the other speak first—in some cases, literally.[34] Rather than judging TV from a predetermined theological norm, it is only after listening—and listening well—that the church speaks into the conversation.

Dialogue and Content

A number of theologians and church leaders have recently voiced a similar approach to that of Ong and McLuhan by focusing on both the formative nature of TV technology and the narrative content it conveys. For example, pastor and author J. E. Eubanks points out a significant shift in the use of violence and gore in *CSI: Crime Scene Investigation*, a show that features what was once a unique visual aesthetic made possible by digital technologies.[35] Unlike those who fall into the category of caution, Eubanks does not begin with a ready-made ethic in hand. Instead, he locates his analysis firmly within the parameters established by the series itself, noting in particular the ways it developed over the course of its fifteen-year run. According to Eubanks, whereas the show once used graphic images of violence to evoke horror, it now functions simply to incite terror. It is important to point out that he still lands on a critical note here. However, he offers this critique by taking the show on its own terms rather than basing it upon some foreign or abstracted criteria. Citing TV critic Matt Zoller Seitz of *Vulture* magazine, he calls out the formal distinction between horror and terror: "'The terms are often used interchangeably, but I wish they wouldn't be. Where horror is driven by psychology and philosophy and sometimes theology, terror is driven by fear of violence, period.'. . . Why, one might ask, would CBS allow (or even encourage?) one of its anchor shows to devolve in this way? Seitz suggests the answer to that, as well: 'CBS is in the fear business. Terror is one of their most reliable profit centers.'"[36]

What Eubanks provides is a theological engagement that ultimately questions the ethics of the show's use of graphic violence, but only after letting *CSI* speak first. And this is the fruit that is born from a posture of dialogue. Engaging in theological dialogue with TV does not mean the absence of critical conversations—quite the opposite. In the case of *CSI*, it opens us up to the real source of tension between the show and a Christian ethic. That is, it isn't the violence that should disturb us theologically; it's the uncreative storytelling.

This kind of dialogical approach helps not only to focus and rightly orient our theological criticism; it also shapes the church into a more credible conversation partner. For example, Shane Hipps (*Flickering Pixels*), Craig Detweiler (*iGods*), and Brent Laytham (*iPod, YouTube, Wii Play*) all interact with emerging media like television from the standpoint of a constructive dialogue.[37] Each assumes that digital technologies are actively shaping the humans who use them and thus shares some concerns about the ways this technology might be forming individuals and communities. But on the whole, they see the formative work of TV technology as rife with possibility, so they commit themselves to a give-and-take conversation with TV rather than a one-way monologue directed at TV. That is, instead of condemning television as morally problematic from the outset and judging it as a "success" or "failure" through a purely ethical lens, they present a compelling case for engaging in a mutually beneficial dialogue between the church and television, asking how we might both celebrate and critique the medium.

Craig Detweiler is one of the more gifted conversationalists when it comes to engaging film and TV stories theologically. His ability to engage in dialogue is not simply due to the fact that, unlike many others, he is a trained screenwriter, director, and theologian (although that certainly doesn't hurt). It's because his interaction with television begins by taking it on its own terms, thus allowing TV to determine the shape of the conversation. As his understanding of *The Wire* demonstrates, Detweiler also has a keen ability to discern the ways in which a show that contains few if any explicit theological or religious references is actually inviting viewers into a profoundly theological dialogue.

Unlike the cop shows and crime dramas that are typically featured on network television, *The Wire* is complex, ambiguous, and often unresolved. As such, "*The Wire* subverts the Western myth of good and evil."[38] For Detweiler, the subversive nature of the series allows it to function prophetically, chipping away at our casual indifference to the racial injustices that have come to mark urban life. "Like the biblical prophet Jeremiah, [it] seeks the welfare of the city, reminding us, 'When it prospers, you will prosper.'"[39] In other words, after listening—really listening—to the show's prophetic critique, Detweiler allows that critique to inform and enrich his theological reflection.

For some, the possibility that a TV story might shape one's theology is too much of a risk. But just as it is with any form of dialogue, unless we are willing to open ourselves up to our conversation partners—to take the risk of being affected, informed, and enriched by them—it is difficult for any real conversation to take place. As Detweiler's analysis of *The Wire* suggests, the goal of dialogue isn't about getting a point across or winning a debate about ethics. It's about mutual transformation: "I write about *The Wire* because it reminds me of my own commitment to lived religion. It assaults my indifference. If *The Wire* is merely studied or admired, we all lose. *The Wire* gnaws at our national conscience. It gets me off the couch and back into urban America. The characters on *The Wire* may not win the game, but they are committed to playing. Am I? Are we?"[40]

Detweiler's commitment to dialogue might be challenging for some, but it is by no means new. As early as 1950, Edward Carnell reflected upon the relationship between the church and television in his *Television: Servant or Master?*[41] Coming at TV from an explicitly theological perspective, Carnell could neither condemn TV nor unthinkingly praise it. Television was not wholly good or wholly bad but a "mixture" of both.[42] In fact, the real problem with TV was not TV at all but the flawed and disoriented humans who used the technology for destructive purposes.[43] Thus, in Carnell's estimation, "interpreting, directing, and understanding television is the responsibility of *this* generation."[44] Given television's seemingly limitless possibilities for both good and evil, the community of faith simply has no other option but to think theologically about this new medium in ways that neither view TV as too "worldly" nor encourage people to just "turn it off."[45] Much has changed in the world of television, the church, and the broader culture since 1950. Indeed, Carnell wrote at such an early stage in the development of TV that few shows even existed for him to analyze, much less engage theologically.[46] However, his basic approach toward television, which was dialogical to its core, established a key model for contemporary theologians and church leaders like Detweiler, Laytham, and Eubanks, who are operating in a context that is now overwhelmed by television content.[47] And in this way, Carnell turned out to be both influential and prescient.

Appropriation

Appropriation and Technology

As we move through the typology from dialogue to appropriation, another interesting inversion takes place. That is, those who are suspicious of TV content produced by major networks and therefore either avoid television altogether or assume a cautious approach toward TV are sometimes the very same people who willingly appropriate television technology in order to communicate the gospel. This inversion has existed throughout the history of the church's engagement with television, and it reveals a somewhat reduced understanding of what TV actually is and the world it creates. As we continue to see, then, little has changed over time because many of the same assumptions about TV programming and technology that were present in the early days of television are still in operation today. These commonly held assumptions are evident among both mainline and evangelical Protestants, but it is evangelicals who have been the most enthusiastic in their appropriation of TV technology.

We are using the term "appropriation" to describe those who believe television has the capacity to provide a transformative experience for the audience. Regardless of whether a program or series is intentionally or even explicitly making reference to religion or the Christian faith, it can realign, challenge, or broaden one's understanding of life, offering up greater possibilities for being human in an often-inhumane world. Historically speaking, evangelicals have been suspicious about these kinds of vaguely spiritual and often ill-defined experiences of transformation, especially when they occur outside the church and without reference to the gospel. In contrast, they have been far more comfortable with "direct communication—clear, concise, propositional, easily understood expressions of the Christian gospel, grounded in simple words."[48]

In spite of these general misgivings, evangelical broadcasters have been more than willing to appropriate the technology of TV, especially when delivering content designed to serve as an alternative to network programming. Indeed, as some have argued, "evangelicals love television. Scholars have suggested that perhaps there is a mythos that surrounds television—an overwhelming faith in television technology itself—that breeds this mindset."[49] This enthusiastic embrace of TV technology has been driven in part by the fact that TV's privileged position within the home grants content producers access to a domain that was once inaccessible to religious institutions. But it also traffics in various assumptions regarding the primary language of TV and how this medium-specific language affects an audience. Theorists like Quentin Schultze suggest that the inherent biases of television—its "immediacy" and "live-ness"—seek to establish an unparalleled depth of intimacy with its audience.[50] Thus, for anyone concerned with communicating the gospel story over and against other possible narratives, television is uniquely able to prepare the hearts of individual viewers for a genuinely transformative experience.

Programs such as Pat Robertson's *700 Club* have appropriated TV technology to deliver explicitly Christian content to the at-home audience. Perhaps best known in the broader culture for his unsuccessful bid for the US presidency, Robertson balked when journalists described him at the time as a "televangelist." He was much more comfortable with the title of "religious broadcaster." The distinction here is important to maintain because it highlights the primary difference between those who appropriate TV technology and those who see it as a form of divine encounter (our final category). To be sure, Robertson is in fact a broadcaster. He not only hosts his own TV and news program (*700 Club*), but he also founded the Christian Broadcasting Network (CBN) and CBN cable network, which became ABC Family Channel when he sold the company. But the primary reason Robertson does not envision himself as a "televangelist" is because his principal approach to television technology is that of appropriation—leveraging the medium of TV to deliver countercultural visions of human flourishing directly into the home.

In a similar vein, Ben Armstrong, in his book *The Electric Church*, goes so far as to claim that cable television would become "a revolutionary new form of the worshipping, witnessing church that existed twenty centuries ago."[51] Although writing in the late 1970s, his vision for appropriating TV technology reflects a trend within the history of the church's engagement with television that is as consistent as it is pervasive. That is, those who fall into the category of appropriation have generally embraced an instrumental view of technology and a determinist conception of TV messages. In other words, in the hands of these practitioners, TV technology is seen as a value-neutral tool for transmitting value-laden content.

Appropriation and Content

A more recent and, in fact, less common approach is to consider the ways in which network programming itself might crack open new possibilities for TV viewers to experience a reorientation of their life and world. Among evangelical critics and theologians, this kind of appropriation could just as easily be described as "The Gospel according to." Building on the success of Robert L. Short's *The Gospel according to Peanuts*, Mark I. Pinsky offered a similar take on *The Simpsons* that underscored the show's clear affirmation of faith and family, even when it was embodied by cynical and seemingly profane characters like Bart and Homer Simpson. The title of Pinsky's book was, of course, *The Gospel according to "The Simpsons,"* and it suggested that both the explicitly religious elements in the series (like the evangelical Ned Flanders) and its sincere explorations of fatherhood, family, and morality allow viewers to catch "glimpses of faith that the spiritually faithful have been trying to communicate for years."[52] In other words, even when it is not trying to be spiritual or religious, *The Simpsons* offers viewers new ways of understanding a world marked by the same cynicism and irony that the show mocked.

The Simpsons was always positioned as a kind of antidote to family-friendly programming. Fox even moved it from Sunday night to Thursday night to directly compete with the wholesome and generally accessible *Cosby Show*. But the Simpsons were the complete opposite of the Huxtables. One was an upwardly mobile, respectful, honest nuclear family; the other was "struggling, skeptical, disrespectful, ironic, hopeful."[53] Not everyone recognized this subtle turn toward hope. Many evangelical leaders dismissed the program as crude, offensive, and sacrilegious. In response to a concerned parishioner, Lee Strobel, pastor at Willow Creek Community Church, even preached a sermon titled "What Would Jesus Say to Bart Simpson?" Interestingly, while they were responding to the same content, Pinsky's read of *The Simpsons* is far more generous than Strobel's, and it may be that this difference is due, at least in part, to Pinsky's basic posture of appropriation.

We will return to *The Simpsons* again, but for now it is enough to say that Pinsky is helpful because he is a bit more evenhanded in his approach than those who have reacted critically to *The Simpsons* over the course of its nearly three-decade run. Even Robert Short, the original "Gospel according to" author, became a convert: "I've never been much of a TV watcher. It's against my religion, as they used to say. But now Mark Pinsky's *The Gospel according to 'The Simpsons'* has made me at least a partial convert. I was blind, but now I see that, in *The Simpsons* anyway, there is goodness galore—intelligence, hilarious writing, insight, telling social criticism and commentary, and plenty of helpful hints for spiritually challenged people like me."[54]

Numerous others have emulated Pinsky's appropriation of television under the general concept of "The Gospel according to." Chris Seay wrote *The Gospel according to "Lost,"* and along similar lines, Tim Wesemann penned *Jack Bauer's Having a Bad Day*, and Jana Riess wrote *What Would Buffy Do?*[55] Pinsky himself authored *The Gospel according to Disney*, and, more recently, Blake Atwood released *The Gospel according to "Breaking Bad."*[56] In every case, the common thread is a shared posture toward television content that conceives of these narratives (whether they are explicitly religious or not) as filled with potential for expanding the imaginations of viewers and offering them insight into their common humanity and the world in which they live. Or, to use the words of Robert Short, those who assume a posture of appropriation recognize that many TV programs are filled with "goodness galore."[57]

Divine Encounter

Divine Encounter and Technology

Our final category includes theologians, church practitioners, and Christian "media moguls" who believe that television has the capacity to provide the viewer with an experience of transcendence—a divine encounter. Throughout the medium's short history, those who have approached TV technology in this way have often been known by another name: televangelist. The designation itself is revealing as it highlights the historical tendency among certain evangelical churches and individuals to embrace modern technology as a divinely appointed instrument for gospel proclamation. Indeed, their zeal for the possibilities of TV technology has often reached a fever pitch. For example, in 1986, "televangelist Jimmy Swaggart told his viewers that it was 'D-Day or Delay.' Either they supported his goal of communicating the gospel via television to all nations on earth, or they were delaying the salvation of mankind. Pointing to his colorful map of the world, Swaggart repeatedly told viewers that money was the only obstacle to global evangelization; the technologies were already in place."[58]

Something more than crass pragmatism is going on here. In Swaggart's mind (or at least in his practice), TV actually bears a kind of metaphysical significance. And he is not alone in this view. There are almost too many examples to list, but some of the more notable church leaders who have also embraced TV technology as a mediator of the divine are Fulton J. Sheen, Oral Roberts, Jerry Falwell, Jim Bakker and Tammy Faye Bakker Messner, and more recently Joel Osteen, T. D. Jakes, and Robert Schuller. It is interesting to note that many of these TV evangelists have also been leaders of rather large congregations or Christian organizations, which means that their primary method of evangelism was to broadcast sermons that were originally intended for a particular Christian community. This is not to say that all televangelists operate with identical theological paradigms or apologetic strategies. Rather, what unites them is simply a willingness to leverage the technology of TV as a means for communicating some version of the gospel message.

Television is thus pictured as a value-neutral tool—a mere "instrument"—that expands the preacher's capacity to convey (gospel) information, which serves as a kind of antidote to the otherwise destructive content communicated by mainstream programming. It is this somewhat inverted approach toward TV technology, on the one hand, and TV content, on the other, that allows a televangelist like Jerry Falwell to reject a program such as *Teletubbies* as damaging to the moral lives of children while, at the very same time, employing the instrument of television to deliver content that reflects his own religious commitments.

> When the church responds to TV technology in this way, both preexisting theories of communication and particular conceptions of the gospel are in operation: [This] segment of Christianity has been quick to grasp every new communication technique as it came along—first radio, then short-wave, motion pictures, television, and, more recently, cable, satellite TV, and videocassettes. Theirs is the "pipeline" theory of communication: when the Christian message is reduced to a set of unvarying verbal formulas, the only question is how to build a bigger and better "pipe" through which to deliver the message to the recipient.[59]

So the approach of the televangelist, borrowing as it does from radio evange-lism and even revivalist preaching, is not necessarily unique to the twentieth century. Nevertheless, it provides a concrete example of one way in which the church has responded specifically to TV technology—a response that ultimately reduces the Christian message to a dataset and embraces (often uncritically) the value-laden technology delivering that message.

Ostensibly, the goal of communicating the gospel through TV technology is some sort of transformation—a fundamental change within viewers that is brought about by their encounter with the gospel message. In the days of Oral Roberts, this transformation involved nothing short of conversion to Christianity. However, more recent televangelists like Joel Osteen approach transformation in far more therapeutic (and perhaps more palatable?) terms. Rather than "making a decision for Christ," viewers are encouraged to dis-cover their "best life now."[60] In either case, though, one of the problems with this approach is that it is not always very effective—at least not in the broad, sweeping terms that many televangelists use to describe the impact of their ministries. Although notable exceptions certainly do exist (e.g., Billy Graham's televised crusades), a key difficulty is that information alone is rarely capable of shaping people's behavior—regardless of how compelling or "life-changing" it may in fact be. And even if we are to assume that gospel information is unique in its ability to transform its hearer (and we think it is), the larger problem for the televangelist is that almost everyone who consumes Christian media is already a Christian.

This trend supports most of the available social-scientific research on the subject.[61] For example, one study of the 700 Club revealed that the majority of its members were indeed already Christians. Perhaps even more surprisingly, the study found that a good number of these "faithful viewers" were not actu-ally viewers at all. Instead of watching the program, they simply supported it financially. Indeed, "all of the contributors were convinced that by supporting this ministry on the important, national, cosmopolitan medium of television, they were ensuring the ultimate triumph of their worldview."[62]

This pronounced difference between the stated goals of televangelists and the ways that actual audiences make use of evangelistic programming recalls our discussion in chapter 3 of how viewers often find television meaningful in ways that run counter to the intentions of its creators. It also suggests that, in many cases, one of the primary impulses standing behind the production and consumption of televangelism is not theological but political. It reflects both a perceived loss among certain evangelicals regarding their sense of cultural prominence and a desire to carve out a space within the broader culture for a return to a position of stature and authority. At the very least, it is an attempt to exert some measure of influence on public life. So regardless of whether televangelism is in fact an effective tool for conversion, it functions incredibly well in marking out a specific "brand" of evangelicalism for its own adherents.

Creating explicitly "Christian" media has always involved a balancing act of sorts. It is no small task to develop compelling TV content that is religiously faithful without it becoming pure propaganda. It's also fairly difficult to distribute this programming in ways that are financially sustainable (i.e., profitable) while, at the same time, serving the primary (not-for-profit) mission of the ministry. As a result, many would question whether this approach to TV has been worthwhile in purely pragmatic terms.[63] Others have raised theological concerns (and in many cases, they have been right to do so). It is surely apparent by now where we stand in relation to this approach. However, the point here is not to make any final judgments one way or the other but simply to describe one of the more prominent ways in which the Protestant evangelical wing of the church has responded to TV. And in anticipation of where the constructive portion of our theological exploration is heading, it is worth noting here that, because this diverse and sometimes problematic history has to do at its core with what it means to be an "evangelical," we would do well not to be dismissive of certain groups simply because their approach differs from our own. For if we are incapable of affirming and reclaiming the voices within our own tradition, it is hard to imagine that we will ever be able to engage constructively with the great diversity of voices that speak to us from outside our tradition.

Divine Encounter and Content

The typology we have been using to categorize the church's response to TV features two distinct but overlapping lines (one designating the church's response to TV content and the other to TV technology [see figure 5.3]). However, the on-the-ground reality is far less linear than these lines suggest, and this is nowhere more evident than in the category of divine encounter. From the outset, certain individuals and groups have sought to communicate something of a divine encounter to at-home viewers by televising sermons, worship services, and the like. But within the last decade, an increasing number of lay and professional church leaders have begun to explore the ways in which mainstream TV programming might offer an occasion when viewers are able to experience a moment of transcendence. Needless to say, this is a decidedly different approach than that of the televangelist and a decidedly different conception of what constitutes a "divine encounter."

The church's increased interest in the transcendent potential of television follows a broader shift in the kind of TV programming that is now being produced for the viewing public. For example, when a show goes by the name *Supernatural*, it is explicitly and intentionally raising theological if not downright metaphysical questions from the start. Also, shows like *The Book of Daniel*, *Joan of Arcadia*, and *Saving Grace* feature some kind of divine encounter within the narrative itself. In each of these series, individuals who literally see and hear God or a divine messenger are forced to navigate a world where the divine is otherwise not a viable option. Interestingly, though, few of the shows that traffic in "transcendent" themes gain enough traction with audiences to keep them on the air, even when they are well produced and expertly written (one notable exception being *Touched by an Angel*, which was both well received and well written). So while they certainly provide Christians a valuable resource for engaging TV theologically, we can say that, in general, what these explicitly transcendent shows primarily offer is a starting point for talking *about* the divine more so than an actual experience *of* the divine. As a result, they invite the kind of theological "dialogue" we discussed above.

In contrast, it seems that the episodes and series that address matters of spirituality or transcendence indirectly are the ones that generate the most potential for a divine encounter. While exceptions certainly exist, they also seem to generate the most faithful and active fan base. These programs are "spiritual" not because they deal with religion or the supernatural explicitly but because they explore the human condition with sincerity and authenticity, acknowledging both its beauty and its messiness. By doing so, they open up viewers to something "more"—a kind of fullness or a sense of flourishing that has its source "beyond" the confines of our immanent frame. Viewers—whether traditionally religious or not—are encountering these TV programs in a way that evokes a kind of meaning-making that is somehow deeper than their lived experience.

One need look no further than the numerous books that have been written in response to the series *Lost* to see that Christians are increasingly asking what this general interest in spirituality means not only for modern persons and the broader culture but also for the church. By the end of the series, more than three dozen books had been published about the show's philosophy, spirituality, and fundamental mystery.[64] Some authors, such as Christian Piatt, engage in a theological dialogue with the show. His book, *Lost: A Search for Meaning*, is "less an effort to stake claims about truth either in the show or in scripture than it is an attempt to stimulate thought, reflection, and discussion."[65] Others offer something more along the lines of what we have described as appropriation. Chris Seay's *The Gospel according to "Lost"* suggests that *Lost* is able to bring about a transformation within the audience because it neither downplays complexity nor explains away ambiguity. Just as the characters in *Lost* experience growth and transformation in the midst of their chaotic and mystery-laden environment, so too do the viewers.

All these conversations concerning the cultural significance of *Lost* underscore our earlier point regarding the importance of attending to viewer responses (i.e., "practice") in our critical analyses. That is, in an attempt to understand a series theologically, we must always take the audience into consideration, not just the show's "trace" elements. And when it comes to *Lost*, it is Christian viewers in particular who seem to have "found God" in the show.[66] Indeed, the tidal wave of books about *Lost* can be understood as a response to what these Christian leaders perceive to be a divine encounter mediated by the series. Whether that encounter took place within the author's own experience or their community's or the culture at large, the influx of writing and reflection on *Lost* demonstrates an attempt to make sense of a profound spiritual experience— an experience that is, at its core, open, mysterious, and difficult to put into words. So for those who approach TV in terms of its potential for opening up a divine encounter, the particular experience that televisual content creates is as important as the content itself.

In this way, *Lost* exposes the fragility of our typology, or at least reveals it to be far more fluid than we would like to imagine. It is perhaps fitting that when it comes to how the church has responded to a nonlinear, open-ended, and spiritually ambiguous show, our categories (which are linear, closed, and clear) prove to be a bit too rigid. In fact, as Piatt's and Seay's books demonstrate, many of those whose primary response could be described as dialogue or appropriation would also fit comfortably within the category of "divine encounter."

In *What Can Be Found in "Lost": Insights on God and the Meaning of Life*, John Ankerberg and Dillon Burroughs offer a prime example of those who believe that TV can open viewers up to a divine encounter.[67] As such, they also bring our historical examination of the church's response to TV into the present. In their 2008 text, Ankerberg and Burroughs examine the numerous references to God, spirituality, and the divine in *Lost*, placing those themes into conversation with the biblical text and, in some cases, the Christian theological tradition. Using the categories we have laid out, their interpretive tendency is to see the dialogue between theology and TV as one that moves from Scripture toward television and not the other way around. Thus, their stated goal is to "note what God's Word, the Bible, says about each issue, with an emphasis on both the positive and sometimes cautionary aspects that connect with the show. . . . We hope to help you understand these issues from God's perspective and to live in a way that lines up with the truth of the Bible."[68]

Even though Ankerberg and Burroughs are attempting to leverage the spirituality of *Lost* to explicate Christian doctrine, their hope is for readers to consider a question that Rose, one of the many characters living on the island, asks: "What does God have to do to get your attention?" In other words, their basic assumption is that viewers can and do encounter God in and through this TV program. Like others who approach TV in terms of the divine encounter it potentially opens up, the question Ankerberg and Burroughs are placing before us is not whether God speaks in *Lost*. Instead, the question viewers must answer is the same question posed to all the survivors on the island: Are we listening?

Looking to the Future by Looking to the Past

The historical development of how the church has responded to TV is all fine and well, but only if it somehow informs where we go from here. In an important sense, we are entering uncharted territory. So much is changing within culture, and the rate of these changes seems only to be increasing. We struggle at times to know whether "television" is even a helpful term in the current climate of technological convergence. Yet at the same time, we cannot avoid the reality that there is more "TV" available than ever before, and it is now a part of our lives in a way that it has never been before. So as we move forward, how might the church respond to TV in ways that are not only faithful (i.e., rooted in our historical tradition) but also life-giving and constructive? Let us consider four broad areas that will serve as an outline for the remainder of the book.

First, we need to reconsider how we think about the "commercial" nature of television. While fully recognizing the problematic aspects of consumer culture, we need to forge a more constructive, even sympathetic, understanding of TV as a commodity—one that is part of a larger system of production and consumption. It is not enough to simply decry TV's commerciality as an inherent deficiency, especially when an argument could easily be made that modern folk philosophy is structured and funded primarily by the resources of advertising. In a sociocultural context where our view of the world is shaped by media that make us feel something and draw us into affective alliances through the power of audiovisual narratives, the church needs to develop a theological vocabulary that speaks to commercially shaped modern persons in life-giving ways.

Second, we need to move beyond the inadequate dichotomy between content and technology that has existed throughout the history of the church's engagement with TV, especially when it comes to the ritual elements of TV viewing. We have used this dichotomy in the current chapter in an effort to accurately describe the various ways that the church has conceived of TV in the past. But it is ultimately an unhelpful distinction. Television is a "medium" because it generates an entire ecology—a symbolic world—that always involves both a communication technology and the content it delivers. The two simply cannot be separated without remainder. And this raises one of the more interesting ethical questions to which we will return. That is, running counter to the argument we have put forward so far, could it be that, in some cases, we would do well to assume a posture of avoidance, or at least caution? If TV is a world-generating medium that shapes the ritual lives of viewers, has the church thought critically enough about the role of television in the home? Television was originally embraced as a domestic appliance almost without question. It set up shop in our living rooms as one of the givens of modern life. But now that it has moved into every room of the house and calls to us from every screen we carry with us, is it enough to continue with the same lack of thoughtfulness that first allowed this pervasive medium to move into our domestic space? In other words, how might we become more proactive concerning the ritual nature of television viewing as a part of our domestic life?

Third, both lay and professional theologians who are interested in engaging culture need to develop a theology of television's narrative content that is medium-specific. We have sought to lay the groundwork for this kind of endeavor in the first section of the book by considering the various analytical categories that are necessary for understanding television on its own terms. But now, as we move more decidedly from critical analysis to interpretation, it will be important to demonstrate the value of locating this project within a larger theological framework. Up to now, the bulk of those who have been thoughtfully engaged in theological dialogue with television are approaching the conversation from the standpoint of communication studies and media studies. For one reason or another, they are also predominantly Reformed in their theology. But given their commitments to other critical methodologies, their theological paradigms remain either under-explored or uncritically embraced. Thus, rather than allowing other critical projects to drive our exploration of the cultural significance of television, what is needed is a way of framing our entire understanding of TV narratives in theological terms.

Finally, following directly from the last point, it seems that Christians need to reconsider their understanding of communication on a very basic level. In part, this revisioning must rely on the shifts that are taking place within communications theory—from a "transmission" view of communication to a "ritual" view, for example. But if we are to develop a truly theological understanding of communication (and communication technologies like TV), we need a different and more varied set of resources than what is commonly found in communications theory and media studies alone. A theology of communication must recognize that, ultimately, communication is about not only information or even ritual practices but also communion. It is an encounter between two freedoms, a merging of two horizons, a meeting that can only occur between an "I" and a "thou," to use Martin Buber's terminology. Or to borrow from Walter Ong again (who was also explicitly referencing Buber), a work of art "can never get itself entirely dissociated from this I-Thou situation and the personal involvement which it implies."[69] This is a fundamentally relational and even "incarnate" view of communication that, by necessity, requires a deep well of theological resources to develop. And it will be the aim of the next chapter to do so.

6

channeling theology

tv and God's wider presence

For fans of Joss Whedon's *Firefly*, this chapter will feel strangely familiar. It is brief (some might say tragically so). It raises a number of questions while only hinting at the answers. And just like a series that is cut short long before its time, this chapter will (we hope) leave readers asking for more—much more. In some respects, this is simply the by-product of interdisciplinary work. For it to be a theology *of* anything, we not only have to develop the critical tools necessary for understanding a particular cultural artifact or phenomenon, but, at the very same time, we must also root this critical work in a fully orbed theological paradigm of some sort. The inherent risk is that something receives short shrift along the way—that we run out of space or time or audience share and are thus forced to cut the story short just when things are getting interesting.

Thankfully, we know from the very start that our time is short, so unlike the writers who worked on *Firefly*, we have some control over how and when things will end. Even so, it is important to point out that, when it comes to the vast stream of discourse otherwise known as the theological tradition, we are simply dangling our legs over the dock and letting our toes test the waters. Readers are therefore encouraged to see this chapter as a springboard for further examination and discovery of their own. Each of the theologians and theological concepts we discuss below are part of an expansive historical conversation, the full breadth and depth of which we cannot possibly unpack in these pages. Instead, what we offer here is a collection of dialogue partners who, together, will help us locate our exploration of television and televisual culture within a larger theological framework.

In the previous chapter we considered the historical development of the church's response to television. An important insight that emerged was that Protestants in general and evangelicals in particular have, to varying degrees, been held captive by a correspondence theory of truth and a transmission view of communication. As a result, the "truth" of the gospel is reduced to its propositional content—its core "message"—and the primary task of the Christian faith is conceived as the transmission of this information by any means (or media) necessary. The problem with this picture is that the gospel is more than a proposition. It is first and foremost a story, and, as such, it bears an aesthetic truth that cannot be reduced to its content alone. As James K. A. Smith has suggested, the gospel story is "not just a vehicle for ideas; it means both *more* than that and *differently* than that."[1]

Setting aside for a moment the theological difficulties that these assumptions about communication and propositional truth present, they are of immediate concern here because, as we made clear in chapter 1, television traffics in stories. It is a narrative medium through and through. Even when the programming is not scripted (e.g., the nightly news, live sporting events, or home improvement shows on HGTV), it is always already narrating the world to us. To be sure, these narratives are mediated by an increasingly wide range of communication technologies, are bought and sold as one of the principal commodities of the United States, and function as a primary portal for our ritual lives. But TV stories are more than the sum of their parts. These narratives—consumed through various media and ritually incorporated into our lived experience—shape our basic awareness of the world.

As it currently stands, the theological tradition seems ill equipped to engage television on this nonpropositional level, which is to say nothing of its technological, ritual, or commercial levels. So at least part of our task must be to undo the ways in which theology has become bound up with certain theories of communication and human knowing that are as reductive as they are unhelpful. In order to do this, though, we must identify those resources within the theological tradition that will uniquely enable us to make sense of this hybrid, adaptive, and world-creating medium—to address TV as TV. Thus, our goal in this chapter is not only to locate our exploration of TV within a larger biblical and theological framework but also to forge some pathways through which television might actually expand and enrich our theological categories.

Augustine and Communication

Admittedly, there is an irreducible ad hoc–ness to our approach, but this does not mean that we are moving forward as if untethered from the theological tradition. If anything, it is very much the opposite. Just as it is with players in a jazz ensemble, we are improvising, but our ability to contribute something meaningful (besides just dissonant noise) to this collaborative project does not occur by happenstance. It requires a great deal of preparation—an intentional and practiced interaction with the tradition. Likewise, in order to engage meaningfully with our (post)postmodern world in a way that is both theologically nimble and adaptive, we must become practiced in the wisdom that has preceded us. It is for this reason that we start not with a contemporary theologian but with one whose work has endured through many technological, industrial, economic, and ecclesial upheavals: Augustine.

Augustine was one of the early architects of Christian theology, and his work has left an indelible mark on the shape of Western thought more generally. But Augustine himself knew nothing of the digital mediascape in which we presently live, so our first step is simply to consider the ways in which his ancient wisdom might inform and give shape to our decidedly contemporary concerns. However, we also want to understand how contemporary theologians have received and appropriated Augustine, especially in those realms that directly impinge upon our exploration of televisual media and culture. Because of these dual aims (one ancient and the other modern), we will barely be able to scratch the surface of the individual theological projects we are engaging. The goal here, however, is not to engage in a comprehensive survey but to acquire the kind of theological clarity that comes about only through a convergence of multiple perspectives.

As we noted earlier, almost every available exploration of the theological significance of TV and TV culture has come from the perspective of communication studies or media studies. To some degree this makes perfect sense. Before it is anything else, television is a communication technology, so it is appropriate to ask what communication is on a fundamental level and how we are to understand the significance of both what and how TV communicates. However, what these studies have been unable to do is articulate an actual *theology* of communication—one that prioritizes the theological tradition as its primary critical framework. And as it turns out, Augustine provides us with a number of invaluable resources for engaging in this kind of constructive theological project.

In *On the Teacher*, Augustine reflects on the means by which humans are able to communicate with one another and, perhaps more important, how they know whether the ideas they are communicating are true or good.[2] As a former rhetorician and propagandist for the Roman emperor, Augustine considered words to be the primary means by which humans were able to communicate and, ultimately, to learn.[3] Words could inspire the hearer to seek out the truth.[4] But as a thoroughgoing Neoplatonist, Augustine also believed that nothing of "eternal value" (i.e., the "True" or the "Good") could be contained in these words because they issued from our physical bodies.[5] As language is anchored in the material world, it is a mediating instrument that, by its very nature, is one step removed from the immaterial source beyond being. "No-thing" is actually communicated through language because the "really real" is an immaterial reality. Thus, according to Augustine, even though humans were able to communicate directly with God and one another prior to their fall from grace, they are now limited to the confines of their bodies. Words, signs, gestures, and sounds—these are all embodied forms of communication that set us at a distance from the world and one another, mediating, as it were, what was once an immediate relationship.[6]

Augustine develops these thoughts on human communication along similar lines in *On Music*, but with a slight twist.[7] In this treatise, "Augustine stretched his rhetorical training and its emphasis on words and broadened language to horizons beyond the verbal to symbols, gestures, and sounds—all of which are vehicles for communication between human beings and between humanity and God."[8] So Augustine presents us with something of a mixed bag. On the one hand, given his Neoplatonic commitments, he operates with the assumption that mediated, embodied forms of communication are fundamentally inferior or "less-than-real"—a reflection of humanity's fallen-ness and the loss of our eternal unity.[9]

On the other hand, mediated communication is, for Augustine, a basic element of the concrete human experience. It is simply the way things are. Not only does mediated communication define our everyday interactions between persons, but it is also one of the avenues through which humans are able to ascend beyond the confines of the sensible world and return to the realm of the eternal and immaterial. The idea of moving through the material world toward the immaterial realm is certainly a reflection of Augustine's Neoplatonic commitments. But Augustine also believed that physically mediated communication was the very means by which God chooses to communicate with humanity. God condescends toward humanity and communicates in ways that humans can understand, even when they encounter the otherwise ineffable. Just as the apostle Paul suggests, the Spirit intercedes for human beings with "groanings too deep for words" (Rom. 8:26 ESV).

To be sure, it is important that we move beyond Augustine's (and really, Neoplatonism's) strict equation of mediated communication with fallen-ness and un-reality. From the perspective of the biblical witness, our creaturely embodied-ness is neither a product of sin nor something for us to escape. In the creation narrative of Genesis 2 (prior to the tragic expression of humanity's will to power), humans are not given bodies; they *are* bodies, animated by the "breath" of God.[10] And along with the rest of creation, God calls these human bodies "very good" (Gen. 1:31). We could go on, but the point here is that Augustine's suspicion of physical, bodily life is something for us not to uncritically embrace but to acknowledge as a source of a continued ambivalence within the Christian tradition regarding bodies and physicality.

That being said, Augustine is still quite helpful for our present purposes because he introduces us to two important concepts regarding human communication. The first states that because it is anchored in our bodies, all human communication is mediated to some degree or another. Even among individuals inhabiting the same physical space, their interactions are always mediated by their bodies. As a result, from an Augustinian perspective, mediated communication is a fundamental element of what it means to be human, a basic component of our life-in-the-world. It is the avenue through which we express our subjective experiences, convey conceptual categories, and, ultimately, relate to others (both human and divine).

Second, Augustine sketches out a theory of communication that makes room for the multidimensional nature of human interaction. Communication is never simply about conveying propositional information. In some important respects, especially when it concerns language, communication will always involve the transmission of some kind of content—thoughts, concepts, and abstractions. But it should never be reduced to these categories alone, nor should it be evaluated only in these terms. As humans are very basically sense-making creatures, says Augustine, human communication is more than mere transmission. It necessarily involves symbols, gestures, and sounds as well, for certain groanings of the human spirit can never be fully expressed in words; certain longings will always exceed the grasp of the propositional.

If, as we suggested earlier, the medium of TV is in fact an adaptive hybrid that is at once a communications technology, a narrative art form, a commodity, and a portal for our ritual lives, then Augustine helpfully informs our understanding of television as a communications technology. For example, much has been made recently about the pace at which television technology is both changing and expanding and how these changes have shifted our basic understanding of what television is.[11] What is more, the relatively recent proliferation of the internet has not only permanently severed the tie between TV programming and its delivery system (historically, a TV set), but it has also generated a seemingly infinite demand for more content. As a result, a whole host of new distribution platforms have emerged, each of which can be accessed through a number of communication technologies, whether that be a phone, a computer monitor, a tablet, or an actual television. Increasingly, companies that were once content distributors (Hulu, Netflix, Amazon Prime, and even YouTube) now feature original programming that is accessible anytime and virtually anywhere because it is available for consumption on any media device.

A significant subset within the Christian tradition would interpret these various levels of mediated interaction negatively. We considered some of these voices in chapter 5. The argument goes something like this: Because it mediates the world to us through a technological apparatus, television moves us away from rather than toward genuine community and relationship.[12] As a result, the very act of engaging in mediated entertainment is inherently deficient when compared to face-to-face interaction. Television's lone saving grace was that it once required viewers to gather together in the same location to watch the same programming at the same time. Now, though, regardless of our physical proximity, we are only ever "alone together," separated from other human beings by our increasingly pervasive (and invasive) media devices.[13]

If Augustine is correct, though, the question we should be asking is not whether we should engage in mediated forms of communication but rather to what degree does the mediating work of a modern communication technology like TV lead to genuine human interaction. A robust theological anthropology recognizes that all human communication is mediated by materiality to some degree, and the chief example of this is our physical bodies. From a theological perspective, then, rather than conceiving of a communication technology like TV as inherently flawed or duplicitous, we can reclaim its value as an extension of our fundamental humanity.[14] It is simply part of what it means to be a human being. Rather than write off TV technology because it encourages humans to communicate indirectly, we ought to be asking how various kinds of media relate us to one another and, by extension, what the gains and losses are for both the individual and the community. Put differently, our theology should not be anti-technology or anti-mediation per se but rather pro-human.[15]

We of course acknowledge that some TV technologies can and do discourage authentic human communication (i.e., communion), but we want to emphasize that this is not necessarily (or even usually) so. For example, we considered earlier fans of the show *Glee* (known as "Gleeks"). Interacting as they do almost exclusively through social media, this network of passionate viewers is profoundly mediated—almost by definition. But their relationships with one another and the ways in which they forge their communal identity are not inherently deficient just because they are mediated. They are simply different.

As such, they call for a different kind of evaluative criteria that acknowledge both the benefits and the deficiencies of this particular mode of communal life.

Some believe that digital communities like these are on the verge of replacing physical relationships altogether, fueled as they are by mediating technologies. But this fear is somewhat misplaced. It also happens to be reductive and overly simplistic. Once again, Augustine is helpful here. We simply cannot communicate directly, so it is unhelpful to decry TV based simply on the fact that it sets us at a distance from one another or from "reality." Even if we somehow could communicate immediately, and the best thing for us all was to throw our media devices in the recycling bin and meet at a coffee shop with "real," flesh-and-blood human beings, it is important to note that, on the whole, TV viewers' digitally mediated relationships are not replacing but are augmenting their physical relationships. In many cases, digital forms of communication are actually encouraging and fueling relationship building and communal identity formation in the physical world.[16] As such, these mediated networks are as significant and formative as any other community in the "real" world.

None of this is to suggest that television communicates in entirely unproblematic ways. Television certainly has the capacity to disrupt authentic communication and inhibit human flourishing. But if embodied mediation itself is not the problem (as Augustine's Neoplatonism might suggest), then it is possible for theology to consider the ways in which different modes of communication might lead to different modes of human relationality and community. Thus, television is theologically significant not simply because it is capable of transmitting information to our brains. It is both more than and different from that. It is significant because it engages the whole of our embodied being through multiple modes of communication—through words, sounds, symbols, and gestures. As a result, the body and, by extension, each of our mediated interactions with the world become potential sites for genuine human connection and, very possibly, for an encounter with reality itself.

Communication as Ritual Formation

If communication is more than simply the transmission of information, then what exactly is it? And how might a broader theological conception of human communication enrich our engagement with the medium of television? Just as before, Augustine's thought proves invaluable. One of his best-known lines comes from the opening of *Confessions*, which in many ways encapsulates Augustine's theological anthropology: "our heart is restless until it rests in you."[17] To be human, for Augustine, is to desire—to be motivated by what we love.

Yet because of human sinfulness, our love has become disoriented and mis-directed, which is all the more tragic because we don't even realize that this is the case. Our desires are now directed toward something other than the true Source of all our affections.

Even though Augustine recognizes humanity's basic *disorientation*, in no way does he urge the Christian to stop loving or desiring. This would be to abandon what makes us human. Rather, he suggests that we Christians ought to love ourselves and others "in God" and "for the sake of God."[18] Instead of denying our erotic impulses (*eros*) in order to love faithfully (*agape*), Augustine suggests that *agape* is rightly ordered *eros*.[19] So for Augustine, the problem is not desire itself. Instead, what holds humanity hostage is disoriented desire, an impulse no longer tethered to the Origin for which it longs.

Augustine's picture of the human being as fundamentally a desiring crea-ture is particularly helpful for our purposes because it offers a theological conception of how human communication works that is not limited to trans-mission alone. Interestingly enough, Augustine's premodern notions of com-munication (as mediated by the body and driven by desire) anticipate recent developments within the humanities and the arts more broadly. Namely, there has been a decided shift among those exploring the significance of popular culture from a transmission view of communication to a "ritual view." As noted in chapter 3, Clive Marsh and Vaughan Roberts have outlined some of what this shift entails:

> The ritual view focuses more on the relationship between communication and the culture of a *gathered* community. Much greater emphasis is placed on embodi-ment and body language, drama, visual elements, and use of space and time. . . . The move from a transmission view to a ritual view of communication means there is a shift away from the *content* of what is believed to *how beliefs are shaped* within religious communities. What people believe seems to matter less than the fact that a believer is a community member and an active participant in that community's ritual practices. Believers receive communication by virtue of their participation. This shift recognizes (again) the importance of religious *practice*, as opposed to simply religious *belief*.[20]

Despite our modern tendency to use metaphors taken from the world of digital technology, communication is not simply about "downloading" bits of information onto a hard drive. It has to do with the way that embodied human beings are shaped by their ongoing, routinized participation in the life of a com-munity. From this view, rather than the extension of messages through space or the act of imparting information from one brain to another, communication is the enactment of shared beliefs that function to guide and maintain society.[21]

Enter James K. A. Smith. Not only do Augustine's notions of embodied communication and human desire serve as the starting point for Smith's theological engagement with culture, but the entire focus of his project reflects these broader shifts toward a ritual view of communication. The first two books in what will eventually be Smith's three-volume project dedicated to developing a "liturgical theology of culture" are *Desiring the Kingdom: Worship, Worldview, and Cultural Formation* and *Imagining the Kingdom: How Worship Works*, both of which we will briefly consider here. At his best, Smith is an elegant philosopher and theologian. His thought is both provocative and creative in all the right ways. At times, he is downright brilliant. Without question, he moves us in the right direction. But it is in those moments where we depart from Smith that we will discover some of the more interesting points of conversation, especially as it concerns our understanding of a highly ritualized yet thoroughly commercial medium like television.

In *Desiring the Kingdom*, Smith follows Augustine closely and suggests that love or desire is what principally drives us.[22] According to Augustine's theological anthropology, humans form their basic awareness of the world affectively. We are not fundamentally thinking machines. Rather, ours is an embodied, emotional, gut-level "understanding" of our being-in-the-world. Because our default way of "intending" the world is not a cognitive "knowledge of" the world but is actually noncognitive and pre-reflective, Smith suggests that it is wrong to reduce human communication to the transmission and processing of information.[23] Genuine communication takes place as one participates in the (trans- and de-)formative practices of a particular community. For Smith, these are "meaning-laden, identity-forming practices that subtly shape us precisely because they grab hold of our love—they are automating our desire and action without our conscious recognition."[24]

Concerned as he is not simply with what people believe (i.e., content) but with how they are formed in contemporary culture (i.e., practice), Smith spends the bulk of his time in *Desiring the Kingdom* suggesting that humans are, at their core, "liturgical animals" (*homo liturgicus*). Humans simply cannot help worshiping something—whether that something be the God of orthodox Christianity or the god of American consumerism. In turn, those worship practices habituate us, says Smith, teaching us not only how to love but what to love. "Liturgies—whether 'sacred' or 'secular'—shape and constitute our identities by forming our most fundamental desires and our most basic attunement to the world."[25] Put differently, liturgies are formative because they are ultimately "pedagogies of desire."

Smith develops this idea further in *Imagining the Kingdom* by exploring how liturgical practices (both religious and secular) actually go about shaping our desires. In short, the argument Smith puts forward is that ritual practices direct our love by capturing our imagination. As he states it, "The way to the heart is through the body, and the way into the body is through story."[26] By drawing on the language of the "heart," "body," and "story," Smith intentionally uses "imagination" in broadly aesthetic terms. Imagination for Smith is "a quasi-faculty whereby we construe the world on a precognitive level, on a register that is fundamentally *aesthetic* precisely because it is so closely tied to the *body*."[27] Smith is not using the term "aesthetic" here to denote a preoccupation with art or even "the beautiful." Instead, our imagination is fundamentally aesthetic for Smith because it is an intuitive, affective way of understanding our being-in-the-world—a bodily attunement to the world that precedes and thus underwrites "objective" knowledge and intellectual reflection.

Because our imagination is rooted in how our bodies make and experience meaning, liturgies capture our imaginations by engaging our bodies and in-corporating them into a larger communal "body." As a consequence, they are able to orient us physically, affectively, and even erotically toward the world. So the content of ritual practices becomes "true" for the participant not when an abstract proposition is subjected to enough critical analysis and syllogis-tic reasoning that it can pass through some threshold of believability. It is true because it makes sense of our discrete, seemingly random experiences aesthetically—in a register of meaning that concerns our basic "feel" for the world. And according to Smith, it is this deep, affective way of attending to the world that ultimately shapes our action in the world: "What's ultimately at stake in a liturgical anthropology is a philosophy of action. Liturgical formation is a way of describing the intense formative dynamic that shapes our imagination and forms our background horizons, which in turn affect how we constitute our world and thus what we feel ourselves *called to* in the world."[28]

Given our interest in constructing a medium-specific theological framework that makes sense of television as both a communications technology and a portal for our ritual lives, it should be fairly evident how Smith's reading of Augustine connects to our project. In particular, Smith's liturgical theology of culture provides us with language to speak of communication in broader terms than simply the transmission of information from sender to receiver. Smith offers a convincing rationale for the ritual dimensions of communication and the for-mative nature of embodied, ritual practices. What is more, Smith also develops a theological anthropology that conceives of these rituals as engaging human beings primarily (and nearly exclusively) through their imaginations—through their affective sensibility toward life and the world. In this way, rituals (whether secular or religious) bear an aesthetic truth that does not abide by the same "logic" as propositional truth, yet they offer a particular disposition toward the world that would be otherwise inaccessible. Smith is not writing about TV per se, but he certainly has cultural practices like TV watching in mind when he talks about imaginative, embodied, formative rituals that capture our passions and direct our desires toward a particular end.

Smith's understanding of the formative nature of secular liturgies provides explanatory power for a number of cultural expressions and artifacts, and the ritual practice of TV watching is no exception. However, one of the most obvious examples of how it applies to television is related to America's obsession with football. So devoted are fans to college and professional football that it is almost inaccurate to describe the rituals dedicated to the game as "secular," for they are nothing of the sort. Hundreds of thousands of fans flock to the temples otherwise known as stadiums to attend games in person. But more than any other professional sport, football is a game made for TV. Indeed, Americans watch more football on television than just about anything else. The next closest competitors in the TV marketplace are shows about football. In fact, so compelling is the at-home viewing experience that the NFL is now making plans to retrofit its stadiums with individual, in-seat HD screens and interactive apps that mimic the home viewing environment.[29]

To be sure, the practice of watching football on TV is connected to the basic elements of sports fandom, but it is also much more than that. Using Smith's terms, the routinized consumption of televised football functions as a "pedagogy of desire." It not only orients our desires but actually shapes what it is that we love. And if Augustine is correct, we are what we love. Or to put it somewhat differently:

> The NFL is, in a real sense, our civic religion. It has Sunday worship services, midweek Thursday celebrations, patron saints (Hall of Famers), and a liturgical calendar that begins with the NFL draft (in April) and ends with the Super Bowl (in February). The NFL even has a robust small group network (Fantasy Football leagues) dedicated to studying every nuance of every play of every game. The catechesis process is rigorous, but the various avenues for inclusion are generous (notably, women are the fastest growing demographic of NFL fans). And the result is a profoundly football-literate community that is also devoted—yes, devoted—to interpreting the significance of this game for our life and the world. Little else in our culture has so fully captured the American imagination and compelled so many people to orient their lives around it.[30]

This way of understanding the practice of watching football on TV is meant neither to minimize religion nor to overstate the cultural significance of televised football. Rather, it is simply to say that Smith is correct: rituals habituate us. They capture our imagination through aesthetic means and orient our desires toward a particular vision of the good life that in many ways determines how we act in the world. Through the medium of television, Americans have become devoted to football because the rituals it provides shape their desires. Far beyond the transmission of some kind of football "content," the "truth" of their devotion follows an emotional, intuitive, and precognitive logic rather than the logic of "reason." This goes a long way in explaining why, in spite of several recent revelations regarding brain damage to athletes, domestic abuse among players, and economic structures that radically favor a wealthy minority, the popularity of football is at an all-time high. It's because we love it. And that love is inscribed into every fiber of our being.

The genuine sense of devotion that football engenders raises a number of related questions that we might explore. However, the primary question we need to address is not so much whether the televisual liturgies of the NFL are effectively shaping our desires. We are in basic agreement with Smith that they are. Instead, the real question is, from a theological perspective, whether the formative work of these secular liturgies is or even can be good. It is in answering this question that we depart most noticeably from Smith's liturgical theology of culture.

The Poetics of Consumption

Smith is quite helpful in sketching out the basic conceptual categories we need in order to understand the formative nature of television as a portal for our ritual lives. So it is all the more interesting that, despite our agreement with his project on numerous levels, we diverge so noticeably in terms of how we finally understand the theological significance of contemporary cultural rituals like TV watching—a "secular liturgy" par excellence. And this divergence is perhaps most clearly seen in our evaluation of consumer culture and the rituals of consumption it entails.

For Smith, "our [i.e., the theologian's] cultural criticism should be discerning to what ends all sorts of cultural institutions are seeking to direct our love."[31] Of this much we can agree. But Smith goes on to claim that "from the perspective of Christian faith, these secular liturgies will often constitute a mis-formation of our desires—capturing our imaginations and drawing us into ritual practices that 'teach' us to love something very different from the kingdom of God."[32] In other words, because rituals orient us according to their built-in *telos*, secular liturgies almost always deform and misdirect us. To be fair, according to Smith, this critique of secular liturgies as de-formative is not "total," but in actual practice, it would be almost impossible using his categories to identify a secular liturgy that functions in constructive ways.[33] Smith's posture toward cultural liturgies is thus fundamentally antithetical, and it is here that we most decidedly part ways with his critical evaluation. He is explicit about this "read" of culture and makes no apologies for it (nor should he). Cultural rituals stand in diametric opposition to the rituals of "Christian worship," which leads him to the logical conclusion that "worship functions as counter-formation."[34] That is, in a cultural context that seeks to de-form and mis-direct our desires through its ritual practices, Christian worship moves us in the opposite direction, shaping our passions into what Augustine would call "the right order of love."[35]

It would be nice if we could simply chalk up our departure from Smith to a matter of differing emphases. After all, Smith is primarily concerned with the formative nature of ritual practices and Christian education, whereas we are concerned with a robust understanding of television—a multifaceted cultural form that includes but also extends beyond its ritual dimensions. However, the difference between Smith's approach and ours has to do more fundamentally with a different set of theological assumptions regarding both the nature of worship itself and the ways in which Christian rituals are always already implicated in the broader web of ritual practices in which they are located.

At issue is the significance of the particular form that Christian rituals assume and how that form affects their ability to rightly order our desires. For Smith, form matters "because it is the form of worship that tells the Story (or better, *enacts* the Story)."[36] Rather than a disposable "husk" that can be changed at will in an effort to more effectively communicate the core message of the gospel, the meaning of worship, like the meaning of a poem, "is ineluctably bound up with its form and is not reducible to what can be propositionalized or paraphrased."[37] Smith is far too nuanced a thinker to reduce this to an issue of style—guitars over organs, choirs over worship teams. Instead, he is concerned with the historic elements that constitute the particular narrative arc of a worship service.[38] He thus "testifies to a common 'shape of liturgy' that represents the accrued wisdom of the church catholic, led by the Spirit, regarding what we might call 'the narrative sense' of Christian worship."[39]

What is problematic about the way that Smith employs this line of thinking is not his suggestion that the church has historically found certain forms of Christian worship to be routinely efficacious (e.g., the Lord's Supper and baptism). Nor is it wrong to suggest that form does indeed matter in worship. It surely does. Rather, the problem is the totalizing nature of his claims. For Smith, certain forms of worship are considered universally normative because they are thought to reflect or enact a divine ordo.[40] There is a kind of idealism in play here, for just like the heavenly practices they supposedly mimic, certain Christian rituals are treated as if they too operate in a kind of "untouched" or "unfallen" state. That is, their efficacy in shaping our desires according to the "right order of love" hinges on their formal connection to a fixed, supratemporal form.

But they are "untouched" in another, less theological sense as well. Smith operates as if Christian worship is somehow wholly distinct from the broader ritual landscape that constitutes modern life. He seems unconcerned with the ways in which the participant's symbolic practices outside Christian worship necessarily shape both what and how worship means. Even if the form of Christian worship were indeed fixed, its ritual meaning (and thus its *telos*) would shift for those involved according to how (and not just what) their symbolic practices mean (conceptually and ritually) beyond Christian liturgy. And this is to say nothing of the fact that the forms of life that are found within Christian liturgy often traffic in symbolic cultural resources that are shared among multiple groups, some of which are decidedly not Christian. In what sense, then, can Christian worship be understood to be "counter-formation"? Counter to what? In other words, Christian worship, however "ideal" its form, does not exist in a vacuum, and neither do those participating in worship. Just as people are enculturated, so too are their ritual practices.

As a consequence, the Spirit's very presence in worship becomes contingent.[41] Smith seems to suggest that, rather than indwelling the gathering of the community, the Spirit's presence is restricted to (and determined by?) certain ritual forms. Not only does this conception run the risk of isolating the liturgical act as the sole locus of divine encounter within the life of the church, but it also disregards the reality that the Spirit might very well be present outside Christian liturgy.

All of this comes to bear on Smith's understanding of secular liturgies like watching televised football as primarily de-formative. If only certain ritual forms can orient our desires toward the *telos* of God's *shalom*, and the Spirit is only ever present in these fixed formal arrangements, then it stands to reason that any ritual practice that takes place outside these parameters will be at best theologically meaningless and at worst destructive. This obviously presents us with a number of difficulties if one of our goals is to identify the value and possibilities of television as a portal for our ritual lives. At least on a surface level, television rituals are neither fixed in form nor directed toward the same end as Christian worship. So the question we need to consider is how we might make use of Smith's understanding of the formative nature of secular liturgies while, at the same time, moving beyond his construal of those ritual practices as fundamentally distorted and distorting.

Helpful in this regard is the recent work of Bill Dyrness, who, interestingly, starts his "poetic theology" in the same place as Smith: with Augustine's notion that "our heart is restless until it rests in you." Dyrness calls his theological project "poetic" because he is concerned not with aesthetics per se but with the poetics of everyday life—the symbolic objects and practices that embody our desires and thus orient our lives. For Dyrness, both our desires and the practices that enact these passions have a theological referent:

> To be sure, sports, fishing, and the arts are not religious in any traditional sense, but, for many of our contemporaries, they have *taken the place of* religious practices. And like religious practices, they have become things for which they live—and perhaps for which they might even die! Indeed, the argument I want to develop will go further and argue that the significance they derive from these activities has not only a human meaning but a possible theological reference as well. That is, the drive that moves them to pursue the goods associated with their passions is a movement of the soul that, if nurtured more deeply and oriented rightly, would lead them to God.[42]

The contemporary practice of consuming TV could certainly be included in Dyrness's list of everyday practices. In the context of late capitalism, this routinized pursuit of televised goods cannot be detached from the larger commercial structure that both undergirds and in some senses animates modern life. Smith would agree. In fact, he even suggests that, given its recognition of the human being as a desiring creature and its ability to shape our basic habits into a never-ending cycle of consumption (desire-consume-desire-repeat), capitalism has a better anthropology than the Christian tradition.[43] But Smith takes this one step further and suggests that the bent toward consumption embedded within secular liturgies is the very thing that directs human beings toward a vision of the good life that stands in direct opposition to one oriented toward God's kingdom.

It is at this point that we find Dyrness a more sympathetic dialogue partner than Smith. According to Smith, human desire is part and parcel of the structure of what it means to be human—and nothing more.[44] Our passions are human passions and thus lend themselves to misdirection. For Dyrness, however, God is always already deeply involved in human life—including our passions and the pursuit of goods associated with our desires.[45] There is simply no such thing as a purely human endeavor wholly detached from God's involvement. What this means theologically is that, given the contemporary context, even the desires marshaled by capitalism and the "secular" devotional practices it promotes serve as a possible locus for God's presence and activity in the world. And if this is indeed the case, then we are free to affirm these "secular liturgies" as places in the modern world where God is actively present. Our consumptive habits can certainly become disoriented and have the potential to promote rival visions of human flourishing. But this is neither necessarily nor always the appropriate way to construe these practices. What is more helpful is a way of understanding commodities like TV that recognizes the very practice of consumption (and the devotion that energizes it) as theologically significant—as inextricably related to the work of God, who is present in the midst of our mundane, everyday pursuit of goods.

Modern Family's "Connection Lost" episode (season 6, episode 16) offers a helpful illustration of our point. Claire Dunphy is stuck in an airport terminal while on a business trip. As faithful viewers of the show already know, in addition to her day job she is also a loving wife and mother. So she attempts to navigate the complexities of her family dynamics from a distance, which is only made possible by the digital media at her disposal. In an interesting twist to TV conventions, even the audience is "mediated" by her communications technology. The entire episode takes place on the screen of Claire's laptop as she attempts to contact her older daughter through instant messaging; makes purchases on various websites; video-conferences with her husband, younger daughter, and other members of her extended family; and logs in to a social media website under a pseudonym. This frames Claire's family as truly a "modern" family, but it also shines a light on the broader cultural context of the audience—one that is hyper-mediated.

ABC/Photofest © ABC

Combined with the episode's various levels of mediation is its explicit branding. The Dunphys do not communicate with one another on generic computers operating unaffiliated applications or media devices. Every piece of technology they use is made by Apple. This choice by the show's creators is significant in how we understand the episode, for it not only brings the

Nolan Gould and Julie Bowen as Luke and Claire Dunphy in ABC's *Modern Family* "outside" world of commerce into the narrative through product placement but it also draws upon the symbolic capital of Apple's affective economics. As with most major corporations, Apple's mission is first and foremost to cultivate a brand identity. It doesn't sell products; it sells a way of being in the world. And this way of being in the world has a decidedly aesthetic shape. The "instruments" that consumers buy from Apple are simply everyday tools—phones, music devices, word processors. But they mean so much more than that because they also embody to some degree our desires to live a beautiful and elegant life. To be sure, Apple leverages its deeply emotional, identity-shaping relationship with consumers for economic gain. But to construe the practices of consumption as nothing more than a depraved and egocentric pursuit of "stuff" is to fundamentally misunderstand the ways in which consumers meaningfully incorporate these commodities into their lives.

It is true that, like every "modern family," the Dunphys are located within a wholly commercialized world where their ability to interact with one another is not only mediated but also bound up with the affective economics of corporate branding. But it also happens that the aesthetic truth of their human interaction cannot be reduced to crass marketing techniques or the acquisition and maintenance of wealth. They are genuinely connecting, relating with one another, and interacting—in other words, communicating—not in spite of but in and through their mediated, branded practices. Along with Smith, we could construe this interaction as deficient either because it is mediated or because it is thoroughly commodified, but neither the practices depicted on the show itself nor the audience's practice of watching the show suggests this kind of understanding. Instead, what we get is a narrative that simply assumes the concrete realities of modern life yet nevertheless offers an optimistic and even hope-filled vision for the value of family and the possibility for community in a branded, technologically mediated society.

Reworking a phrase we used earlier, this is not a story about a family that is unwittingly "alone together." Rather, the narrative of the episode actually hinges on the fact that, even though the Dunphys are separated by physical distance—even though they are "alone"—they are still very much together. This isn't a pale reflection of a "real" family or a substitute for a more "authentic" togetherness. Actually, in a very real sense, there is no family (modern or otherwise) without the MacBooks® and iPhones® and FaceTime® apps. These people have not been consumed by their practices of consumption. They do not, in the words of Smith, "foster habits of self-display that closely resemble the vice of vainglory."[46] Nor do their branded interactions "amplify the self-consciousness and ironic distance that characterize late modern capitalism—to a debilitating degree."[47] Rather, their consumption of these technologies (and our mediated consumption of their story) has created avenues for genuine human connection. And we can and should affirm this impulse theologically—celebrate it even. But this is only possible if we root our everyday practices of pursuing and consuming goods within the larger framework of God's presence and activity in the world. In doing so, we are able to move beyond Smith's negative construal and reclaim consumption as a location for the activity of God—as a site where our desires can be positively directed toward humanity, toward community, and even toward beauty.

God's Wider Presence

In the midst of our effort to discern and affirm what is potentially good and true and beautiful about television and TV culture (as opposed to merely adjudicating what is morally bankrupt, false, and grotesque), we have intentionally raised questions about God's presence and activity within the contemporary spaces where individuals are discovering and creating meaning. Whether our focus has been the technology of television, the ritual practices that TV mediates, or the contemporary patterns of consumption it encourages, what we have really been asking is this: How broadly are we willing to conceive of God's revelatory presence in the world?

Interestingly, even though both Smith and Dyrness answer this question by starting with Augustine (the patron saint of Reformed theology), they each arrive at very different places regarding the Spirit's presence (or lack thereof) in culture. For Smith, the Spirit is inclined toward particular ritual forms that are found (exclusively?) in the historical liturgy of the Christian church. Rather than as a movement of God in one's life, he conceives of our desires as an enduring structure of human longing. Dyrness, on the other hand, has a more expansive view of the Spirit's active engagement in our "everyday poetics." But because his project has more to do with theological aesthetics than revelation per se, the intimate connection between human passions and the presence of God in our everyday practices serves primarily as one of his operative assumptions. The points of divergence between the two theologians, then, are not so much about their individual views on the human being as a desiring creature or the formative nature of rituals but rather are related to a different set of core theological assumptions about God's presence in the created order.

Along parallel lines, we have also been exploring what it would look like to expand our theological conception of communication (to include transmission, ritual, and consumption views), and how a broader notion of communication might inform our understanding and engagement with television. As a consequence, the final element of our framework that we will sketch out in this section has two interrelated functions. First, it provides us with biblical language for speaking of the manners in which God is indeed present and active in and through cultural forms like TV narratives. Second, it pushes us to consider communication in a way that exceeds the limits of the critical methodologies employed by media theory and ritual studies.

Our final dialogue partner is theologian Robert K. Johnston, and the touchstone for our conversation is his recent work, *God's Wider Presence: Reconsidering General Revelation*.[48] We have already highlighted the ways in which Johnston's *Reel Spirituality* laid much of the groundwork for our present discussion of theology and TV. But the constructive theology he presents in *God's Wider Presence* opens up the dialogue in some helpful ways. The reason Johnston seeks to "reconsider" general revelation is because it is a theological category that has become muddied to the point of being unhelpful and possibly even misleading. Perhaps unsurprisingly, theologians within the Reformed or Calvinist traditions have done the most significant work in the area of God's general revelation. Following in the footsteps of Augustine (who else?) and later Calvin, Reformed theologians have taken seriously the biblical witness and its testimony to God's "common grace" as it occurs outside the church and without reference to Jesus Christ.[49] Indeed, it is this commitment to grappling with the biblical text that is one of their greatest contributions to contemporary constructive theology.

Yet as Johnston rightly notes, it is also the case that the theological conversation about God's general revelation has been overly focused on the more propositional and didactic passages of Scripture such as Romans 1 and 2. When viewed only through the lens of these passages, general revelation is typically understood to be a "cup half empty" in comparison to the special revelation found in Jesus and the community of faith. It is treated as either merely "preparation" for the reception of the gospel message or the mechanism by which humans are left "without excuse" for denying what creation has routinely made clear to them (Rom. 1:20). At best it is insufficient (because the revelation is not "special" enough), and at worst it works to condemn all humanity (i.e., it is "general").

Johnston too is concerned with situating the biblical text at the center of contemporary theological reflection. But Johnston himself is not Reformed, so he is free to move beyond this tradition by highlighting the nonpropositional portions of Scripture that testify to God's wider presence and activity in the world. He explores songs such as Psalm 19 where the heavens declare God's glory, and stories about foreign kings like Melchizedek (Gen. 14) and Abimelek (Gen. 20), who both serve as conduits for God's blessing by "acting in the integrity of [their] own beliefs."[50]

In addition to these texts, Johnston turns to the collection of sayings in Proverbs that have their origin outside the believing community. These serve as evidence that the Bible itself comprises (and thus affirms) the revelatory insights of those outside the covenant community. He also points out God's somewhat surprising yet consistent tendency to appoint outsiders as divine messengers. "Of particular interest . . . are the accounts of King Necho [2 Chron. 35] and of Balaam son of Beor [Num. 24]. For in the narratives surrounding them that are given by the biblical writers, these two foreigners, both clearly outside of the people of God, nevertheless hear God speak to them directly."[51]

Drawing from both the biblical record and various streams within the theological tradition, Johnston sets forth his understanding of "general revelation":

> It is my contention that God's wider revelation is not something that is available to all humanity through the *imago Dei* based on our human capacity. Rather, with [Karl] Barth, we must say, first, that revelation always needs the Spirit as Revealer—it is event. Secondly, with [Friedrich] Schleiermacher, general revelation is not first of all accessible because of our rationality, but rather is rooted in that intuition of Something or Someone beyond us and our feeling that results from this encounter. And third, with [C. S.] Lewis . . . general revelation is not merely a trace, something largely insignificant given Christ or incomprehensible because of our sin, but the experience of the wider Presence of God through his Spirit mediated through creation, conscience, and human culture.[52]

Building upon Johnston's understanding of God's wider presence, it is clear that our contention about the Spirit's presence in cultural artifacts and practices is in no way a "natural theology" that conceives of the human person as capable of acquiring an objective knowledge of God through some form of rational inquiry. Instead, the Spirit's revelatory presence concerns the imaginative, affective, embodied experience of God's very self that is mediated by humanity's various creative endeavors. In this view, TV-consuming habits, TV technology, and even ritualized TV practices all serve as potential locations for the Spirit of God to speak in and through these contemporary forms of life.

We can go one step further and say that a robust theology of the Spirit also has the potential for expanding our understanding of communication. In terms of God's wider revelation, communication is something more than the transmission of content or the enactment of a particular narrative. It is an encounter between an "I" and a "thou" (to borrow once again Martin Buber's phrase). In other words, when placed in a larger theological framework of God's revelatory presence, communication is, at its core, communion.

As George Steiner has suggested (although somewhat provocatively and not without his detractors), creators create primarily for the sake of communicating with an "other." But Steiner is not alone in speaking of the artistic enterprise in this way. Jaron Lanier, avant-garde musician and father of virtual reality technology, agrees: "There are areas of life in which I am ready to ignore the desire for connection in exchange for cash, but if art is the focus, then interaction is what I crave. The whole point of making music for me is connecting with other people."[53] Although not a theologian, Lanier comes very close here to describing what the theological tradition calls communion. The audience (whether real or imagined) is the "other" with whom the artist seeks to connect. We can accept or reject this invitation, but either way, the aesthetic exchange expresses a core reality. That is, "the experiencing of created forms is a meeting between freedoms."[54]

If in fact our experience of created form involves a meeting between two freedoms (the freedom of the artwork and the freedom of the audience), then the process in which we consume TV narratives might best be understood as an encounter—one in which we enter into a personal relationship with a televisual story. As Steiner rightly suggests, this aesthetic form of relationality naturally leads to transformation, for anytime we encounter meaning that has been given form (*poiesis*), we are opened up and laid bare before the other. This ontological encounter changes us because it involves an expansion of our very selves—a fusion of horizons, to use Hans-Georg Gadamer's language, or a "refiguration," to use Paul Ricoeur's. There are no empirical "proofs" to validate this reality because its truth is fundamentally intuitive, metaphoric, and impressionistic. The experience itself bears a subjective immediacy that outstrips our words to describe it. But this is exactly the point. If there were some kind of externally verifiable evidence for this transformative encounter, the narrative would in fact be robbed of its world-making power.

Speaking of "sensed immediacies" in this way will do little to refute logically or objectively the challenges of the ardent materialist. But that is not our goal. Instead, we simply want to present a particular "take" on the power of TV narratives and see if it feels right to some readers—if it resonates with their lived experience on an affective, intuitive level. For example, the way in which a TV story can tap into a deeply felt aesthetic register of meaning is likely apparent to any parent who has ever watched the NBC show *Parenthood*.[55] This particular series follows the life and travails of the extended Braverman family. In terms of genre, the show is technically a comedic drama, but there are moments when it is far closer to a "melodrama." This is especially the case during those episodes when certain plot devices are injected into the narrative in order to boost the series ratings. After all, many families have dealt with the challenges of raising children on the autism spectrum, struggled with overcoming breast cancer, lost jobs due to economic collapses, or wrestled with the consequences of unwanted pregnancies and absentee fathers. But very few families are like the Bravermans and are forced to endure all these trials at once. Fans will of course forgive this inclination toward the melodramatic as more a function of market demands than a product of its overarching narrative.

Nevertheless, if we consider the show from a series level, *Parenthood* is actually permeated not with melodrama but with the everyday and the mundane. Outside the occasional outlier during sweeps or at the end of a season, nothing really extraordinary ever happens over the course of its six seasons. Instead, the Bravermans simply experience ordinary life. To be sure, there are highs and lows, but the series is mostly a slow and meandering walk through what we might call "the everyday." Children are born (and adopted), marriages are forged and dissolve, and siblings interact as both friends and competitors. Along the way, the audience discovers what it means to be and become a family in the midst of the ebbs and flows of life. And it could be for this very reason that, even though the show never had a huge audience, it still managed to develop a passionate fan base. Indeed, many parents who attempt to articulate their experience of the show point out its ability to tap into untold reservoirs of meaning—a deeply emotional, aesthetic truth that resonates with their own lived experience in ways that are actually impossible to articulate. As one TV critic put it, "Though it has recently become an altar of catharsis, with its own tear-duct-based rating system—pooling tears, falling tears, choked sob, full sob, hysteria—'Parenthood' was never built to go viral. There are no OMG moments, and it's hard to live-tweet when both hands are full of tissues."[56] In other words, it seems that, in its depiction of mundane parenting reality, *Parenthood* encounters the audience (especially parents) and "seizes" them through largely affective means.

That the narrative of *Parenthood* is capable of laying hold of the audience in this way—possessing them even—is a kind of given for those who find it meaningful. But exactly how this takes place we cannot say with any sort of certitude, for it leverages an aesthetic power that cannot be captured in words. The show's emotional truth is one step beyond language (both the "language" of TV and human language) and, as such, a step toward the transcendent. Again borrowing from Steiner, "the embarrassment we feel in bearing witness to the poetic, to the entrance into our lives of the mystery of otherness in art and in music, is of a metaphysical-religious kind."[57] In other words, in our encounter with contemporary televisual narratives, we apprehend an aesthetic presence that invites us to respond—to become "respond-able." And when we locate these aesthetic encounters within the larger theological framework of God's wider revelation, we are able to construe them as both a mechanism and a location for a potential encounter with the Spirit of God. They provide an occasion for entering into communion with the transcendent in and through the immanent frame.[58] In doing so, they underscore the reality that all good art does indeed start in immanence. But it almost never stays there.[59]

Learning to Breathe in a Televisual World

If the medium-specific theological framework we have been piecing together in this chapter were the house of a well-known sitcom family—say, the Flanders home from *The Simpsons*—then Augustine brings us to the metaphorical doorstep by highlighting the mediated nature of human communication. Smith opens the door with his emphasis on the ritual shaping of our desire. Dyrness carries us across the threshold by encouraging us to see the poetics of our everyday lives. And Johnston opens the windows and lets the Spirit breathe life into our otherwise humdrum existence—an animating presence that permeates our domestic space. Like the faithful Ned Flanders knows all too well, this Spirit not only energizes one's personal devotional life but also ushers us beyond our white picket fences and into the messy, complicated, and uncomfortable world of our neighbors—one populated with misbehaving kids named Bart and beer/doughnut-obsessed parents named Homer.

So the kind of theological framework we have introduced here, although only briefly outlined, is meant first of all to help us make sense of TV as a complex, ever-evolving form of contemporary life. However, it also has potential for contributing to theological reflection beyond the medium of television. For instance, as we consider more broadly the ways in which our basic awareness of the world is shaped by our ritual practices, and how those cultural rituals are efficacious primarily because they so fully capture our imaginations, we can more fully value those modes of truth that are poetic before they are propositional, affective before they are cognitive, and sensual before they are rational. This is not to disregard or downplay cognition or rationality or propositions. It is simply to say that our lived experiences—the ways in which we live and move and have our being in the world—cannot be understood in their fullness through a single modality. We are certainly more than our bodies and feelings and imaginations; but we are surely never less than that.[60] Theology would do well to recognize this cultural reality both in the way it articulates the Christian faith and in its choice of the channels by which it communicates that articulation. The gospel "message" still matters, but if it is to be in any way meaningful in the contemporary world, it must make sense on an affective, embodied, aesthetic level before it makes sense as a piece of information to be analyzed and processed.

Our framework also opens up a kind of theological freedom that we should not treat too lightly. If in fact the Spirit of God is present and active in cultural products and practices to such a degree that God can and does speak through them, then we are free to explore and even affirm culture without fear or trepidation. Certainly we need to proceed with wisdom and discernment, but the very fact that God's revelatory presence necessarily involves an encounter with a transcendent Other means that any "truth" or "untruth" we discern will emerge from this intersubjective encounter rather than an ideational abstraction that exists simply to be uncovered. In other words, truth—even theological truth—is fundamentally dialogical.

The lack of doctrinal tidiness implied by this dialogical approach might make some uneasy. However, it is actually an opportunity, if only we could see it as such. In the first place, remaining open to hearing God speak through the voice of the other provides us with an avenue for engaging in the important process of self-critique. Our theology is often wrong and simply misguided; of this we can be sure. But we will never be able to hear a word of correction if our preconceptions regarding who God is and how God operates are beyond critique. What is more, though, an approach of this sort also encourages us to engage the broader culture with a sense of anticipation and discovery, always seeking the unexpected ways in which God might be moving, given our ever-emerging contexts.

The questions we raised regarding the theological possibilities of consumer culture offer a prime example of how we might explore the theological significance of cultural practices without fear. What if, rather than rejecting modern capitalism as wholly depraved, we asked where the Spirit was present and active in our consumption? What if it is not the process of production and consumption itself that is theologically problematic but rather a particularly insatiable system of production and consumption—one that generates an endless cycle of unmet desire and restlessness? In this view, we might affirm the human impulse to produce and consume created goods as appropriate and even beautiful, but at the same time, construct pathways for the faith community to consume in ways that are shaped not by the insatiable demands of late capitalism but by the creational rhythms of God's Sabbath rest. If God is indeed present and involved even in our purchasing habits, then we cannot simply write off consumption itself as an expression of misdirected desire. We have the freedom to imagine ways in which our consuming practices can in fact be committed, involved, fully present, and oriented around Sabbath rest—a basic posture toward commodities (and commercial life) that seeks the well-being of our neighbor rather than anxiously hoarding up capital at our neighbor's expense.[61]

Of course, we want to say more than that God is simply present and active in the midst of our consumption; we also want to ask in particular what God is doing and how TV might serve as a means for God's (trans)formative grace—a topic we will take up in the next chapter. But without a basic openness to the ways in which God might be moving unexpectedly, this possibility is simply unavailable to us.

In all of this, what we are moving toward is really a more appropriate theology for living faithfully in a post-Christian and increasingly post-secular context. These terms don't mean the same thing to everyone, but they do express a basic reality that the church now exists on the margins of society. Wherever the center may in fact be, and whether or not the fragmented nature of modern life even allows for one, the church is no longer there. However, as is always the case, God remains present and in active conversation with people beyond the walls of the church. And if history is any indication, there is much to be gained from this set of circumstances. In fact, it turns out that some of the more creative and enduring forms of Christian life have emerged from similar contexts of marginalization.

Yet whatever paradigms we construct moving forward, a robust theology of God's wider presence suggests that our approach needs to be rooted in humility. We simply do not know what our digitally mediated culture will look like in six to twelve months, much less six to twelve years. And we certainly do not know how God will choose to be involved. All that we can say with any confidence at this stage is that, given the way the Spirit has moved in the past, it will be surprising, unsettling, and very possibly scandalous to those who haven't the eyes to see—or the screens on which to watch.

7

ethics

is there anything good on tv?

In the spring of 2012, *Saturday Night Live* featured a skit poking fun at *Game of Thrones*, the critically acclaimed HBO series that had just aired the premier episode of its second season. Based upon the novels of George R. R. Martin, *Game of Thrones* had gained some notoriety for its use of graphic and pervasive nudity. The show is also incredibly violent, but it was the on-screen depictions of sexuality that caught the eye of the long-running sketch-comedy series *SNL*.

As one of its many "digital shorts," the *SNL* spoof offered a compelling theory concerning the seemingly gratuitous sexuality in *Game of Thrones*. Framed as a behind-the-scenes look at the creation of *Game of Thrones*, the skit suggests that the "artistic vision" for the series was due in large part to the collaborative work of George R. R. Martin and . . . a thirteen-year-old boy. The digital short depicts Martin on the set to ensure that the series stays true to the novels upon which it is based. Similarly, the adolescent Adam Friedberg (played by Andy Samberg) is present to "make sure there are lots of boobs in the show." After a giddy Friedberg describes in detail one of the many hyper-sexualized scenes that actually took place in the HBO series, he sums up the situation well: "And all of that aired on TV—right after *Rango*. It's HBO!"

The irony (and to some the travesty) of the *SNL* parody is that it's funny because it's true. While there is no actual thirteen-year-old managing the creative direction of the show (at least we don't think there is), *SNL* didn't have to exaggerate at all to make its point. Despite its critical acclaim and its passionate fan base, *Game of Thrones* was apparently operating in some ethically murky waters, to such a degree that its artistic merit was being called into question—by *Saturday Night Live*. But the skit also raised questions about HBO's responsibility in the matter, especially concerning the larger narrative flow that the network was constructing. Indeed, *Rango* is an animated children's movie about a chameleon. And HBO placed this content immediately before *Game of Thrones*, a dark and seedy drama for adult audiences. In response, this ninety-second skit on late-night television raised an important ethical question: How should we as a society understand and respond to HBO's decision to create this content and distribute it in this way? After all, if *SNL* thinks a show might be over the line, something must really be wrong.

None of this is to suggest that *Game of Thrones* is so morally bankrupt that it has no aesthetic merit. Rather, it is simply to say that, when it comes to our understanding of televisual culture, it is difficult to come to an understanding of "what is good" (i.e., aesthetics) without also asking "what is good for us" (i.e., ethics). It's almost as if questions of ethics are built in to any consideration of aesthetics, which is why, without any sort of religious conviction whatsoever, the TV series *Saturday Night Live* explored a decidedly ethical question by commenting ironically on another TV series. Through the unique power of parody, it highlighted the moral shortcomings of both *Game of Thrones* as an artistic creation and the audiences who consumed it.

These questions are of particular concern for Christians not only because aesthetics and ethics are inherently related but also because any robust dialogue between theology and TV should be able to generate some kind of common vocabulary for discussing societal values and human flourishing—for exploring the question that has been asked since Aristotle: What is the human good?

Having said this, readers will recall our discussion in chapter 5 regarding the various ways that members of the Christian community have responded to TV throughout the medium's history. In particular, we suggested that those who engage television from a posture of "avoidance" or even "caution" are often focused on "ethical" questions (see figure 5.3). As a heuristic device, this way of framing things was helpful at the time because we were attempting to distinguish between the various approaches one might take toward televisual media. But like any typology, it has its limits. One of those limitations is that "ethics" can become a kind of shorthand for a very limited understanding of how TV media or any cultural artifact relates to human flourishing.

So now that we have a few more tools at our disposal, we want to expand the possibilities for engaging TV ethically. Some critics and theologians who operate with an avoidance strategy often allow their ethical questions regarding TV to be framed only in terms of the sex, violence, and vulgar language that is depicted on-screen, which ultimately "encourages a truncated understanding of a [show's] ethical significance. It falsely narrows the ethical field, allowing other depictions with ethical import often to come in under the radar."[1] In distinction from this rather reductive approach, we want to engage in a more expansive process of ethical discernment—one that requires us to look with new eyes and listen with new ears, to appreciate before we appraise, and to enter empathetically into uncomfortable truths and disturbing realities.

In this chapter, then, we develop further our medium-specific theological framework by considering the various ways in which people might actively respond to the Spirit's presence and activity in and through TV and TV viewing. Building upon our interaction with James K. A. Smith, we are concerned here with the ways in which the ritual practices associated with TV might encourage particular kinds of human action and whether those actions are contributing to the common good (i.e., whether they might be considered "ethical").[2] Also, though, by developing the work of William Dyrness and Robert Johnston, we are continuing to explore how the Spirit might be present and active in these symbolic practices. That is, we are asking what it is that the Spirit intends to do to us and with us as we watch TV and as we incorporate it ritually and symbolically into our lives as a meaningful practice.

In some respects, our approach finds a home in what many ethicists would call "virtue ethics." The virtue approach recognizes that "*right actions* are a natural outgrowth of being *the best sort of person*. To become the best sort of person, valuable character traits like honesty, courage, fair-mindedness, generosity, self-discipline and even-temperedness are to be cultivated."[3] But our concerns are not only about cultivating specific virtues that will lead to right action. We are also interested in the ways that virtue-forming practices can serve as a location where contemporary persons might initially recognize God's presence in their lives or, on a more basic level, sense their need for something they desire but are unable to describe—an itch they haven't the resources to scratch. Some might call this an experience of transcendence or grace. Others might call it insight or revelation. We are fond simply of "presence."

We are thus operating with a theological assumption that can be summarized as follows: the Spirit's presence shapes us through certain symbolic practices into certain kinds of people who understand (i.e., see/hear/feel) the world in certain ways and thus relate to it (i.e., act) accordingly. And while this claim is fine and well, it immediately raises a series of questions that strike at the heart of a robust Christian ethic: What are the criteria that allow us to determine whether our TV watching (in general and of specific shows) is functioning as one of these theological practices or not? Where might we celebrate, affirm, and delight in television as an inspired practice that moves us toward the common good? And on what grounds should we critique, protest, and seek to transform TV, recognizing those places where it serves as an impediment to human flourishing?

Borrowing again from Dyrness, we might say that humans are involved in various creative projects, and that each has various levels of compatibility or resonance with God's project in the world. Watching TV is but one of those many projects. So we want to consider the ways in which television might be functioning as a theological practice that resonates with the Spirit's presence and activity. It would be tempting to start by identifying a series of biblical/theological propositions that could serve as our basic criteria for ethical discernment, asking whether a show's content aligns with and/or validates our preconceptions. But these criteria would be a cultural abstraction; they would be external to our lived experience. They would also reflect a failure on our part to acknowledge that the resources for moving a society toward wholeness and flourishing already exist within that cultural context.[4]

So just as we have done throughout the book, we start in this chapter from the ground up, allowing TV to speak first. Rather than imposing categories upon TV, we want to begin by discerning the ethical shape of TV and allowing it to expand our vision. In doing so, we are demonstrating what Gordon Lynch calls "ethical patience," cultivating "the ability to hear and understand popular culture on its own terms before seeking to critique it."[5] By taking this approach, we will be able to demonstrate more fully how the symbolic practice of TV watching has not only ethical significance but also theological significance. That is, by first considering how particular TV programs and TV viewing habits might promote human flourishing in their own right, we open up a more hospitable space for relating these practices to the project of God in the world.[6]

Moving beyond Content Analysis and the "Big Three"

Before turning toward a few concrete examples, a caveat is in order. As we noted in previous chapters, any attempt to understand TV "on its own terms" requires careful consideration of a program's sights, structures, and sounds (i.e., its "trace"). The same can be said regarding a show's ethical import. However, this kind of critical analysis should not be confused with "content analysis," the process whereby a piece of media is divided into discrete data points that are then organized and measured according to a number of representative types (usually the "big three" of language, sex, and violence).

As we hope we have made clear by now, there is often a world of difference between what a show depicts and the overarching shape of its narrative—between its content and its meaning. What a TV show "means" is of course a matter of interpretation, which is why some cultural critics and theologians are simply not comfortable with a hermeneutic approach to media. Coming to terms with the meaning of any artwork is an ongoing, dialogical process that is open, contested, and continually up for negotiation. There are always loose ends. In contrast, "content" appears on the surface to be more fixed, concrete, and, perhaps most important, measurable. For this reason, one of the most common approaches among those who are concerned about the ethics of television is to quantify the frequency and duration of TV content in order to evaluate its effects.

There are religious and nonreligious, liberal and conservative examples of this approach, but on the whole the primary focus of content analysis concerns the ways in which violent, sexual, or vulgar TV content influences its audience—especially children. Indeed, the potentially hazardous effect of exposure to media content was the central concern of the Telecommunications Act of 1996, which called upon the entertainment industry to create and implement a voluntary rating system for television broadcasts. The TV Parental Guidelines were created to provide parents with advice and guidance on TV content so that they could make informed decisions about what their children might watch. Developed in conversation with the Federal Communications Commission and based upon the already familiar MPAA ratings used for film, it is unsurprising that both the rating categories themselves (TV-Y, TV-Y7, TV-G, TV-PG, TV-14, TV-MA) and the individual content descriptors focus exclusively on language (D, L), sexuality (S), and violence (V, FV).[7]

Few would disagree with the need for parents to be well informed about the media their children are consuming. But a system designed primarily to prevent children from being exposed to inappropriate content does not provide us with adequate criteria for developing a full-orbed ethical engagement with television. Unfortunately, though, for a number of lay and professional theologians, the TV rating system (along with its focus on the "big three") has become the ethical standard for Christian engagement, thus making it difficult to move beyond these content-based criteria.[8]

The broader aim of content analysis is to determine more clearly how media shapes society as a whole—for good or for ill (but mostly for ill). It is an intrinsically ethical approach, for it assumes that the media content we consume shapes how we see the world and, by extension, how we (ought to) act in it. Indeed, for some, even "the most innocuous sitcom carries messages about how our society works and how its citizens should behave. . . . According to television's creators, they are not just in it for the money. They also seek to move the audience toward their own vision of the good society."[9]

There can be some value in compiling statistical data of this kind, especially as it concerns the ways in which media might reflect or even prompt changes within the broader cultural imagination. However, the downside is that it tends to reduce the formative work of TV to little more than the content it conveys. It assumes that the mere transmission of discrete pieces of data from a sender to a receiver is all that is required to shape people into ethical (or rather, not-so-ethical) agents. In other words, it mistakes the content depicted on television for its meaning, giving little attention to TV's formal dimensions, the process by which it was created, or the various contexts of its reception.

However, what is perhaps even more problematic about empirical research is that, when it comes to TV content, it is largely inconclusive. Some remain convinced that the cumulative effect of exposure to ethically dubious content shapes how people actually behave in the real world.[10] Depictions of violence either spawn violent behavior or desensitize viewers (again, especially children). Pervasive sexual content generates a laissez-faire attitude toward traditional sexual mores and an increasingly promiscuous society. So forth and so on. Others completely disagree, though, pointing to the impossibility of directly connecting the consumption of media content with specific behaviors. There are simply too many other contextual factors in play to "blame" TV.

Interestingly, advocates for both positions are analyzing the same empirical data, yet they arrive at very different conclusions. Jolyon Mitchell has noted this disparity among those concerned with violent media content: "The study of media violence, and the many forms that it takes, has a long history. It has been and remains one of the most hotly debated topics in media, communication and cultural studies. Questions such as 'to what extent, if any, does media violence influence viewers?' have provoked countless quantitative and qualitative studies. Some argue there are no or very few discernible causal effects, while others posit significant and specific impacts."[11]

We haven't the space here to rehearse the details of these competing arguments, but even if we could, it would be a bit of a distraction from our primary concern. From a theological perspective, content analysis alone is simply inadequate. On its own, it is a limiting and, at times, possibly even misleading approach to constructing a robust Christian ethic. Indeed, in some cases, it actually blinds us to the deeply ethical discourse that is arising from television itself. This is not to say that depictions of language, sex, and violence should be of no concern to Christians. Rather, it is simply to say that, when we allow depictions of language, sex, and violence to co-opt the ethical conversation, we are operating with an impoverished view of TV's ethical import. Our ethical vision becomes impaired, myopic even. We see problems where there are none and, at the very same time, fail to see what is truly problematic.

Thus, to develop an ethical vision that allows individuals and communities to interact creatively and wisely with TV, we need to consider more fully the ways in which TV stories engage viewers' imaginations, ritually orienting their passions toward a particular vision of the good life and thus shaping their actions. Because our lived ethic is always an on-the-ground reality, this kind of ethical discussion begins with a consideration of the larger ethical tone and intention of a particular TV story. However, given the medium-specific theological framework we described earlier, we are also concerned with the formative nature of TV watching practices and how this process of ritual formation might very well serve as a location where the Spirit of God is uniquely present and active, constantly moving viewers toward an awareness of that "something" for which they long but cannot quite name. So as we turn toward a few concrete examples, our hope is to do more than simply identify and describe the ethical shape of a particular show or series. We also hope to redescribe it theologically in terms of the Spirit's presence and activity.[12]

Witness: Cable News and *The Daily Show*

One of the more noticeable effects of the ever-evolving TV landscape has been the proliferation of twenty-four-hour news networks and, along with it, the rise of entertainment journalism. The advent of cable television in the early 1980s created both a delivery system and a market for this nonstop supply of information-based programming. In more recent years, the expansion of online media outlets has only added fuel to the fire, providing consumers a seemingly endless feed of "breaking news." Every moment of every day, the networks' quest to capture the largest audience share meets with TV's voracious appetite for a constant stream of compelling content. The end result of this perfect media storm is that the very notion of what constitutes a story as "newsworthy" is being stretched to its limits.

A somewhat recent example can be found in the way that numerous cable news networks covered the fiftieth anniversary of Martin Luther King Jr.'s march from Selma to Montgomery, Alabama. Journalists from almost every major news network (CNN, MSNBC, Fox News, CBS, NBC, ABC) broadcast live reports from the now infamous bridge where Alabama state troopers used clubs and tear gas to brutalize marchers trying to cross over the county line. In the days prior to round-the-clock news, this kind of on-location commentary would likely have served as one small part of a much larger and more comprehensive piece. But the need to fill countless hours of programming blocks with content (newsworthy or not) has generated a radically different kind of journalism.

As a result, it became difficult at times to discern whether the stories being reported from the eponymous bridge were about the Selma-to-Montgomery marches at all.

For instance, throughout the day, CNN produced various segments about the aerial drones they were using to capture footage of the bridge, along with live commentary and analysis from their embedded reporters. In other words, CNN's leading story on the anniversary of "Bloody Sunday" was not about the Selma marches, MLK, or the fractured history of civil rights in America. It was about a flying robot, attached to a camera, taking "exciting" video of a bridge. Given the amount of airtime dedicated to these toy helicopters, it was clear that the "breathtaking" and "never-before-seen" footage provided by the drones was the truly compelling content of CNN's coverage. Apparently, the dawn of the modern civil rights movement just didn't have enough drama of its own to keep audiences interested all day long.

This assessment might strike some as overly cynical or critical, but it may not be cynical enough, especially when we consider the broader cultural ramifications of the shift in how networks produce news and how audiences consume it. Even before the rise of twenty-four-hour cable news, Neil Postman voiced serious concerns about what happens to public discourse when the lines between news and entertainment are blurred. Postman wasn't anti-entertainment, nor was he suggesting that all news should look like what we find on C-SPAN. Rather, his primary concern with television as a medium was its tendency to turn *all* public life into entertainment, thus undermining our ability to engage in thoughtful reflection either individually or as a public. According to Postman, "The problem is not that the television presents us with entertaining subject matter but that all subject matter is presented as entertaining."[13] More so than anything else, argued Postman, TV news epitomizes the totalizing effects of the medium, for television has radically altered the form, content, and purpose of journalism. News is now a format for entertainment. It provokes applause, not reflection.

As we have already noted, we are generally far less critical of television's cultural influence than Postman. But when it comes to the current state of news media, he was more right than wrong. Initially, the move toward cable news seemed to reflect an incredibly democratic impulse within the industry. Consumers were now no longer dependent upon the "big three" networks (CBS, NBC, ABC) as the sole providers of information, for the expansion of cable news outlets created opportunities for them to get their news from alternative sources—to hear a different set of stories that did not always share the same ideological commitments as the big three.

At least in theory, this diversity of options provided access to an equally diverse set of perspectives on the various events taking place around the world.

But in 1999, the FCC made a historic decision that forever changed the face of US media, allowing individual firms to own more than one TV station in a market. Almost without our knowing it, every TV network, film studio, music company, internet provider, and online distribution platform quickly came under the control of no more than seven (seven!) privately owned corporations. Significantly, theorists and practitioners of diverse political and religious stripes all point to the increasing concentration of media ownership as a profoundly ethical dilemma that must be addressed.[14] Some would even go so far as to say that it is *the* ethical dilemma facing modern society.

So many otherwise divergent voices share concerns about the ethics of media ownership because there is a fundamental contradiction between the communication requirements of a for-profit, highly concentrated, corporate media system and the communication requirements of a democratic society. A well-informed public is the backbone of a healthy democracy. Yet, as with every other genre of televisual media, TV news is in the business of communicating not just information but stories. No program or newscaster is ever simply transmitting "the facts" to an audience. He or she is always already locating this information within a larger narrative, which is why it is appropriate for us to consider the ethics of TV news in a book that has been focused mostly on fictional stories. Indeed, the parallels between the two are striking. Like fictional stories, TV news does not objectively present us with reality but rather "frames" reality—both metaphorically through its ongoing narrative work and literally through its positioning of the camera. Audiences only ever see part of the picture.

There is nothing inherently wrong or unethical about framing reality through narrative means. It simply reflects the way humans understand and make sense of their life and the world. The problem comes when information is narrated in such a way that it creates the illusion of understanding but is actually leading one away from understanding. For example, when a news program or network obscures its narrative work (intentionally or unintentionally), it is operating as if its particular take on reality is not a "take" at all but is simply "the way things are."

Even more problematic is when a small group of media magnates not only profits from this illusion but also maintains its power by successfully sustaining it. Within this kind of economic system, which in some respects is unique to the United States, journalism has little to do with the public interest or the common good. It has to do more with turning a profit. And the best way to turn a profit in the current structure of corporate control is not to keep the public informed but to captivate a faithful audience by reinforcing a consistent and compelling narrative across multiple media platforms.

Under the guise of "integrated marketing," a few multinational conglomerates frame every piece of information we encounter within a broader but often hidden narrative designed to encourage our continued consumption of their own media products. It doesn't matter if the content is newsworthy or not. It doesn't matter if the reporting is fair or balanced, whether it offers legitimate critiques of those in power or simply props up the status quo. It only matters that it keeps the audience coming back for more. In this way, it seems that, just as Postman feared, public discourse has been co-opted by the logics of commercial entertainment, and audiences couldn't be more pleased.

It is perhaps fitting, then, that one of the more compelling critiques of these powerful narratives comes not from the realm of journalism or politics but from a half-hour "fake news" program on cable TV, otherwise known as *The Daily Show*. Hosted for sixteen years by comedian Jon Stewart, *The Daily Show with Jon Stewart* figured prominently in the pop-cultural imagination, especially among the coveted eighteen to thirty-nine–year-old demographic. On the one hand, it is an ironic, self-referential parody of current events. On the other hand, it is a serious commentary on contemporary culture in the form of absurdist humor. In other words, it is infotainment as satire. Recognizing it as such is a key element in understanding the show's power and meaning, especially as it concerns its ethical intentions.

In terms of its trace, *The Daily Show* still airs four nights per week (with new host Trevor Noah) and features a fairly consistent format. Stewart typically opened the show with an extended monologue on current events, shifted to a second segment where he interacted with correspondents in "the field" (who were actually on a green screen in the studio), and then ended the program by interviewing a celebrity or political figure (or sometimes, when the stars aligned, a political celebrity). All told, each episode contained only twenty-two minutes of content, but this content was intentionally divided into distinct segments, each of which existed beyond the original broadcast in a variety of digital contexts. Also, supplemental content such as extended interviews were accessible online, which only complicates our ability to say with any kind of finality or certainty what a particular show or segment meant or how exactly it functioned in the broader culture. In other words, as with much modern television, *The Daily Show* assumes a form that is designed for maximum "spreadability."[15]

Because *The Daily Show* is first and foremost satire and because its narrative flow encourages us to understand individual segments of the show as unique embodiments of a much larger narrative that is told over the course of numerous seasons, we can focus our analysis on how particular segments stand in critical contrast to the larger narrative work of the network and corporation. In the case of the Bloody Sunday commemoration, Stewart dedicated the entire

The cast of Comedy Central's *The Daily Show with Jon Stewart*

opening segment of the March 9, 2015, episode to calling out the absurdity of CNN's obsession with its drones. At one point, he even riffed on MLK's "I have a dream" speech: "I have a drone! That a news channel would be judged not by the content of its . . . content, but by the uselessness of its gizmos."

Stewart's satirical diatribes were meant to do one thing: to expose the constructed nature of contemporary news media and to challenge the totalizing narrative of an increasingly consolidated media ownership. This is not to say that *The Daily Show* is somehow free from the narrative work of its own network or parent corporation (Comedy Central is owned by Viacom, the sixth-largest mass media corporation in the world). In fact, the show's creators don't even attempt to be objective. Instead, they intentionally highlight the fabricated and thus ideologically loaded nature of all media—including their own. *The Daily Show* is not "news"; it is "fake news" distributed by Comedy Central. The correspondents are not "journalists"; they are "The Best F#@king News Team Ever."[16] And it is this very self-consciousness that enables *The Daily Show* both to expose the otherwise invisible operations of corporate narratives and to demand that cable news do more than simply entertain.

Whether one agreed with Stewart's politics or not is almost beside the point. What is more important is that The Daily Show was voicing a critique almost identical to Postman's, which is that entertainment should be entertainment and journalism should be journalism. When journalism functions according to the logics of entertainment, it inhibits our ability to engage in constructive public discourse. Indeed, Stewart has voiced this perspective in other settings as well, including CNN. According to Stewart and the creative producers of The Daily Show, it is nearly impossible to maintain journalistic integrity when broadcasters are required to meet the demands of profit-driven, multinational media corporations. As a result, cable news programs are forced to obscure the larger ideological work of the network and corporation, offering to the public information that is often ideologically shaped misinformation.

The Daily Show, however, is explicit about its political and ideological commitments, a freedom it has primarily because of its genre (satire) and the larger narrative flow of its network (one oriented toward comedic entertainment). To be sure, it is not consistently an "equal opportunity offender" as some of the show's creators claim. However, viewers are able to discern more accurately what is and is not "factual" or "actual" because the show makes its ideological commitments clear; at no point does it even suggest it is offering anything but a biased interpretation of events. Depending upon one's political leanings, this in-your-face perspectivalism can be either frustrating or welcome (or both at the same time). Regardless, by calling out the constructed-ness of all media narratives and being up-front about its own political biases, The Daily Show provides its audience with a (not uncomplicated) avenue for both understanding reality more clearly and critiquing media representations that traffic in un-reality.

It might go without saying, but desire for clarity of vision is a decidedly ethical impulse. So too is the critique of harmful media representations. In fact, as Jolyon Mitchell notes, "Many Christian ethicists now speak of the importance of vision, and by extension learning to see, to understand and to describe the world correctly."[17] The Daily Show does not shy away from the fact that it is "framing" the news in very specific ways and thus presenting viewers with its own limited view or "vision" of reality. But in doing so, its goal is actually to reframe events in such a way that audiences might be able to resist the totalizing narratives of corporate news—narratives that would have us believe that the "reality" it presents is the complete and unfiltered truth. And if these categories of vision and cultural critique do indeed define the ethical import of The Daily Show, then the moral discourse that the show provokes has almost nothing to do with its various depictions of language, sex, or violence. Rather, we need to ask how audiences are formed as moral agents by watching the show and how that formative process resonates with the intentions of the Spirit, who is present and active in and through this symbolic practice.

According to Mitchell, the collective cultural expectations regarding journalistic integrity represent a wider set of shared practices that reflect what the Christian tradition calls "witness."[18] That is, "while many journalists would not claim to be working as Christians, they can manifest several Christian virtues, including compassion and the desire to bear witness to the truth."[19] So even while we must acknowledge that every journalist cannot help reporting the "facts" through his or her own skewed perspective, journalists still serve an essential public role in describing and communicating truth to those who are unable to witness significant (and even not-so-significant) events firsthand.

But what happens when this kind of witness is co-opted by powerful entities that are less concerned with laying bare the truth than with producing must-see television for the sake of maintaining their corporate interests? How might we engage and understand this circumstance ethically? It is interesting to note here that both the Jewish and the Christian traditions provide a number of resources for remembering, reframing, and redescribing reality when those in power are working hard to obscure it. Indeed, much of what is known in both the academy and popular culture as "cultural criticism" is actually parasitic on the prophetic tradition's critique of oppressive power structures and the systemic injustices perpetuated by their ideological commitments. But as it concerns our consideration of TV ethics, what is perhaps even more interesting is the mode in which the prophetic tradition often voiced its criticism and bore witness to truth: satire.

In *Satire and the Hebrew Prophets*, Thomas Jemielity suggests that the prophetic literature of ancient Israel, although predating satire as a formal literary category, provides ample evidence of the satiric. Prophetic speech is entertaining. It is funny. It praises, extols, and teaches. But it also ridicules and blames. It is biting in its humor. Think of Hosea making fun of the carved wooden phallic symbols worshiped by a high priest of the northern kingdom (Hosea 4:12), or Elijah suggesting to the prophets of Baal that their god might be too bathroom-occupied to hear them (1 Kings 18:27). In this way, Hebrew prophecy demonstrates "the laughter of attack, the laughing at that characterizes satire."[20]

According to Jemielity, prophetic literature calls upon the satiric so often because the prophet's goal is to subvert the closed and self-satisfied system of the institution, and satire is particularly effective in this regard. "The forms of prophetic speech must shatter the forms of moral complacency: the prophetic word, like the satiric, must attack language itself and the forms of language because they shelter the customary and the complacent."[21]

Even within the biblical witness, prophetic satire is unapologetically entertaining. It is laugh-out-loud funny (consider Haman in the book of Esther, who tries every trick in the book to bring down the Jews, only to have it all backfire on him in rather ironic ways). But it is also a profoundly ethical mode of discourse, bearing witness as it does to uncomfortable truths that its hearers would rather simply ignore. It is not difficult to recognize the resonance here with modern-day satires like *The Daily Show*. For what it's worth, Stewart and company were also attempting to shatter our moral complacency and bear witness to truth in a form (and format) that could possibly wake us from our entertainment-induced slumber. And as Jemielity makes clear, satire is particularly well suited for this kind of prophetic witness because it both critiques and clarifies at one and the same time: "Satire compels because of its morally imaginative power to picture the consequences of irresponsible behavior that speak to and yet transcend the circumstances of their time. . . . Keen insight, not clairvoyance, is the key."[22]

If TV programs like *The Daily Show* do indeed shape viewers into people who understand and thus behave in the world in certain ways, and if the Spirit of God is an active agent in this process, then we might say that the Spirit is shaping people through satirical fake news, teaching them how to see the world more clearly and, as a result, compelling them to actively resist the powers and principalities that would have them mistake an illusion for the truth. In a context where every piece of information is always already "framed," the first step in voicing a prophetic critique is to point out that all of reality is being framed, especially by the powerful few who would have us believe that their version of the story is either complete, comprehensive, or even just the way things naturally are. The second is to reframe reality in a way that encourages rather than inhibits human flourishing. Using biblical language, this means remembering and redescribing reality not according to the logics of entertainment but according to the logics of *shalom*.

In this way, the ethical shape and intentions of *The Daily Show* expand our theological vision by encouraging us to shift our focus from depictions of sex, language, and violence to a consideration of how that content is framed and by whom. Like any other show, it of course fails nearly as often as it succeeds and, in some cases, even contributes to the problem. Yet what should trouble the Christian ethically is not first and foremost the content of *The Daily Show* but rather a media environment that leaves the public with no other choice but to consume increasingly narrow and incomplete representations of the world in which we live. For the lay and professional theologian, then, we ought to confidently affirm and celebrate those media that seek to provide not complete objectivity but clarity of vision, even if these media assume the form of biting satire, as does *The Daily Show*. Likewise, we can also critique and resist those news outlets that frame reality in ways that simply perpetuate the desires of a powerful minority at the expense of the weak and the marginalized. In this way, the Christian actually collaborates (sometimes uneasily) with critical voices already present in the broader culture and, in doing so, participates with the ongoing work of the Spirit of God in the world.

Hospitality: *Fresh Off the Boat* and Otherness

Increasingly, large multinational conglomerates exert a significant level of influence on the way that televisual media frames and therefore bears witness to reality. But these corporations (and the executives who run them) are only part of the equation. As we made clear in previous chapters, audiences are active agents in the meaning-making process as well. Reception matters in terms of both what and how a show means, and this is especially true when it comes to the ways in which audiences are shaped ethically in and through their TV consumption.

However, one of the primary ethical critiques leveled against TV media concerns not reception per se but representation. Numerous cultural critics suggest that, on the whole, television fails to reflect the great diversity that exists in the real world. Even when TV images and narratives are diverse in their representations—racial, religious, economic, political, cultural, or otherwise—the various characters that embody these underrepresented people groups are rarely fully realized human beings. Instead, they are often reductive and harmful stereotypes—a kind of generic shorthand for "otherness" that "reinforces the status quo or, at best, gently tweaks hegemonic formations."[23] So the issue is not merely whether certain minority groups are represented but whether they are represented well, that is, in ways that are constructive, life-giving, and good.

In many cases, these concerns about the ethics of media representations assume that studios, networks, and advertisers are primarily (if not exclusively) responsible for what and how diverse groups are represented in and through media. To be sure, as we suggested above, this assumption has its merits. Most of the content that makes it onto screens of any kind serves the interests of a powerful minority. But given the evolving nature of TV storytelling, the proliferation of options for customizing one's TV viewing practices, and the shifting power dynamics between producers and consumers, we cannot conclude so simply that the problems with TV representations are related only to its producers. These problems also have very much to do with consumers. Or, to put it somewhat differently, we as viewers cannot ignore our own share of the responsibility when the television we consume radicalizes otherness at the expense of our common humanity.

To reiterate, we are intentionally expanding here what it means to engage television ethically, attempting not only to discern the ethical tone or intention of a particular TV program but also to consider how it functions within a larger cultural context. And at least in the United States, one of the more salient examples of the way in which TV's ethical significance is bound up with its cultural context concerns the representation of race. Interestingly, on the surface, it would seem that there are now more options than ever to encounter the racial "other" in healthy and constructive ways on television. In fact, a number of programs have recently emerged that depict racial diversity in increasingly broad and textured ways—from shows that feature racial minorities as leading actors and actresses (*Scandal*, *How to Get Away with Murder*), to those with an intentionally diverse cast (*Community*, *Grey's Anatomy*), to those that tell the stories of historically underrepresented groups (*Cristela*, *Black-ish*).

In the not-too-distant past, though, the TV landscape was far less colorful. A program like *The Cosby Show* was heralded for its sympathetic portrayal of a black family in part because it was such an anomaly. Bill Cosby's brand of humor and the show's otherwise endearing qualities were surely what made it one of the most popular shows of the 1980s and early 1990s, but its unabashedly positive depiction of black persons and communities was still quite rare at the time. In fact, some critics even voiced concerns about the Huxtables. While they were certainly a heartwarming bunch that was accessible to the dominant (i.e., white) culture, the question was whether a family with a medical doctor and a lawyer as parents could faithfully represent the experience of most black families living in America. Were they a "real" black family, or a disingenuous representation of blackness designed to be more palatable to white audiences?

The Cosby Show was one of a few tipping points in the history of TV's depiction of race. It not only made possible subsequent shows with largely African American casts like *A Different World* and *The Fresh Prince of Bel-Air*, but it also paved the way for the current slate of racially diverse programming. The show's influence simply cannot be overlooked or disregarded, even when we take into consideration Bill Cosby's now-tarnished reputation. But despite all the good that *The Cosby Show* has brought about in terms of representations of race, the question voiced by its critics remains equally pertinent today. That is, if television does in fact function as a common vocabulary for discussing what we as a society value, should TV narratives and characters represent race in terms of *what actually is* or *what ought to be*?[24]

This question is certainly reasonable, but it is also somewhat problematic because it tends to overlook an important detail: the audience. For instance, even before families were gathering together every Thursday night to watch the Huxtables, Norman Lear was pursuing conversations about race in America with his *All in the Family*. Interestingly, while the show itself offers a scathing critique of Archie Bunker's explicit racism, its popularity suggests that some viewers saw in Bunker not a bigoted buffoon but someone just like them. Regardless of Lear's intentions, viewers could see in Archie a humorous affirmation rather than a satirical critique of their own prejudices. In an important sense, this inclination to legitimize one's racist attitudes is to be expected. After all, TV stories depend upon the willingness of viewers to emotionally bond and identify with a protagonist (however unlovable). As a result, "although the script made it abundantly clear that Archie's behavior was reprehensible, the Norman Lear approach was basically to humanize bigotry in order to poke fun at it."[25]

All in the Family thus serves as a reminder that, especially when it comes to representations of race, audiences do not always decode TV narratives in ways that align with the intentions of narratives' creators. Some proponents of *All in the Family* suggest that the show actually did function "prophetically" by opening viewers up to a larger moral landscape: "Archie Bunker can be interpreted— and rightly so—as an icon of white racist attitudes in North America. Archie's character is not celebrated by the show's producers, but repeatedly mocked. Along the way, the audience is invited to confront their own stereotypes and ignorance. The show, then, can be seen as a subtle form of prophetic mockery."[26]

However, it is important to keep in mind that this is not always or even necessarily the case. Some viewers can and do "read against the grain," internalizing and making use of TV narratives in ways that are as unpredictable as they are uncontrollable.

None of this is to suggest that *All in the Family* was an ethical failure. In fact, like *The Cosby Show*, it too served as a watershed moment in television history. However, the various ways in which audiences have accepted and understood *All in the Family* highlights the reality that, because the practice of meaning-making is so multilayered and complex, a truly robust ethical conversation cannot be concerned only with questions of representation. It must also engage issues of reception.

Even with the best of intentions, TV producers haven't the capacity to "solve" something as fraught as race relations in the United States. What they can do, however, is immerse viewers in narrative worlds where they regularly encounter the other not as a prejudiced reduction or a generic caricature but as fundamentally human. In other words, TV has the potential to help people envision their world differently. Thus it is important for Christians to be critical of both grossly negligent racial stereotypes and overly sanitized versions of race that obscure reality in order to make it more viewer friendly.

Yet, from a theological perspective, *how* we watch TV is just as important as what we watch. Those who are interested in the ethical significance of TV often overlook the various modes by which contemporary audiences consume television, which suggests that we have more work to do in terms of developing an ethic of reception. For example, even if TV programs could do the hard relational work of racial reconciliation for us by offering a perfect balance of "brutally-honest-but-also-uplifting-and-positive" depictions of diverse people groups, audiences simply have too much control over their viewing practices. The emergence of new TV technologies and distribution platforms has shifted the dynamics between producers and consumers, creating an environment in which the viewer—and not the network—ultimately determines what makes it (and more important, what doesn't make it) onto the screen.

The premier season of the ABC show *Fresh Off the Boat* offers an interesting example of this producer/consumer dynamic. Featuring a cast comprising almost exclusively Asian American actors (Randall Park as Louis, Constance Wu as Jessica, and Hudson Yang as Eddie), *Fresh Off the Boat* is based upon the Eddie Huang memoir of the same name. Set in the mid-to-early 1990s, the show explores cultural difference, otherness, and the complexities of racial identity by telling the story of the Huangs—an Asian American family living in suburban Orlando, Florida. In its pilot episode, the narrative addresses race and race relations directly, culminating with an African American classmate telling the young Eddie, "Oh, it didn't go well? The white people didn't welcome you with open arms? You're the one at the bottom now. It's my turn, chink!"

Needless to say, the show is daring in its willingness to address race with raw (and sometimes brutal) honesty. It is also funny, well written, and features superb acting. But given the constraints of a network television sitcom, can we say that it is good? That is, does it actually invite viewers to confront their entrenched stereotypes and see the racial other in a way that promotes human flourishing?

Perhaps unsurprisingly, much like the conversations that surrounded *The Cosby Show*, some believe that *Fresh Off the Boat* is a beacon of moral progress, while others are critical of its "stereotypical" representation of race. One prominent TV critic praised the show, suggesting that no sitcom could ever be "authentic" or true to life, but that this should in no way diminish its cultural significance or its ability to advance conversations about race in America:

> [*Fresh Off the Boat*] has the burden of representation. Because there are so few series with Asian regulars—it's the first Asian-American family sitcom since *All-American Girl* two decades[!] ago—*Fresh* is inevitably going to be scanned for stereotypes and generalizations. Seen through that frame, Jessica does sometimes

evoke tiger-mom stereotypes, and Louis does recall pop-culture images of the nice, unthreatening Asian man. . . . At the same time, they feel like distinct, realized individuals. . . . That there aren't more Asian, especially East Asian, stars on American TV is a problem—and, historically, an embarrassment. But it shouldn't rope *Fresh*, a show that's trying to tell a story about the messiness of multiculturalism, into responsible dullness. . . . I doubt any network sitcom is going to prove very true to Eddie Huang's life, or any real person's. But in a way, that may be fitting for a show whose themes are about combining authenticity with artifice. . . . "True" or not, *Fresh off the Boat* could prove to be distinctive, funny and lasting—and yes, even important—if it stays true to itself.[27]

Eddie Huang himself has offered a similarly ambivalent take on the show, noting that, despite the fact that his story "had become an entertaining but domesticated vehicle to sell dominant culture with Kidz Bop, pot shots, and the emasculated Asian male," it nevertheless matters that the Asian American experience is being taken seriously on a national stage.[28] So even Huang himself wrestles with the question of whether *any* kind of representation is better than no representation at all.

Like the many other TV narratives that feature families of color, *Fresh Off the Boat* raises questions about representation, authenticity, and stereotypes that we must all take seriously if we are to discuss race with any kind of sensitivity or thoughtfulness. But given our theological commitments, our process of ethical discernment cannot stop here. So as we consider whether a TV show is representing the other in constructive ways, we also need to ask whether viewers within the dominant culture are even seeing the other at all.

As we noted in previous chapters, the broadcast model that once defined TV production, distribution, and consumption has now been replaced by a "narrow-cast" model—one in which producers strategically create content that is targeted toward niche audiences. Whereas a huge hit like *The Cosby Show* was garnering audiences of thirty to forty million viewers at its peak, a show in the current climate can generate an audience of two to four million viewers (or even fewer) and still be considered a "success." This is not to say that fewer people are watching TV—quite the opposite. Viewers simply have access to innumerable options for their TV consumption that can be customized in highly individualized ways. In fact, streaming services like Netflix automate this customizing work for us, constantly suggesting to us what we might "like" based upon our prior viewing habits.

All this is to say, even with the recent proliferation of programming that is constructively engaging issues of racial diversity and otherness, it is nevertheless possible (and now quite easy) to avoid these diverse representations altogether. What is even more problematic is that this narrowing of the audience's moral field of view usually isn't—or at least doesn't have to be—a conscious act. Without doing anything other than accepting the "friendly" recommendations of Netflix, viewers are able to construct a TV experience in which they see, hear, and encounter only what they already like and know. Alternative accounts don't even appear as available options. We can now go days, weeks, or even months without interacting with a single vision of reality that might challenge our own. In the process, our basic awareness of the world becomes ever more rigid and absolute. Otherness is not merely marginalized; it is literally rendered invisible. The other is customized out of our queue and thus out of existence.

Of course, not everyone's preferences will lead him or her to delete shows like *Fresh Off the Boat* from their Netflix queue. Nevertheless, the point we are making as it concerns TV technology is that theology needs to do more than simply celebrate the existence of ethically robust representations of race on TV. It also needs to advocate for a conscious and proactive engagement with television that pushes viewers beyond what they already like or prefer. In doing so, it can affirm those televisual encounters that expand rather than restrict our moral vision, shaping us in ways that are more open and hospitable toward the other in our midst.

This movement toward an ethic of reception resonates with the broader theological reality of the Spirit's presence and activity in the world. Indeed, as the biblical witness makes clear, the Spirit moves in ways that are particularly inclined toward acts of hospitality. In concert with the writer of Hebrews, who was glossing on the story of Abraham and Sarah receiving divine messengers in Genesis 18, an ethic of reception encourages us to "not forget to show hospitality to strangers, for by so doing some people have shown hospitality to angels without knowing it" (Heb. 13:2). We can thus confidently affirm those broader cultural practices that shape us into people who demonstrate hospitality, for the Spirit is uniquely present in those spaces where otherness is not simply depicted, but overcome.

It may be, however, that we have been entertaining the wrong stranger. Most Americans (including those who are a part of the Christian community) have integrated TV technology into their domestic lives without any question at all. Indeed, "in richer parts of the world houses or flats are filled to overflowing with different media. Computers, televisions and radios are welcomed into every conceivable domestic space. They are permanent guests and taken-for-granted members of the family. They are often invited into the most private spaces without a second thought."[29] It would seem that we have uncritically embraced television technology as a fixture of modern life, choosing to focus our ethical energies only on the content that television mediates rather than the technology itself.

Yet when it comes to the very real and urgent task of grappling with the ethics of racial representation, our theological commitments simply do not allow this kind of uncritical embrace of TV technology. In fact, these commitments demand that we practice an alternative form of hospitality—one that is both more unsettling and more embodied than our Netflix preferences might allow. In the first place, for TV to shape our imaginations in ways that promote the human good, we must resist the tendency to allow user interfaces to dictate our viewing habits. Despite the overwhelming morass of digital content and the seemingly "intuitive" nature of our online profiles, we can—and should—make the curation of TV content an integral part of our TV-consuming practices. Curation will become increasingly important in an age when TV content no longer disappears after it is released but only piles higher. Indeed, given the recent surge not only in the amount of TV programming that is being produced but also in the quality of those stories, developing our capacity to identify what is worthy of our time and attention is of paramount importance. Yet to do this—to assume a posture of reception that refuses simply to consume whatever Amazon or Hulu or Netflix suggests—requires us to engage television with far more wisdom, insight, and, indeed, humility than our usual TV-watching practices allow.

It is also essential that we keep in mind how the author of Hebrews expands upon the notion of hospitality: "Continue to remember those in prison as if you were together with them in prison, and those who are mistreated as if you yourselves were suffering" (Heb. 13:3). In other words, while we may be unknowingly entertaining angels, it is far more likely that our commitment to Christian hospitality will require us to enter willingly into the suffering of the other, bearing the burdens of those who are imprisoned, mistreated, and suffering in our society. But to be a people capable of remembering those who suffer "as if you yourself were suffering" is first to see the other not as "other" at all but as fundamentally human.

By establishing TV-watching practices that might expand rather than constrict our vision of racial otherness, we do so with the recognition that these practices are shaping how we see the world and, in turn, how we act toward the other as moral agents. Intentionally developing this kind of ethic of reception is neither natural nor easy. As James K. A. Smith would say, it involves a basic reworking of our habituated tendencies and thus a reordering of our desires. So being proactive about our ethical engagement with TV is not just about what we watch or even how we watch it. It's about what—and even who—we love.

As a consequence, one of the major ethical tasks before us is to open our domestic spaces not only to *narratives* of otherness made available by TV but to the *actual human other* in our midst. Television consumption can be and often is an incredibly isolated and highly personalized activity. But this does not have to be the case. Television programs like *The Cosby Show* were once able to gather human beings together in real time and space around a common narrative. Things have since changed, but not because shared stories are less culturally significant than they once were. Rather, it's because the distribution model and the technology have changed. Sure, *The Cosby Show* was recorded before a studio audience, but it was no more a "live" broadcast than *Fresh Off the Boat* is. The key difference is that the network determined when we watched *Cosby* (Thursdays at 8 p.m.), and the technology determined where we watched it (on a TV set in our living rooms).

Contemporary TV viewers now have far more control, which means that the audience is responsible for dictating not only what but also when and where to watch. This flexibility presents viewers with numerous possibilities for constructive engagement, not only as it concerns questions about race and racial identity in American culture but also in regards to gender, religion, sexuality, and socioeconomics, among other issues. Television producers have created a helpful avenue for engaging in these conversations. But it is up to consumers of TV to take advantage of these opportunities by gathering others together not only to watch TV in physical proximity with one another but to engage in a genuine dialogue about how TV representations affect society as a whole. In fact, we want to go one step further and suggest that an ethic of reception rooted in the s/Spirit of hospitality demands that we create these spaces for encountering the televisual and human other, inviting them into the most intimate regions of our lives.

Of course, if we absolve ourselves of the responsibility that comes with a fully developed ethic of reception, TV will only ever be a source of comfort and complacency. It will show us a picture of the world that is racially, economically, politically, and, worst of all, theologically homogenous. But if we reconsider not only what but also how we watch TV, this otherwise unwieldy medium has real potential for helping our increasingly diverse society enter into a robust moral dialogue on a variety of matters, race relations being only one of them. And if this is truly the case, TV might do more than shape us into people who see the other differently. It might very well serve as a location for the Spirit to work, shaping us into a people whose moral imagination allows for no other option except welcoming and embracing the other in self-giving love.

Friendship: *Friends* and Encouraging Empathy

Astute readers will notice that our consideration of the ethical shape of TV has followed closely the critical approaches we outlined in chapters 2 and 3. While our discussion of cable news and fake TV news focused primarily on the process by which TV producers construct televisual media, our exploration of racial representations and their connection to customized viewing habits was concerned with the practice of TV watching. In this final section, then, we focus on the trace of TV, placing a number of sitcoms into dialogue in order to discern the ways in which TV's ethical significance emerges over time and in conversation among a number of other TV narratives. In particular, we are concerned here with TV's moral imagination regarding friendship, and whether certain TV programs might be shaping viewers in ways that are reflective of the Spirit's ongoing, formative work in the world. Take the NBC sitcom *Friends* as an example. As Jolyon Mitchell notes,

> *Friends* was one of the most watched television programs in the United States between 1994 and 2004. Its 233rd and final episode attracted over 60 million viewers in the USA alone. In these twenty-two-minute comic dramas six twenty-somethings share their lives, loves and heartbreaks in Manhattan, largely untroubled by violence and global injustice. . . . Friends become confidants and lovers, drinking partners and betrayers. This is a world full of laughter, fun and playfulness. How these friendships actually shape their characters, form virtues or develop towards an end beyond narcissistic fulfilment is less clear.[30]

Indeed it is. And the reason that it remains unclear whether a series like *Friends* actually forms virtues (in the characters or the audience) has a great deal to do with the conventions of the sitcom genre.

In the first place, because *Friends* operates with the same narrative principals as nearly every other sitcom (i.e., conflict-tension-resolution), each episode seeks to maximize tension and heighten conflict among characters, only to resolve it in the end. Often, the conflict is built into the characters themselves, existing as they do in binary opposition to one another. Whereas Joey is a fun-loving but dense out-of-work actor, Chandler is a responsible though uptight businessperson. And if their diametrically opposed personalities were not enough to generate conflict on an episode-to-episode basis, Chandler and Joey are also roommates, a circumstance that only adds to the comedic effect of their relationship.

The basic plot of the episode "The One Where No One's Ready" demonstrates well how the narrative tension in *Friends* is often produced by simply placing characters in the same living quarters and allowing their opposing personalities to run wild. Early in the episode, Joey steals Chandler's seat while Chandler is in the bathroom. When Joey refuses to move after Chandler returns, Chandler hides all of Joey's underwear, thus forcing Joey to wear a rented tux while "going commando." In an effort to exact revenge, Joey aims to do the very opposite to Chandler, so he puts on every article of clothing in Chandler's closet. Their ensuing dialogue not only underscores the kind of absurdist humor that sitcoms are able to produce by establishing conflict between characters, but it also explicitly states that their core conflict is rooted in the fact that they are binary opposites:

> Joey: Okay, buddy-boy. Here it is: You hide my clothes, I'm wearing everything you own.
>
> Chandler: Oh my God! That is so not the opposite of taking somebody's underwear!
>
> Joey: Look at me—I'm Chandler! Could I *be* wearing any more clothes? Maybe if I wasn't going commando!

Throughout the series, a number of relationships develop along parallel lines among the six principal players in *Friends*. In almost every case, the tension that already exists because of their conflicting character traits is heightened by the setting—a small, shared living space in the middle of the Big Apple. Monica, who is borderline obsessive-compulsive, shares an apartment with Rachel, a bourgeois socialite who never worked a day in her life until she moved in with Monica. Monica's brother, Ross, is a lovelorn paleontologist (with a PhD!) who chronically dates women and, in at least three cases, marries them (and then gets divorced). Phoebe, on the other hand, was educated on the streets and, as a result, has serious commitment issues. As a vegan, bohemian musician who embraces new age spirituality and frequently questions the "facts" of science touted by Ross, Phoebe serves as his countercultural foil. Over the course of ten seasons, each of these characters does more than exchange witty banter about assigned seating. They live, laugh, mourn, and dance together. They make fun of one another. They give and take relational wounds. In some cases, they even share sexual partners. And they do all of this within a genre that demands a timely resolution to every episode in order to set the stage for the next narrative cycle of conflict-tension-resolution.

Given their extreme differences, it's no small wonder that this group of friends, while seemingly at peace with their long history of significant relational conflict, eventually dissolves. The series ends with Monica and Chandler moving to the suburbs, Phoebe getting married to a guy named Mike, Joey still a single womanizer heading to Los Angeles, and Ross choosing to commit to Rachel (who is the mother of his second child) only at the eleventh hour. Rather than becoming better human beings, the characters in *Friends* actually become caricatures of the people that we first meet in the pilot episode. The end result is that Ross, Rachel, Monica, Phoebe, Chandler, and Joey seem to devolve into exaggerated types of their most conflicted selves. Although *Friends* began as a story about a group of young adults forming a proxy family while trying to find meaning amid the chaos and clamor of modern life, it concludes on a much different note. They are surely a gracious and forgiving group of people given all they have done to one another, but have these characters actually developed character? That is, are their quests for fulfillment or their visions of flourishing any less self-directed than they were before?

The lack of change or development among the characters on *Friends* is not an isolated incident. It is actually par for the course for the majority of television series, especially those produced in the United States. In fact, "while it may seem that a pleasure of serial narratives is watching characters grow and develop over time, most television characters are more stable and consistent rather than changeable entities."[31] It's not that characters don't experience major events and traumas. It's just that they "accumulate" these narrative experiences more than "change" from them. Any real or substantive change would mean interacting with the narrative world and other characters beyond the preestablished limits of the sitcom, which could potentially undermine the premise of the entire series. Imagine if Joey and Chandler developed the wisdom and maturity to recognize that their chair-based conflict was both childish and unhelpful for the community as a whole. This would certainly signal growth on their part. But it wouldn't be funny at all. Worse yet, it would effectively eliminate the basic source of conflict that provides the narrative momentum for every episode. Like all episodic narratives, sitcoms demand a return to the status quo each week, and by definition, the greatest threat to the status quo is change.

So the sitcom genre itself is somewhat restrained (or constrained) in its ability to move characters toward moral insight or transformation. Hour-long dramas are decidedly different in this regard. In sitcoms, though, only so much can change before the storytelling structure collapses in on itself. Developing characters along moral lines is especially difficult when the characters are originally conceived as unkind, hypercynical, or simply self-absorbed. Think of Michael Scott from *The Office*, Kelso from *That '70s Show*, or, well, just about any character from *30 Rock*. But the stability and consistency of sitcom characters over time isn't a problem per se. It's part of why we connect with these shows on deeply emotional levels, forming a kind of allegiance with certain characters—even the least likable ones. Like our own lived experience, growth happens in fits and spurts if it happens at all, and more often than not, we find ourselves struggling with the same core issues throughout our lives.

Rather than a limitation, then, the unchanging nature of characters in sitcoms allows for a different kind of development—one that is less about transformation than revelation.[32] That is, over the span of numerous seasons, the audience comes to know increasingly more about a show's characters. It's not a transformation or "change" within the character per se. It's the slow unveiling of a depth—a disclosure of the various nuances, subtleties, and textures that are required to truly "know" another human being. In many ways, this unfolding of a character's attributes directly reflects the process by which we come to know another person in the real world. As a result, the "revelatory" dimension of TV characterization serves as one of the key narrative devices by which TV engages viewers powerfully and encourages them to form empathetic bonds with all kinds of people—from the noble (Jerry Seinfeld) to the nefarious (Newman!).

That the disclosure of a character's inner qualities successfully induces empathy among viewers is also supported by the work being done in cognitive psychology and neuroscience. Christian Keysers is a research scientist who specializes in the study of "mirror neurons" or "shared circuits," the parts of the human brain that fire when we either do a certain action ourselves, or when we observe another person engaging in that same action, or both. This function of the brain, which is in operation whether we are observing "real" or "fictional" people, is directly related to the development of empathy and, by extension, ethics. For Keysers, our ability to empathically mirror the experiences of others is a basic part of what it means to be human: "Empathy is deeply ingrained in the architecture of our brain. What happens to other people affects almost all areas of our brain. We were designed to be empathic, to connect with others."[33] Because our empathizing involves our conscious awareness, we are able to regulate the degree to which we empathize with others. However, our ethics (i.e., how we act toward others) are largely determined on a preconscious or subconscious level, motivated as they are not by our rational faculties but by our empathetic impulses: "Psychology and neuroscience now tell us a different story. Shared circuits might be much more powerful than intellect when it comes to morals. We do not primarily think about whether it is right or wrong to make people suffer. We feel it."[34]

On narrative, psychological, and neurobiological levels, then, our years-long journey with TV characters is about more than entertainment. It involves the ways in which the very structures of our physical bodies allow us to form empathetic and ethical bonds with other human beings. And if this is indeed the case, then our primary concern regarding TV characters is not so much whether they develop moral insight or transformation but whether the empathetic mirroring that takes place when a character's attributes are slowly revealed forms us into more empathetic people. In other words, our questions about growth and development should be focused not so much on the characters that populate TV narratives as on the development of character among the audience. Does *Friends*, for example, invite us as viewers to be and become better—to grow in moral insight and become kinder, more compassionate, more peaceable people? And does it prod us to do the same for others—to be a community that bears witness to the truth, extends hospitality to the outcast and the other, and demonstrates self-giving love for the sake of one's friend (and even one's enemy)?

The question of friendship is significant here, and not just because TV sitcoms so often tell stories about friends (or would-be friends). In an important sense, both the practice of bearing witness and the practice of hospitality that we discussed above are rooted in a prior commitment to being and becoming friends. Indeed, Jesus's words in John 15 underscore friendship as a central tenet of Christian faith and practice: "There is no greater love than to lay down one's life for one's friends" (John 15:13 NLT). Just as hospitality depends upon the kind of love that sees the other as friend (even if that other is in fact our enemy), bearing witness to the truth of violence, injustice, and oppression begins and ends with a willingness to give up one's life for those friends whose voices have been silenced.

Jesus's words about friendship have thus echoed throughout the history of theological reflection. Borrowing from Aristotle's notion of friendship as central to the development of virtue, Augustine understood friendship to be a school in Christian love and virtue. So from a theological perspective, genuine friendships are those that shape us into people who place the interests of others before their own. They stretch us, confront us, and challenge us to assume a posture of self-giving love. Friends make us better. As Mitchell notes,

> Christian friendship is neither possessive nor utilitarian, seeking to build a network of friends so that they can be useful in the future. . . . Friends, from both the past and present, can stretch our vision of God, ourselves and the world we live in. Friends can challenge us to reconsider how we live, how we spend our time and money. Wise friends confront us with the truth. Good friends help us not to take ourselves too seriously. Caring friends support us through heartbreak or encourage us to grow in faith, hope and love.[35]

Few TV narratives are able to explore such notions of friendship, in part because, as we mentioned above, ongoing conflict is integral to episodic storytelling. Character traits like compassion, hospitality, and self-giving love do little to generate or sustain this tension. In fact, they do the opposite. The same can be said for humor. It's really difficult to be both funny and kind. But there are certain series that manage to maintain a comedic sensibility and a narrative trajectory that are marked by kindness and sincerity rather than mean-spirited cynicism. *Parks and Recreation* serves as an example of a show that managed to generate both critical acclaim and a passionate audience for this very reason. Significantly, though, *Parks and Rec* debuted at the height of *The Office*'s popularity, airing on NBC as part of the same prime-time lineup. And just like *The Office*, *Parks and Rec* is a single-camera "mockumentary," features no laugh track, and stars Rashida Jones, the actress who also played a key character in *The Office*. It was even advertised by NBC as created by "the people who bring you *The Office*." So comparisons between the two shows are appropriate. In fact, early reviews were less than glowing because of the many similarities between the two series. During its first season, it was difficult to see how *Parks and Rec* was anything but a slightly less funny spinoff from *The Office*. As one review put it, "Parks and Recreation: Like The Office but . . . Well, Just Like The Office."[36]

But not so fast. Even in the early stages of its development, something was different about *Parks and Recreation*. In the words of Christopher Rosen, managing entertainment editor at the *Huffington Post* at the time, the key difference between the two shows was their tone:

> Whereas on its best days, *The Office* is inherently mean and nasty—most of the humor derives from people doing or saying awful things to other people—*Parks* is surprisingly . . . nice. Leslie [Knope]'s worst crime is that she's a wild over-achiever trapped inside an institution that frowns on that sort of behavior. She gets mocked, but none of the digs feel hurtful. On *Parks*, the only truly mean person is Tom, and even he comes off like a bratty kid in the back of the class-room more than anything else.[37]

Over the course of its seven seasons, *Parks and Recreation* made good on its commitment to "niceness." In contrast to *The Office*'s Michael Scott, Leslie Knope (played by Amy Poehler) is a boss who is genuinely kind, compassionate, and empathetic toward those under her charge. Unlike Michael, who is desperate for friendship as a way of abating his deep insecurities, Leslie seeks friendships not for the sake of her own sense of fulfillment but for the sake of others. And she is all these things in a context known for none of them: local government.

Leslie's unflagging optimism does not ultimately transform the people in her department or even revitalize the parks system in Pawnee, Indiana. But it does cultivate a space where the libertarian Ron Swanson, the entrepreneur Tom Haverford, and the dark and brooding April Ludgate can become more than coworkers. Under the leadership of Leslie Knope, they become friends. It is thus unsurprising that the series ends with each of the characters sacrificing something for the sake of another. Andy brings his Johnny Karate show to an end in order to support April's move to Washington. Donna uses her commission money as a successful real estate agent to start a nonprofit learning initiative called "Teach Yo' Self." Ron resigns from his dream job at the Very Good Building Company to become the superintendent of the Pawnee National Park (a job that Leslie coordinated). And Ben, Leslie's husband, gives up his own bid to be governor of Indiana in support of his wife's campaign.

If doing what is ethical is actually a function of being the best sort of person, then it is Leslie's character—her virtue—that provides her with the necessary resources for placing others before herself. And by the time the series reaches its finale, this selflessness has added up to something much more than the development of Leslie Knope as a character. Hers is no passive acquiescence to the whims and desires of a stronger personality. Instead, her kindness actively discloses the good that was always already residing within her coworkers, prompting them to be and become the best possible version of themselves. Virtue, it would seem, begets virtue. Because it is still a sitcom, this revelation of virtue does not come in the form of a radical transformation on anyone's part. Nevertheless, a slightly clearer picture comes into view concerning the employees in Pawnee's Department of Parks and Recreation. That is, it is only in community—among friends— that these people catch a glimpse of who they truly are and how they might actually flourish. And it's only in the context of these self-giving relationships that they discover not only what friendship is but what it requires.

If Augustine is correct, then we would do well to affirm a show like *Parks and Recreation*, for it encourages viewers to empathize with this collection of characters by revealing the genuine friendships that prompt them to pursue the well-being of the other. Yet given the way that our brains forge these empathetic bonds, we

Rashida Jones and Amy Poehler as Ann Perkins and Leslie Knope in NBC's *Parks and Recreation*

also need to recognize that *Parks and Rec* is not simply offering viewers an imaginative construal of what a community of friends might look like. It is far more than that. It is transforming their very understanding of the meaning and value of friendship by providing these friends an opportunity to feel it on a deeply embodied level. The decision to lay down one's life for a friend is almost never based upon purely logical or intellectual criteria. Cold rationality is inherently self-preserving. Actually being a friend, though—that can only come from a place of empathy, feeling the feelings of another and responding in kind. And in the Christian tradition, this self-denying commitment to one's friends serves as the greatest demonstration of love—both human and divine. As such, the practice of watching and empathizing with TV characters opens up possibilities for the Spirit to move, shaping viewers into people who actively reveal the virtue in others by laying down their lives.

TV Ethics as Neither/Nor

When discussing media ethics of any kind, theologians and cultural critics generally fall into one of two camps. Some are prone to suggest that a TV show is either good or it is not. Plain and simple. After all, questions of aesthetics are irrelevant when the Christian's purity is at stake. This group often turns to Philippians 4:8 as the primary source for its ethical criteria, noting that Christians are called to focus on "whatever is pure." Others are a bit more comfortable with ambiguity and paradox. Although they recognize that TV contains morally problematic content, they also question how any story can be told honestly or with any measure of depth without addressing the raw and unpleasant aspects of lived reality. Coincidentally, they too point to Philippians 4:8, noting that Paul's exhortation begins with a consideration of "whatever is true." Because it is rooted in concrete experience, the truth of our lives is almost always a mixture of both darkness and light, both joy and sadness—not either/or. To avoid or deny this inherent complexity is, in their estimation, to avoid the truth.

While acknowledging the legitimacy of both approaches, we have suggested in this chapter another way, one that might be called "neither/nor" ethics. As far as they go, the above approaches each has its appropriate place, but they tend to overly focus on TV content and the degree to which it aligns with already established ethical norms. But what if our attempt to engage television with wisdom and discernment is about something altogether different? What if, rather than trying to determine whether a show's content either is or is not (or both is and is not) "ethical," "moral," or "virtuous," we were more concerned with the fundamental mystery lying at the heart of life and how our encounter with that mystery in something as seemingly mundane as a TV show leaves us forever changed—including our previously held conceptions of what is and is not "good"? In other words, what if Christian ethics took our encounter with the Spirit of God in practices such as TV watching as a primary theological source and acknowledged how that encounter is forming us into people who are good, true, and even beautiful?

This might be a somewhat scandalous notion to some, in part because theology still has so far to go in fully developing its pneumatological convictions. But it is an approach that has the potential for being particularly helpful in Western, post-Christian contexts, where the historic practices of Christian worship that once served to shape our common ethic are no longer a part of the cultural imagination. It might also be challenging in another respect, for when theology allows for the possibility that the Spirit of God might be engaged in constructive work outside the institutional boundaries we have erected, we open ourselves up to challenge and critique. We may not be as virtuous as we first believed. We may need to change. And sometimes, we need the likes of a Leslie Knope, a Jon Stewart, or a *Fresh Off the Boat* to reveal to us the true depths of our moral failure. The only question is whether we have the humility to hear this critique and the courage to respond accordingly.

conclusion

the season finale: to be continued

Because this is a book about TV, it is only fitting that we open this final segment with a recap sequence—a brief montage of what was "previously on" designed to bring readers up to speed and prepare them for what's to come. To summarize, then, the basic argument we have developed looks something like this: Television is so ingrained in the fabric of everyday life that it almost cannot help functioning as one of the primary means through which contemporary persons make sense of their lives and the world. Indeed, it is exceedingly difficult to describe (post)postmodern culture, much less understand it, without at least a marginal awareness of what and how TV means. But we have taken our argument one step further and suggested that, as a technology, a narrative art form, a commodity, and a portal for our ritual lives, television actually confronts viewers theologically. Whether or not its content is explicitly "spiritual," TV routinely invites (and sometimes demands) theological reflection. On occasion, it even has the capacity to shape viewers into persons whose lives reflect the broader intentionality of the Spirit of God in the world.

For those who might balk at this final interpretive move, it may be helpful to point out that our religiously oriented take on the broader cultural significance of TV and TV watching is not the product of some kind of theological heavy-handedness. Rather, it simply reflects the many ways that consumers, producers, and critics are themselves articulating the significance of TV in their own lives. As Jason Mittell has noted, "I write as an affirmed atheist but also as a television fan who has experienced awe and reverence at moments of authorial prowess and creation that borders on worship."[1] Even for those who do not ascribe to any theistic framework, television has the capacity to evoke a kind of religious devotion—a reverence for something (or someone) that is deeper, larger, or even more real than reality itself.

Given the increasing prevalence and diversity of these kinds of responses to television, our goal in this concluding chapter is not to offer a series of neat and tidy remarks regarding the "findings" of our study. Rather, we bring our exploration to a close by considering how our engagement with TV might serve to energize and give shape to future theological reflection. Put differently, this chapter is much like the season finale of a serialized TV show. It will surely come to an end, but it remains decidedly unfinished. It is "to be continued."

We of course hope that others will expand, refine, and even correct our initial arguments. However, just as we have attempted to do throughout the book, it is important that TV itself continues to serve as the starting point for any and all of these developments. We must allow television to speak on its own terms. In turn, we must do our best to listen to what it has to say. And if we listen well, we might do more than come to a deeper understanding of TV's meaning and cultural power. We might also discover a valuable resource for developing new theological categories, acquire a unique lens for (re)reading the biblical text, and gain much-needed insight regarding the role of Christian community in a post-Christian world. We may even find ways to connect more deeply with our neighbor. By way of conclusion, then, let us consider a few concrete illustrations that highlight some of the more promising directions that a constructive theological project like this might take.

House of Cards: The (Anti)Hero's Journey

The first and perhaps most obvious way that a robust engagement with television might inform future theological reflection concerns the inherently episodic nature of TV storytelling. At the risk of stating the obvious, the great majority of television narratives unfold over the course of numerous installments. But the individual episodes that compose these narratives rarely if ever attempt to tell the whole story, in part because one measure of success among US series is their ability to sustain an infinite narrative middle.[2] In fact, most programs intentionally avoid certain kinds of narrative progress (like character development) because it would suggest that the story actually does have an "end" on the horizon. And when a TV narrative ends, it effectively eliminates the possibility of creating (and thus selling) more episodes. Taken as a whole, then, these dynamics underscore the need to acknowledge that each episode within a given series possesses a narrative integrity of its own.

At the same time, though, no single episode is completely detached from its ending (whether that ending is an actual series finale or, more commonly, the imagined "end" toward which the larger narrative strives).[3] In an important sense, TV stories are constantly navigating the complex relationship between the continually unfolding narrative elements within each episode and those that have yet to occur (but one day will). Thus, from one episode to the next, these stories invite viewers into a diegetic world that exists "in a state of perpetual limbo and awaiting a possible return."[4]

Consider *House of Cards*, the Emmy Award–winning series starring Kevin Spacey and Robin Wright as Frank and Claire Underwood, a Washington power couple submerged in the murky ethical waters of DC politics. That *House of Cards* premiered as an original series distributed exclusively by the online streaming service Netflix is significant. Netflix releases each season of its original series in its entirety, thus blurring the lines between traditionally conceived episodic or serial narratives, on the one hand, and long-form storytelling, on the other. Because an entire season of *House of Cards* is immediately available from beginning to end, individual episodes relate to their larger narrative context somewhat differently than other hour-long dramas that are broadcast by major networks in weekly installments, at least from the perspective of the audience. Rather than taking shape alongside our own stories, each season of *House of Cards* functions almost like an extended episode, capturing our attention for a brief but intense period of time.

Nevertheless, while the Netflix distribution model encourages viewers to binge-watch, they are not required to do so, which means that we should not overestimate the significance of these differences. What is more, at the time of this writing, the series itself was still being made, so anything we say about *House of Cards* must remain provisional and incomplete. The truth of the matter is that the end, once it is fully realized, might change everything we presently know about the narrative. For now, though, what we do have are the individual episodes that together compose each of the first few seasons.

By emphasizing the ways in which the individual episodes and seasons of *House of Cards* relate to the larger whole, we are able to identify hints of where the story is heading. It's a way of unpacking the power and meaning of the series that falls under the concept we have called "trace," which we discussed in detail in chapter 2. When we focus our analysis on these formal (trace) elements, we are also able to see how this form of storytelling has the potential for shaping theology's understanding of other narratives with "infinite middles." The show's music is particularly enlightening in this regard, in part because every episode is framed by a credit sequence with the same musical cue. This sequence thus serves as the common thread that unites all the individual segments. In composer Jeff Beal's own words, "There was always sort of this musical joke between major and minor. . . . The bass line in the main title stays in A minor all the way through, but the melody actually goes to A major a couple times. And the tension that creates, that dissonance—even though it's 'wrong,' it's a right wrong note, because it makes you feel a certain way. It's like, 'Oh man, something's weird. Something's off.'"[5]

Something's off indeed. Frank Underwood, the principal character in *House of Cards*, is monomaniacal in his quest for power, whether in politics or personal relationships. He exploits and then discards or destroys anyone standing in his way. What is more, he is continually rewarded for his efforts, rising to the highest office in the land through a series of calculated betrayals, bald-faced lies, and, eventually, murder. So part of the drama and tension that viewers feel is related to the fact that the show's narrative encourages them to take up a similar position to that of an utterly unlikable (and at times downright immoral) person.

But the tension we feel involves more than the general sense of discomfort that arises when we align ourselves with antiheroes. The "wrongness" of *House of Cards* is written into the music that we hear at the beginning of every episode. It's a dissonance created by the collision of major and minor modes—one that offers a yet-to-be-fully-articulated hint concerning the direction this story is headed. Before we see a single frame, the music suggests that Frank Underwood's ultimate fate has already been sealed. Regardless of his stated intentions, he is not on the kind of "hero's journey" described in Joseph Campbell's *The Hero with a Thousand Faces*.[6] His is the antihero's journey—the inverse of Campbell's monomythic archetype. Frank's demise will come, but when and how remain to be seen.

That the music shows its hand so early and so often highlights the fact that, like most episodic stories, every episode of *House of Cards* is haunted by the ever-present *telos* to which the narrative yearns. But each episode and, indeed, each season, remain suspended in an in-between space. The end has not come, so we are forced to deal directly with the ambiguity and uneasiness of an inherently unfinished work. It cannot be that we disregard the power and meaning of these individual episodes simply because the end remains unknown or undefined. Nor can we wait until the end arrives before we even consider what or how the series means. If this were the case, then we could say nothing about the majority of scripted (US) television, for it is only a small number of series that stay in production long enough to reach their finale. In the interim, all we have are the individual episodes, which offer only the faintest hint of a larger narrative trajectory.

For example, the season 2 premiere of *House of Cards* ("Chapter 14") opens with a rather shocking series of events (spoiler alert!). It culminates when Frank

Underwood, now the vice president of the United States, pushes journalist Zoe Barnes onto the train tracks, thus killing her and erasing all evidence of an earlier cover-up for a promising young senator. The murder is as surprising as it is disturbing. It is surprising because, up until this point, Frank has not directly ended anyone's life. And it is disturbing because this act goes so far beyond what is necessary to silence his would-be detractor. To make matters worse, he suffers no consequences whatsoever for his actions, at least not immediately thereafter. Just in case the audience was not already unsettled enough, the episode ends with Frank turning directly toward the camera, as if to step right into our most intimate of spaces. Breaking the fourth wall, he states, "Don't waste a breath mourning Ms. Barnes. . . . For those of us climbing to the top of the food chain, there can be no mercy. There is but one rule: Hunt or be hunted."

No mercy. Hunt or be hunted. The irony in Frank's statement is that, in addition to acquiring power, he is genuinely concerned with government functioning effectively in its organization of public life. To do the kind of good it ought to do, government needs strong leadership, and Frank sees himself as an agent of change in this regard. In his own eyes, he is playing the part of the hero, and this personal vision is reinforced every time he steps into a position of higher power and greater responsibility—regardless of the means by which he acquires this power. The music in the credits sequence of course tells us a different story—one that is about Frank's moral demise rather than his political victories. But the individual episode itself leaves the story in limbo. In his attempt to live the hero's journey, Frank is willing to destroy anyone and anything in his path because he thinks he's on the right side of history. And time and again he succeeds. In fact, he even flourishes.

At the same time that Frank is busy gaining the whole world, the music suggests that he will eventually lose his soul. Indeed, the credit sequence as a whole contributes to this understanding, concluding as it does with the title of the show: *House of Cards*. The tenuous world Frank has constructed is forever on the verge of collapsing. So we as viewers are left with little recourse but to wait for what is to come. But it is in this waiting—in these moments between episodes and seasons—that we are forced to recognize that, at least for now, the wicked prevail and the good do not prosper. And if we gloss over these difficult episodes by moving too quickly to the end that is now only intimated by the music, we fail to see (or feel) the antihero's journey for what it truly is—the unraveling not only of an individual life (i.e., Frank Underwood) but of our communal lives as well (i.e., Zoe Barnes, Claire Underwood, and, indeed, the country). Frank will get what's coming to him eventually, at least if the music in the credits sequence is any indication. But we have missed something central to the story if we overlook the fact that, along the way, he is destroying everyone around him.

Admittedly, it is difficult to understand any narrative entirely within the confines of a single episode. It proves especially difficult when the episode in question hints at its larger narrative context and, at the same time, also demands that the reader/viewer/listener confront the ambiguities of the individual segment in its own right. This holds true for biblical stories just as it does for TV stories. And while we recognize that formal biblical analyses do not follow from formal television analyses in any direct or immediate way, we do want to suggest that there is an analogous relationship between the two. For example, one of the more familiar passages in the biblical text is found in Luke 10:25–37. It is a brief teaching of Jesus more commonly known as the parable of the good Samaritan.

> Now an expert in religious law stood up to test Jesus, saying, "Teacher, what must I do to inherit eternal life?" He said to him, "What is written in the law? How do you understand it?" The expert answered, "Love the Lord your God with all your heart, with all your soul, with all your strength, and with all your mind, and love your neighbor as yourself." Jesus said to him, "You have answered correctly; do this, and you will live."
>
> But the expert, wanting to justify himself, said to Jesus, "And who is my neighbor?" Jesus replied, "A man was going down from Jerusalem to Jericho, and fell into the hands of robbers, who stripped him, beat him up, and went off, leaving him half dead. Now by chance a priest was going down that road, but when he saw the injured man he passed by on the other side. So too a Levite, when he came up to the place and saw him, passed by on the other side. But a Samaritan who was traveling came to where the injured man was, and when he saw him, he felt compassion for him. He went up to him and bandaged his wounds, pouring oil and wine on them. Then he put him on his own animal, brought him to an inn, and took care of him. The next day he took out two silver coins and gave them to the innkeeper, saying, 'Take care of him, and whatever else you spend, I will repay you when I come back this way.' Which of these three do you think became a neighbor to the man who fell into the hands of the robbers?" The expert in religious law said, "The one who showed mercy to him." So Jesus said to him, "Go and do the same." (NET)

So embedded is the story of the good Samaritan within the contemporary cultural lexicon that news outlets often refer to those who help strangers in need as "good Samaritans," and certain US states have "Good Samaritan" laws. In fact, the characters in *Seinfeld* end up in jail in the series finale as a result of a Good Samaritan law. It is important to note, however, that this title is not actually found in the Lukan manuscript. It is an editorial addition inserted by translators and designed to help orient readers to the text. Much like the non-diegetic music in the credit sequence of *House of Cards*, this extratextual title creates an interpretive frame for the story.[7] Before we read a word, it tells us who the (supposed) protagonist is. We are also given the name of the character with whom we are meant to identify. It is of course the Samaritan—the one who came to the rescue of the half-dead man on the side of the road, showing him mercy and compassion in spite of the many cultural taboos that would have him do otherwise.

Because the Samaritan is so obviously the hero of this particular story, there is no question about what Jesus means when he concludes the parable with the command to "go and do the same" (Luke 10:37). Those who wish to "inherit eternal life" by loving God and loving their neighbor (vv. 25–27) must be like the Samaritan. They must look past cultural and religious differences and show mercy to those in need. It's exactly the kind of valor demanded by Jesus's radically egalitarian vision of the kingdom, so it makes sense that we understand his words as encouraging our identification with the heroic Samaritan. It's all fairly straightforward and simple.

But what if it's not? What if we took a cue from the episodic stories that we encounter in TV and made an attempt to understand this unique episode within Luke's narrative as a story with its own internal coherence? Would we understand Jesus's parable any differently? The story actually begins with a (Jewish) expert in (Jewish) religious law asking Jesus to interpret the (Jewish) Torah (vv. 25–26). After reciting the Shema (the central prayer of the Jewish community), the man asks Jesus, "Who is my neighbor?" (v. 29). Jesus replies not by answering him directly but by telling a story about a man traveling "from Jerusalem to Jericho" (v. 30)—that is, a Jew. And this Jewish man is the focus of the entire story. He is the protagonist. He is the character whose actions initiate the plot and whose circumstances eventually bring it to an end. He is the one who is beaten by robbers and left for dead. He is the character whose mere presence causes a (Jewish) priest and a Levite to pass on the opposite side of the road (vv. 31–32). And of course, it is the Jewish man who becomes the object of the Samaritan's kindness. After finishing the parable, Jesus asks the expert in (Jewish) religious law to answer his own question, "Which of these three do you think became a neighbor to the [Jewish] man?" (v. 36). The answer to the expert's question of "who is my neighbor (i.e., who am I to love)?" is now obvious: the Samaritan.

The point in rehearsing these details is simply that, on a purely episodic level, the text is encouraging its readers and hearers to identify not with the Samaritan but with the man traveling "from Jerusalem to Jericho." It turns out that we are not the compassionate hero. We are the helpless victim. The neighbors we are called to love "as ourselves" (v. 27) are those who condescend toward us, and not the other way around. The parable thus confronts the assumption that loving one's neighbor is something that can be done from a position of power or self-importance. Being a neighbor is not about the ways in which the privileged put their various resources to use. It's about accepting one's fundamental weakness, frailty, and helplessness, allowing the religious, political, and cultural other to help us in our time of desperate need. This is what it means to be and become a neighbor.

It's easy to miss the full weight of this inversion if we fail to understand the parable as a fully formed episode in its own right. It is not the whole gospel story, nor does it pretend to be. But neither is it insignificant or without its own internal integrity. In a twist befitting of Jesus's parables, it is only when we are humble enough to allow the other to touch us (and thus to transgress every cultural and religious marker of identity and purity) that we demonstrate our love of both God and neighbor. Or, to put it differently, to truly love our neighbor, we must first be willing to be "neighbored."

At the same time, if we are to understand this particular episode of Luke's Gospel in all its fullness, then it must be related in some way to the overarching narrative in which it is set. Luke intentionally locates this parable within the larger trajectory of Jesus's life, death, and resurrection. And from the perspective of this broader narrative, Jesus does indeed call his followers to care for the poor, needy, and marginalized in ways that are compassionate and mercy-filled—just like the Samaritan. Jesus's command to "go and do the same" (v. 37) is therefore central to Christian discipleship. Nevertheless, as our examination of television stories has made clear, *how* a story means shapes *what* it means, so an episode cannot be entirely subsumed by its larger narrative, especially when the end or *telos* of that narrative is set in a time that is unknown.

And let's be clear. While Luke's Gospel ends, it makes no attempt to conclude. In fact, the book of Acts picks up where the Gospel of Luke leaves off, with Jesus's promise of the sending of the Holy Spirit (Luke 24:49; Acts 1:5). On the heels of the resurrection, the disciples were understandably curious to know if all they had witnessed signaled the arrival of the kingdom, and if not, when it might finally come (Acts 1:6). Jesus's reply is telling: "You are not permitted to know the times or periods that the Father has set by his own authority. But you will receive power when the Holy Spirit has come upon you, and you will be my witnesses in Jerusalem, and in all Judea and Samaria, and to the farthest parts of the earth" (Acts 1:7–8 NET). According to Jesus, the story of God's ongoing work in the world is moving toward a clearly defined end, but its actual consummation will take place in a future that remains unknown to the disciples. So he tells his disciples that, rather than passively wait on an unknown future, they are to bear witness to the coming kingdom as it unfolds before them in real time. Jesus commissions them to proclaim the gospel story until it reaches "the ends of the earth," which is really just another way of saying that his life and work are meant "to be continued."

In this way, by developing our understanding of the power and meaning of television's episodic stories, theology gains a greater capacity to live in the tension of the gospel's "infinite middle" rather than moving too quickly to the resolution or finality provided by narrative closure. By failing to understand an individual episode like the parable of the good Samaritan (or, more accurately, "the beaten Jew") as a story with its own coherence and integrity, we risk not only misunderstanding the biblical narrative but doing violence to the text. We impose categories onto the text that track our identification in unhelpful ways. The end result is ultimately a case of mistaken identity—one in which we constantly envision ourselves as the hero (i.e., the Samaritan) who condescends toward the helpless and hapless other in need.

The hero's journey will always be compelling. The only problem is that it isn't our story.[8] As Frank Underwood's journey makes clear, those who attempt to play the part of the hero are destined to become antiheroes. Even when we are well meaning, our coercive quests to attain honor and influence often bring about the destruction of everything and everyone around us. Although the exact timing remains unclear, it will eventually destroy us too, for we don't possess the capacity to fix the world through our own power, efforts, and initiatives. We are not the good Samaritan. We are the broken and bloodied Jew. And we need the other.

This reading of the biblical text, developed in dialogue with the episodic stories of television, invites theology (and theologians!) to assume a fundamentally different posture—one that is more humble and far more willing to receive. It points toward a mode of theological inquiry that is decidedly provisional and sometimes frustratingly incomplete. It calls for a theological engagement with culture and cultural forms that recognizes our seemingly infinite capacity for self-deception and acknowledges our latent desire to destroy rather than to flourish. And perhaps most important, it is a way of engaging culture that resists the temptation of playing the hero, choosing instead to allow the other to touch, heal, and help us in our most desperate time of need.

The Big Bang Theory: A Community of Misfits

If *House of Cards* is about an individual's quest to seize and exert power at the expense of everyone else, then *The Big Bang Theory* is its polar opposite. This may be one of the reasons that, during its peak, *The Big Bang Theory* was the highest rated and viewed scripted program on television, trailing only *Sunday Night Football* in the coveted eighteen to thirty-nine–year-old demographic. By the end of 2014, reruns of the show on TBS were also the highest rated of all syndicated programming. Created by Chuck Lorre and written in partnership with Bill Prady and Steven Molaro, the series is, in many respects, a fairly conventional sitcom, both in its form and content. It is recorded before a live studio audience, makes use of a multi-camera setup, and is broadcast on a major network on a week-to-week basis (recall our discussion of these elements in chapter 2). So from the camera setup to the presence of the live audience, the show is structured in ways that highlight TV's communal orientation. Indeed, the proof is in the pudding, for even though it reflects a more traditional mode of creating and consuming sitcoms, *The Big Bang Theory* garners as many viewers as *The Cosby Show* did when it aired.

Thinking in terms of the creative process (one of the modes of critical analysis we covered in chapter 3), comedy writers themselves often identify as misfits and oddballs (especially when reflecting upon their youth), so it is unsurprising when the characters they create feature similar traits. But *The Big Bang Theory* doubles down on socially awkward characters by focusing on the lives of theoretical physicist Sheldon Cooper, BS, MA, MS, PhD, ScD, and experimental physicist Leonard Hofstadter, PhD. As we mentioned earlier, the

The principal cast of CBS's *The Big Bang Theory*

vast intellects (and downright geekiness) of these two scientists are routinely contrasted for comedic effect by the mere presence of their neighbor Penny, the actress/waitress/pharmaceutical rep who possesses no formal education but makes up for it with her social aptitude, stunning good looks, and the "street smarts" she acquired while growing up in rural Nebraska.

So what distinguishes *The Big Bang Theory* from so many other sitcoms is not that its writers use a different set of tropes to explore the relationships between Penny, Sheldon, Leonard, and their squad of eccentric scientists. Rather, its distinctiveness has more to do with the particular quality of the relationships that these characters develop over time. To be sure, Sheldon and Leonard's core set of friends direct plenty of sarcastic and condescending humor toward one another. But as the individual episodes accumulate from one season to the next, the show as a whole adds up to something much more generous and self-effacing than any single segment might suggest. From this perspective, the overarching narrative of *The Big Bang Theory* is more about the ways in which an unlikely collection of idiosyncratic individuals are able to recognize their own flaws and assume a posture that allows the group as a whole to flourish.

At first blush, it might seem unrealistic that a woman like Penny would be willing to endure such an inelegant group of people. But this is to miss the point entirely of what makes *The Big Bang Theory* appealing, for something significant is revealed about these characters in and through their unlikely interactions. Whether it is Penny singing "Soft Kitty" to Sheldon while he is ill, homesick, or anxious (e.g., in "The Pancake Batter Anomaly," "The Vegas Renormalization," and "The Cruciferous Vegetable Amplification" episodes), or Sheldon nursing Penny back to health after she dislocates her shoulder ("The Adhesive Duck Deficiency"), or Leonard buying Penny a car when hers breaks down ("The Friendship Turbulence"), it eventually becomes clear that these characters are seeking the well-being of the others. And they are doing so not simply in spite of but in and through their otherwise grating eccentricities. Each individual is both uniquely flawed and uniquely gifted, but they live as if their sum is far greater than their constituent parts. Put differently, these are not just friends, roommates, and lovers. They are an imperfect but thriving community of misfits—exactly the kind of family that TV writers would envision.

Significantly, this kind of functionally dysfunctional community bears a striking resemblance to the way that the apostle Paul imagined the Christian community.

> Just as a body, though one, has many parts, but all its many parts form one body, so it is with Christ. For we were all baptized by one Spirit so as to form one body—whether Jews or Gentiles, slave or free—and we were all given the one

Spirit to drink. Even so the body is not made up of one part but of many. . . . As it is, there are many parts, but one body. The eye cannot say to the hand, "I don't need you!" And the head cannot say to the feet, "I don't need you!" On the contrary, those parts of the body that seem to be weaker are indispensable, and the parts that we think are less honorable we treat with special honor. And the parts that are unpresentable are treated with special modesty, while our presentable parts need no special treatment. But God has put the body together, giving greater honor to the parts that lacked it, so that there should be no division in the body, but that its parts should have equal concern for each other. If one part suffers, every part suffers with it; if one part is honored, every part rejoices with it. (1 Cor. 21:12–14, 20–26)

Paul's notion of the body in 1 Corinthians is perhaps one of his richest metaphors, but it is often understood to be primarily about an individual's unique gifts and how that gifted individual might contribute something significant to the community. And surely this is an appropriate way to understand the apostle's conception of the Christian community—that no role, regardless of its lack of apparent prominence, is insignificant. In fact, according to Paul, those parts that seem to be unnecessary or weak are actually indispensable.

But if we allow our understanding of the body to be informed by the kind of community we see in *The Big Bang Theory*, a slightly different picture emerges. If the Christian community is really a collection of misfits who are simply too quirky or dysfunctional to navigate life as individuals, then it becomes clear that Paul's understanding of a healthy and thriving community is actually not first and foremost about our individual self-actualization. Paul's words are typically taken to mean that a body's wholeness depends upon its individual members identifying and accepting their appropriate role (whether it's a "prominent" one or not). Everyone is important of course, but if each part would just devote itself to doing what it does best rather than trying to be something it's not (eyes are for seeing and not for hearing!), then the body would be able to operate like a well-oiled machine.

But for Paul, the body is a human body and not a machine. Unlike a machine, a whole, healthy, and integrated human body is not something that comes about when individual parts are pursuing their own unique end, regardless of how efficiently those distinct parts may be able to operate on their own. Rather, for Paul, wholeness involves a basic "for-otherness." That is, the body's "parts should have equal concern for each other. If one part suffers, every part suffers with it" (vv. 25–26). We are not only connected but interdependent. At our core, we are persons-in-relation.

Significantly, the community depicted in *The Big Bang Theory* actually helps to shed a unique light on this reality, providing us with a different lens for understanding the biblical text. This group of radically different individuals is able to function as a community not because they are each realizing their own individual potential but because they are willing to assume a posture toward those in need—even when it requires them to be personally less effectual or entirely abandon their own interests for a period of time. For the health and well-being of the whole, they each assume a fundamentally *in*-efficient, *dys*-functional, and *un*-comfortable posture. It is this basic orientation toward the interests of the other that is so often overlooked in the passage from 1 Corinthians. Yet it seems to serve as the central element of Paul's entire metaphor.

So *The Big Bang Theory* presents us with a picture of a community that, like the apostle Paul's, is thoroughly collaborative. It is literally a co-labor-ing—a straining with and for the other. It is also empathetic—an affective fusion between those who are in pain and the other members of the community. Yet as the show progresses from one season to the next and the full depth of the characters is slowly revealed, we realize that this co-laboring offers no easy fixes. The very same ills that beset this community of misfits in the pilot episode continue to wreak havoc in their lives. Like most sitcoms, growth and change, if they ever do come, involve a long and arduous struggle. And even when the end of each episode arrives at its resolution, it is not always clear if progress has been made. Nevertheless, every week the characters return to engage with one another, faithfully and resolutely. So the community we come to know in *The Big Bang Theory* is not only a community of co-laborers and fellow sufferers. It is a long-suffering community too.

It is here that television offers theology a most instructive way forward. Before it is anything else, the Christian story is a story of transformation. However, the great difficulty we face is that the full realization of God's transformative project has not yet arrived. We live in a time that is "already-but-not-yet." Our brokenness is pervasive and our transformation incomplete. The theological tradition often addresses this reality in terms of the distinction between justification and sanctification—the eternally efficacious work of Christ, on the one hand, and the continual process of being renewed, on the other.[9] But on a more concrete and visceral level, we can simply say that even the "best" of us, like the apostle Paul, "do not understand what [we] do. For what [we] want to do [we] do not do, but what [we] hate [we] do" (Rom. 7:15). Just like the characters in our favorite sitcoms, we experience very few moments of radical transformation in our lives. Instead, even though we are already recipients of Christ's gift of grace, we continue to struggle with many of the same "thorns in our flesh" throughout our lives (2 Cor. 12:7). Change, if it happens at all, comes in fits and spurts. Many times one small step forward is followed by two giant leaps back.

It would seem, then, that our exploration of TV communities like the one found in *The Big Bang Theory* calls for a basic shift in how theology conceives of the primary means by which communities of faith flourish and, by extension, how they contribute to the well-being of society as a whole. Because it is fundamentally relational, real growth or change requires collaboration, a striving with and for the other. It's a commitment not to self-actualization but to self-sacrifice. And perhaps more important, it is a long-term commitment—one that manifests itself in what might be called a "long-suffering presence."[10] It almost goes without saying that this is a constructive and appropriate way to relate to others within the community of faith. It is why Paul employed the body metaphor in the first place. But it is a posture that might prove helpful in our engagements with the broader culture as well. In fact, it seems that we would do well to think of the Christian's role in public life as having less to do with "changing" or "transforming" the world and having more to do with the demonstration of long-suffering presence—the kind we have written about on shows like *NYPD Blue* and *Everybody Loves Raymond*.

If the people of God are themselves "not yet" fully transformed into the likeness of Christ, then the most theologically faithful thing to do is not to demand that the broader culture (and TV in particular) demonstrate this kind of radical transformation as a precondition for our engagement but to set aside our own interests in order that we might co-labor with culture. A robust theological engagement with culture, then, isn't first and foremost about shaping public life so that it serves as an ideal environment for Christian communities to thrive. It is about the community of faith assuming a posture that may very well be inept or unproductive so that the other has an opportunity to flourish. It's about seeking the welfare (*shalom*) of the other even if it comes at great personal expense, for it is only in committing ourselves to the *shalom* of the other that we discover our own well-being (Jer. 29:7). By doing so, the other is revealed to be not actually an "other" at all but rather a vital member of a body that will only ever be healthy or whole when its various parts both suffer and rejoice with one another.

Lost: Rethinking Metaphysics

Finally, our exploration of the theological significance of television presses theology to develop a uniquely Christian metaphysic that might resonate with the contemporary cultural imagination. For some, questions about metaphysics and, more specifically ontology (i.e., our outlook on reality), have been rendered irrelevant in light of the postmodern turn. Although a number of compelling arguments to the contrary are currently being voiced, the academy in particular treats ontological claims with equal parts suspicion and indifference.[11] But if we want to understand how actual viewers make sense of their lives in and through the medium of television and allow this everyday meaning-making to inform the way we do theology, we simply cannot discount the ways in which audiences are actively calling upon television to structure their basic outlook on reality. So it is far from insignificant that one of the key ways in which TV viewers construct their awareness of the world is by employing decidedly ontological language and categories. Indeed, what is most striking is that it seems as if they have no other option at their disposal.

This phenomenon is perhaps nowhere more evident than among fans of the show *Lost*. Of course, by concluding our discussion of TV's theological significance with *Lost*, we return once again to the place where we began—with the world-creating power of a serial TV drama. Yet in terms of its reception (i.e., its "practice"), *Lost* functions "as much as a game as a serial narrative."[12] During the time of its original broadcast, the show's highly serialized format encouraged a kind of "forensic fandom," generating a passionate base of fans organized around a common desire to find meaning in the midst of a mystery-laden narrative. And this collective search for significance was made possible in large part by the emerging digital technologies that gave rise to social networking. Indeed, as Henry Jenkins notes,

> This [ability of TV stories to tap into the capacity of networked audiences] is especially the case in an era when people can pool knowledge and compare notes online, as occurred around the development of Lostpedia, a large-scale Wikipedia-like online reference site which was built by the audience of *Lost*. . . . *Lost*'s producers often found themselves balancing the interest of people watching their series week-by-week and those watching many episodes back-to-back on DVD, suggesting their increased consciousness of alternative modes of viewing.[13]

So part of the enjoyment that viewers derived from *Lost* and the various para-texts it spawned had to do with the possibility of joining a community of other fans who were searching for some kind of meaning in and through their engagement with the show—a mode of interaction that the producers of the series leveraged by intentionally obscuring certain elements of the narrative. Each step toward clarity only revealed further riddles that provoked more unanswered questions—questions that *Lost* fans took great pleasure in exploring. What exactly is the smoke monster? Who are "The Others"? Where did the mysterious hatch lead, and who put it there? What is the Dharma Initiative? And why, oh why, are there polar bears on the tropical island?

This collective desire to uncover the mysteries of an otherwise chaotic and fractured narrative paved the way for a strong fan base to develop and for numerous forms of user-generated media to proliferate. Ironically, it also created the very conditions for a divided response among fans concerning the way that the narrative finally came to an end. Rather than offering any detailed explanations or directly answering any of the lingering questions raised by six surreal seasons, the series finale ("The End") depicts the principal characters gathering in what appears to be a multi-faith church (noted by the prominence of symbols from the world's major religions in the stained-glass windows). Notably, they are all seemingly at peace with one another after six long years of struggle and strife. Ben apologizes to Locke for killing him. Desmond reunites with Penny, and Sawyer is once again with Juliet. Claire and Charlie come together over the birth of Aaron. Even Jack and his father have reconciled. Jack's father, Christian Shephard (note the religious implications of his name), sums up the final segment of the episode and, indeed, the entire series by telling his son, "This is the place that you all made together, so that you could find one another. The most important part of your life was the time that you spent with these people. That's why all of you are here. Nobody does it alone, Jack. You needed all of them, and they needed you."[14]

It is significant that *Lost* ends not by solving all the mysteries of the island but with a kind of beatific vision of community, relational reconciliation, and love. Equally significant is that

> for [some] *Lost* fans, too many questions were left unanswered, and the series failed to deliver on its ludic promises, shifting in the end to a faith-based approach to its narrative enigmas—both offering religious faith as an ultimate thematic conclusion and asking for viewers' faith in the series' creators that the resulting ambiguities were ultimately more satisfying than a litany of explicit answers. . . . But for many fans, love was enough. . . . In the end (and "The End") . . . the series was about how flawed people could establish relationships and a community was able to discover themselves, to explore their beliefs, and to ultimately make choices that were noble and/or damaging to themselves and others.[15]

What is important here is not so much which group of fans was "right" or "wrong," either in their expectations about the show's overarching narrative or in their understanding of what would constitute a satisfying ending (although this is precisely what makes talking about *Lost* with other fans so much fun). More important is the fact that these viewer expectations are clearly underwritten by a metaphysical conception of stories and storytelling. That is, fans accepted and understood the narrative of *Lost* in terms of ontological distinctions and discrete categories of existence. Again, citing Mittell:

> It seems clear that for ongoing serial storyworlds, many viewers want to imagine a creator with full knowledge and mastery guiding the outcomes, and in moments of doubt or confusion, they put their trust and faith in this higher power—or renounce such authority and take control in their own transformative hands. The inferred author serves this role, and our faith in the author's ability to shape a well-told story carries us through the serial gaps—or when the story goes off the rails, we might lose faith and abandon a series. This act of faith is a form of subjectification, in which we willingly give over our power to something greater in hopes for future payoffs—for all the expansion in participatory culture and fan production in recent years, there is still an active desire for many viewers to be the recipient of a well-told story, not a productive partner in its retelling. As narrative consumers, sometimes we want to give over some degree of control to authors, placing our attention in their hands to guide as they see fit. If we doubt that they know precisely what they are doing, our pleasures are weakened, losing faith in the coherence and rationale of their narrative vision.[16]

If Mittell's analysis is correct, then *Lost* fans either did or did not find "The End" to be a satisfying conclusion to the story depending upon whether it demonstrated the overarching coherence that they expected and, indeed, demanded. These viewers were insistent that the narrative be coherent because they were operating with the assumption that narratives are only ever meaningful when an actual narrator exists who is guiding the story according to a distinct vision of the end. And as the fan forums on sites like Lostpedia suggest, the reverse is true as well. Namely, in the absence of some organizing force that is purposively moving the narrative toward its *telos*, this story-world appears to many viewers as simply bereft of any intrinsic meaning. This apparent desire to submit oneself not just to a telic story (i.e., a story with an "end") but also to an omnipotent and omniscient world-creator/storyteller has little to do with metanarratives per se, but it has everything to do with a deeply felt need for a meta-*narrator*. It is a way for audiences to make sense of the narrative world by drawing categorical (and even hierarchical) distinctions between those who are telling stories and those who are willingly submitting themselves to an unseen and perhaps even transcendent narrator.

It is important to note that these expectations regarding a competent meta-narrator are not the exclusive domain of *Lost* fans. The story-world of *Lost* actually encourages this "meta" take on reality too. After Jack realizes that he is in fact dead, he asks his father, "Are you real?" His father replies, "I sure hope so. Yeah I'm real. You're real. Everything that's ever happened to you is real. All those people in the church—they're all real too."[17] In other words, Jack isn't dreaming or hallucinating. "The End" of *Lost* is all very much real, even if it is a kind of self-conscious hyper-reality. What is more, this (hyper-) reality that Jack and his father experience together is somehow participating ontologically in Jack's lived experience on the island and his relationship with his fellow castaways. During the final conversation between Jack and his father, Jack remains understandably confused: "They [the friends in the church] are all dead?" Christian Shephard replies, "Everyone dies sometime, kiddo. Some of them long before you. Some of them long after you." Jack asks, "Then why are they all here now?" As if he had just put down Augustine's *Confessions*, Christian tells his son, "There is no now here."[18]

This profoundly theological if not downright sacramental move within the narrative was not lost on viewers, so neither should it be lost on us. If Christian's words accurately describe the larger mythology of *Lost*, then time is neither flat nor purely linear but participates in ultimate reality. Like all existence, time has horizontal as well as vertical dimensions. In an important sense, even time on *Lost* is never actually lost, for temporality itself is shot through with transcendence.

Some fans found this turn toward the "meta" in the finale to be a perfectly fitting resolution for a show that was always playing with the boundaries between what is objectively real and what is merely constructed or "named" by humans. Because this group of fans understood the mysteries of the island as simply a backdrop for the development of the show's characters, they saw little need for explanations or answers that, even if plausible, would have likely been uninteresting or underwhelming. In this view, the lack of clarity provided by the finale comports more fully with lived reality, for existence itself is seen as fundamentally mysterious. Because it is not univocal but porous, textured, and multilayered, there is always a more profound mystery lying beneath or behind or beyond every "answer."

Other fans were far less satisfied with "The End." However, if Mittell's analysis is correct, those who were disappointed with the finale were just as concerned about metaphysics as those who loved it. Because the more critical group of fans approached the narrative of *Lost* with the expectation that it be governed by some organizing force that lies beyond or outside the narrative proper (i.e., the extra-diegetic world), they rejected the finale's turn toward religion and mysticism as a failure on the part of the narrator to tell a coherent and credible story. The critique here was not so much "that could never happen," for nothing is ever really outside the realm of possibility on a time-traveling island. Instead, the accusation was "they are just making things up." So the fact that a deceased Jack Shephard was reuniting with loved ones in some kind of spiritual limbo wasn't the problem. The problem was that, for some viewers, the showrunners were cheating. By refusing to explain any of the mysteries of the island, they weren't playing by the rules of the game that the show itself had established during its six previous seasons. In other words, many fans of *Lost* were simply acknowledging that, on a deeply intuitive level, it is largely unfulfilling as a viewer to submit to a storyteller who makes things up and then calls them coherent or meaningful, much less "real."

Thus, whether they believed the finale worked or not, both sets of viewers were left to ponder the same question that Jack voiced: Is this real? Or is it simply the firing of synapses and the triggering of subconscious memories? Are the supposed mysteries of the island pointing to other modes of existence and forms of knowledge, or can these phenomena be explained by purely natural causes, the mechanics of which will one day be understood and mastered through empirical observation and analysis? These are innately metaphysical questions, and they were routinely and explicitly raised both by the narrative of *Lost* and by the fans of *Lost*. As such, they do more than simply invite theological reflection. They also provide an on-the-ground cultural resource that has the potential for both energizing and giving shape to our constructive theological project.

As it concerns questions of metaphysics in general and ontology in particular, the current conversations within (Protestant) theology seem to follow one of two distinct trajectories. One of those trajectories, motivated as it is by the critical skepticism of Continental postmodern philosophy, would have theology do away with metaphysics altogether and focus only on what is given within the purely immanent frame. Anything else is at best speculative and, at worst, idolatrous.[19] The other trajectory derives most of its energy from the notion that the contemporary cultural imagination is beholden so fully to the project of modernity (and by extension postmodernity) that it is simply no longer compatible with a Christian vision of reality. Theology should thus reclaim the "Platonic-Christian synthesis," or the "Great Tradition" embodied by pre-Enlightenment Christianity as its primary ontological starting point.[20]

In light of our examination of how contemporary persons discover and create meaning in and through televisual media (which often involve metaphysical assumptions), neither of these options offers a completely fitting approach for cultural engagement. Instead, our dialogue with television shows like *Lost*, *The Big Bang Theory*, and *House of Cards* has demonstrated that what is needed is a distinctly theological metaphysic—one that acknowledges and affirms the concrete experiences of modern people who yearn for transcendence in the midst of an otherwise disenchanted world, and then seeks to relate those cultural movements to the real presence of the Spirit of God in the world. We briefly sketched in chapter 6 an outline of what this kind of in-Spirited theology might look like. But much more work needs to be done, for a theological project that can credibly address categories of being and existence within the flattened horizon of hypermodern or postmodern culture will always run the risk of collapsing transcendence into immanence or vice versa.

Moving forward, then, we must resist the easy dichotomy between metaphor and metaphysics. Theology simply cannot disregard questions of ontology, especially when contemporary cultural practices like TV watching are already framing reality in this way. But neither can theology abandon the central role that myth, metaphor, and symbol play in the construction of the modern imagination. What the contemporary situation requires is something along the lines of a mythical-realist ontology. For lack of a better word, we might even call this a "televisual theology." Of course, by using the word "televisual," which literally means "distant vision," we do not mean to imply that theology should offer a comprehensive or complete take on life and the world. Rather, it simply means that theology would do well to encourage the development of a penetrating vision—a form of poetic insight that enables us to see, hear, and feel the world both as it truly is and as it will one day become. Some call this kind of seeing wisdom.

We would of course be fools to claim that we know with any kind of certainty where a theological project of this sort might ultimately take us. Just like the ever-evolving medium of TV, the landscape of contemporary culture is changing at too fast a pace to make any unqualified predictions. Nevertheless, what we do know is that, however our theology takes shape, it must emerge in the context of a collaborative community. So consider these final thoughts to be not a conclusion but a call to participate in a story that is still "to be continued"—an invitation that is as uncertain and hopeful as the one Christian Shephard offered to his son at "The End" of Lost.

Jack: Where are we going?

Christian: Let's go find out.

appendix

theology from tv

Once a year, Hollywood takes to the airwaves to give him thanks. His name is lifted up, and he is praised. He's talked about as the creator of all things, the inspiration behind the artists' work, and the reason that so many of those who work in show business come together in his honor. That the celebrants also put on their Sunday best—and the celebration almost always takes place on a Sunday—should not be overlooked.

The "he" who is thanked and praised is, of course, Steven Spielberg, and the Sunday event is the Academy Awards. A recent study by *Voactiv*, which examined every Oscar acceptance speech ever given, determined that Spielberg's name was evoked forty-two times.[1] In second place was Harvey Weinstein. James Cameron and George Lucas were next in line. God came in at number six.

The fact that God is among those who are routinely thanked on televised awards shows raises an interesting question. That is, what if our only source for theological reflection were TV broadcasts like the Oscars (which continues to rank as one of the highest viewed television events of each year; more than sixty million viewers watched at least part of the show live in 2015)? How might that shape our understanding of who God is, what it means to be human, and who the community of faith is to be and become? A more common way of phrasing this question would be to ask something along the lines of, "If aliens landed on earth, what would TV tell them about human culture?" Of course, we should probably thank Spielberg for inspiring that notion too. After all, he was the one who encouraged close encounters with those aliens in the first place and arranged for a certain E.T. to phone home.

In order to answer our somewhat hypothetical question (except for those on team Mulder, in which case it is not at all hypothetical), we examine in this appendix a few categories of TV programs, including unscripted TV (e.g., sports, news, talk shows, and awards shows). However, our primary interest is in scripted television, with a focus on longer-running episodic series. In the first category are shows that place theology front and center, prominently featuring characters that believe in g/God or practice some form of organized religion (often Christianity). A second category contains shows that depict supernatural worlds with religious elements woven into their underlying mythology. Third, there are shows that either have a religious character as a regular part of the mix or deal with issues of faith, spirituality, and religion because of their setting (e.g., it's hard to do a hospital show without occasionally addressing mortality, belief systems, prayer). Finally, there are shows that express theologically informed understandings of life and the world by altogether *avoiding* religion, spirituality, and transcendence.

Before we consider a few concrete examples, though, it should be noted that a theology that comes *entirely* from television is obviously going to be limited by that which actually makes it onto television, and as we pointed out in our chapter on the process of making TV, various creative, economic and—perhaps most significantly—ideological factors contribute to which shows are seen and which shows are not. But if TV really is shaping the contemporary imagination, then it's important that lay and professional theologians are able to identify and understand the various ways in which TV employs explicitly theological language, symbols, and frameworks. And while theology is by no means TV's primary concern, there is still much to discuss; certainly enough so that a curious alien would have plenty to phone home about if he, she, or "other" was watching (with its two, twelve, or twenty-three eyes) what humans watch on TV.

Religion in the Foreground

In 2014, *The Bible* miniseries (which aired on the History Channel) became one of the more successful series of the year, averaging more than ten million viewers for each of its five nights.[2] Soon afterward, NBC aired the series *A.D.: The Bible Continues*, which could be described as a sequel of sorts but was more technically (as the series' title suggests) a "continuation" of the original series.[3]

Though few series have been as biblical as *The Bible* (obviously), some significant shows have put faith front and center. One of the most successful shows of all time is *Touched by an Angel*. Premiering in 1994, it was one of the ten most watched shows for four of its nine seasons and continues to be viewed via streaming services and in syndication. The concept of the show is not at all complicated: angels in human form integrate themselves into the lives of persons in need, helping them achieve something that they want, or overcome an obstacle, or come to terms with an emotion, and generally comforting them—in essence, doing the kinds of things that many imagine "guardian angels" might do. The show doesn't make any big theological statements. It simply presents the idea that angels are real, that God is in charge, and both have a desire to help people deal with life.

The show's developer and showrunner, Martha Williamson, was sometimes criticized for not being religious enough, or at least for not being religious in the "right" way. Even though Williamson is an outspoken Christian, the name of Jesus is never mentioned, and the whole concept of angels in human form interacting with people in tangible ways is simply assumed. But Williamson had different intentions for the show. Wanting to reach as wide an audience as possible, she strove to produce a show that simply told people, "God loves you." As a consequence, Williamson preferred that the series not get into the specifics of who that God was or what that God's name might be.

Shortly thereafter (from 1996 until 2007), *7th Heaven* emerged as the number one rated show on the WB network. The program—about a pastor and his family of five (and then six) kids and one dog that was so adorable that it was featured in the opening credits—was especially popular with teen girls and women. It also had a larger audience than *Buffy the Vampire Slayer* or *Dawson's Creek*, two shows on the same network. Yet both *Buffy* and *Dawson's* received more attention from the press. Whereas both of the latter shows were featured on the cover of *Entertainment Weekly*, *7th Heaven* never was. The series is still remembered fondly by those who watched the show growing up and the parents who watched it with them. It was then and remains now rare for a television narrative to focus so clearly on people of religious conviction—even though America is a country full of those same kinds of people.

But *7th Heaven* was not initially designed to be a show about them. When Brenda Hampton, the creator of *7th Heaven*, first pitched her idea, her concept was simple: she wanted to do a TV show about a "functional family." The dad was going to be a therapist. But an executive suggested that he be a minister instead, and thus a show (and, eventually, the show's title) was born.

That the series was never meant to be about a religiously devout family becomes evident as *7th Heaven* is watched more closely. Religion hardly seemed to be at the center of this family's life, despite the fact that it's how the father made his living. In the earlier episodes, the church isn't emphasized at all, and it was a few years into the series before the pastor/dad ever appeared in the pulpit, giving a sermon (although, to the show's credit, his wife does deliver a sermon). Eventually, the series did explore the patriarch's "workplace" a little bit more, and one of the daughters followed in her father's "robe-steps" by becoming a minister herself (which, again, is quite remarkable). But the idea that *7th Heaven* was a show about "Christians" or that it was any kind of a "Christian show" because of the profession of one of the protagonists is overstated at best.[4]

From the alien's-eye view, then, what does this say about *these* people? Might it suggest that, for this family, their religious convictions were primarily a "private" matter, operating "in the background" rather than front and center, influencing every aspect of their lives—their decisions, their ethics, the things they did (and didn't) do? The dad who was a pastor might have talked about prayer, but how often did the family actually pray? Were they ever seen in worship? Did they study the Bible or discuss and debate how Scripture was informing their lived realities? It's hard to find moments when they did, if they ever did so at all.

So almost in spite of its explicitly religious content, *7th Heaven* rarely succeeded in presenting a full-orbed picture of a family whose very livelihood was tethered to a worshiping community of faith. It is still embraced by members of the faith community (it is a show about "family values," after all). But it just barely moved the bar in terms of robust representations of religion, religious people, or religious practice on TV, and as of this writing, no show has come along to pick up that mantle, or stand in that pulpit, the way Reverend Camden hardly ever got to do.[5]

Joan of Arcadia might have been trying to go after the same kinds of people who watched *7th Heaven*. Premiering in 2003, the series deals with a teenage girl who started seeing visions of God (who would appear to her in various human forms and direct her to take some sort of action). It took the idea of a divine agent very seriously without addressing or developing any specific doctrines, similar to how *Touched by an Angel* mostly avoided the subject. But it was just as deeply grounded in an exploration of genuine religious devotion.

Joan started out strong, then struggled in the ratings. It was canceled after two seasons, replaced on Friday nights by *Ghost Whisperer*. The head of CBS at the time explained that the demographics of the viewers for *Joan of Arcadia* skewed old (a not-as-desirable demographic for advertisers), and that perhaps the appeal of Jennifer Love Hewitt—and the subject matter of the new show—would attract younger viewers. "I think talking to ghosts may skew younger than talking to God," was one of the reasons he gave for replacing Joan with Jennifer.[6] *Ghost Whisperer* ran for five seasons. As might be expected, neither God nor ghosts ever sat down for an interview to make a case for why they were, in fact, the younger-skewing subject.

Saving Grace, which aired on TNT, had a concept that combined aspects of *Joan of Arcadia* and *Touched by an Angel*. It follows the character of Grace, played by Holly Hunter, who is confronted by a gruff and hardened angel to make changes in her life, which Grace struggles to do. But the angel keeps after her, and she keeps making the effort. The show's creator, Nancy Miller, said that she wanted to do a show that looked at "God, faith, religion and sin through the eyes of a woman who has pieces of all of us in her."[7] The show allowed Grace to stay imperfect and broken and in one sense showed her "wrestling with God" rather than just immediately doing what God wanted her to do (or be who God wanted her to be). It wasn't afraid to let things get messy, the way life so often is. *Saving Grace* had TNT's highest premiere of any show on that network up to that time and ran for three seasons, but the economics of television (which are often dependent on international sales) led to the show's early end. Once again, the bottom line trumped even the most laudable of efforts.

One series that is often overlooked took place in a church and had religion at its center. *Amen*, which ran from 1986 to 1991, starred Sherman Hemsley of *The Jefferson's* as the deacon of a church and Clifton Davis as its pastor, and—much more frequently than *7th Heaven*—actually showed the pastor at work doing the things an actual minister does: preaching sermons, dealing with church politics, and caring for his flock (albeit in a lighthearted way indicative of a sitcom). It was popular, though not a spectacular success. Yet for those who might believe that there has never been a long-running program that showed the inner workings of a church, *Amen* has already filled that gap.

Amen does, however, present us with one of the elephants in this room—or in this sanctuary, to be more specific. That is, TV depicts the religious life of the African American community differently than it does that of white persons of faith. Hollywood writers and executives seem to assume that church attendance is a prevalent part of African American culture, pure and simple. So if one's understanding of the religious habits of Americans was derived exclusively from scripted TV, it would be reasonable to conclude that nearly all African Americans are churchgoers (usually at churches with great gospel music) and most white people are not (and those who are usually prefer singing along to an organ). Religion, then, when it is addressed directly on TV, functions more like a marker of cultural or racial identity than an exploration of actual religious devotion. And in these instances, it ends up leveraging stereotypes that fail to reflect the on-the-ground realities of religion or religious adherents.

Though no religion-centric series have been as successful as *Touched by an Angel*, *7th Heaven*, or *Amen*, quite a few network shows have put religion (and religious people) front and center. *The Father Dowling Mysteries* followed the escapades of a crime-solving priest; *The Book of Daniel* was about a minister who talked to Jesus (who appeared to him in human form); and *The Flying Nun* was about a nun who . . . well, her special skill is right there in the title. *Nothing Sacred* showed the goings-on at a Catholic church, and *Kings* told the biblical story of David in a contemporary, almost Shakespearean style. Comedy

Central aired a show called *Black Jesus*, and Dan Aykroyd played a widowed pastor on *Soul Man*, by the creators of *Home Improvement*. (That show should not be confused with *The Soul Man*, which stars Cedric the Entertainer as a former music star who becomes a pastor and has enjoyed a long run on TV Land.) There was also *Hell Town* (another crime-solving priest), the BBC's *Father Brown* (ditto), and *Rev.* (a pastor rather than a priest; no crime solving involved). And the Canadian show *Little Mosque on the Prairie*, focusing on the Muslim community in a small town, ran for several seasons on the CBC.

The above list is not meant to be complete, but it does demonstrate that religious communities, people, and places of worship do occasionally appear on TV. We just have to look for them a little more carefully.

There are two other significant (and highly popular) TV shows that were not only religious in nature but were also designed to teach and promote the value of a core religious text: the Bible. That one stars a talking dog, and the other features talking vegetables should perhaps put them in a category of their own. *Davey and Goliath* is the one with the talking dog. Produced by the Lutheran Church in America and airing in the early 1960s (then revived in the early 1970s), *Davey and Goliath* is a stop-motion animated (i.e., Claymation) show that depicts the adventures of a young boy and his dog, Goliath. Episodes often deal with spiritual themes, though they are not overtly religious, and some explore serious issues such as death, racism, and religious intolerance. Seventy-five episodes of the show were produced, and those who have seen the show tend to smile just at the mention of its name.

VeggieTales might be considered a descendant of *Davey and Goliath*: a series aimed at kids that gained an adult following as well. Although *VeggieTales* wasn't originally a "TV show" (it was direct-to-video), it eventually found its way to television, with versions of the episodes airing on NBC. Later, in 2014, Dreamworks started producing original episodes for streaming on Netflix. Starring Bob the Tomato and Larry the Cucumber, *VeggieTales* is much more religiously overt than *Davey and Goliath*, offering (in its earliest incarnation) retellings of biblical stories like Daniel and Jonah, as well as original stories that address issues such as fear and forgiveness. Many adult viewers of the show can still sing the various "Silly Songs" that were part of the show, especially when they can't find their hairbrushes.

In 2006, NBC made a deal with the producers of *VeggieTales* to air the already-produced shows on broadcast TV. But NBC made some significant edits. In the original versions, at the end of each episode, Bob and Larry would appear on a countertop and sum up the lesson of the show, often quoting a passage from the biblical text and always ending with, "Remember, kids, God made you special and he loves you very much." But when the show appeared on NBC, those final moments were removed, and all Bob and Larry said was "Good-bye."

Fans took note and inundated NBC with protests, but the network did not change its position. A spokesperson for NBC said, "Our goal is to reach as broad of an audience as possible with these positive messages while being careful not to advocate any one religious point of view."[8] In other words, it was okay for these armless vegetables to act like they believed in God; they just couldn't actually talk about it.[9] By removing specific language from *VeggieTales*, the network put its own theological spin on the show, changing (and possibly even undermining) the original author's intent.

But there is good news for proponents of "freedom of vegetable religious expression." Netflix—perhaps more aware of the *VeggieTales* fan base, as well as the changing (i.e., more segmented) habits of viewers—allows for much more blatant proselytizing on its streaming service. On the show *VeggieTales in the House*, Bob and Larry can speak as they please, quoting the Bible and even saying, "God loves you." It's refreshing to see the vegetables so verbally unrestrained.

Netflix's acceptance of Bob's and Larry's religious commitments might actually be a sign of things to come. As broadcasting gives way to narrowcasting, Netflix and other streaming services are aiming at smaller and smaller pieces of the entire pie, rather than one specific segment of it, the way cable outlets like FX, Disney Junior, and MTV do. It is increasingly likely that programming that appeals to more-specific demographics can and will flourish (and here "fans of vegetables who talk about Jesus" is its own demographic). Whereas NBC might have, rightly or wrongly, assumed that specific language about a specific religion might limit a show's audience, today's streamers and broadcasters can target those segments directly.

Still (at least as of the 2015/16 television season), it remains difficult to find shows in which religion could be considered any kind of major player. Even the few that have been mentioned here rarely address complex issues of theology, and they mostly avoid the intricacies and nuances of characters' beliefs and practices. So any theological reflection based purely upon these shows is going to have a similar kind of simplicity—a reductive conception of reality that verges on misrepresentation. There is something both to celebrate and to critique here. God is occasionally present, and characters are engaged in ongoing conversations about the role of religion and religious practice in their lives. At the same time, the most blatant and in-depth exploration of biblical theology on TV mostly takes place on a countertop, between an animated tomato and his cucumber best friend. So if everything one knew about theology came from watching shows about these faithful few, it would be easy to conclude that the most serious of religious adherents were simply biding their time until they were tossed into a salad.

I'm Spiritual but Not Religious

A few series that are not overtly religious actually address religion in insightful ways, and some even interact with the biblical text in ways that many of the explicitly religious TV characters do not.

Supernatural, for example, invites viewers into a supernatural world (otherwise, the show could have been titled just *Natural*). The main characters investigate strange phenomena that include the appearance of mythical monsters, demons, ghosts, and other spirits. But they also regularly talk about heaven and hell and frequently deal with the idea of Lucifer trying to bring about the apocalypse. That the characters on *Supernatural* quote the Bible more than any of the Camden children from *7th Heaven* is an often-overlooked fact when people are looking for genuine representations of religion on television.

Along similar lines, *Sleepy Hollow* draws heavily from the book of Revelation. There is regular talk about the four horsemen, the coming apocalypse, and the battle of Armageddon. Two-hundred-year-old Bibles and religious artifacts from previous centuries are regularly featured as being items of great value, possibly even holding a key to the survival of the human race.

Buffy the Vampire Slayer offers a clear vision of good and evil (Buffy = good; vampires = bad) and uses the symbols and images of Christianity as a storytelling tool. For example, vampires tend to avoid going into churches, affected as they are by the sight of crosses and the use of holy water. These rules are rooted more in vampire lore than in the religious convictions of the show's creator. Still, the show proceeds on the basis of certain assumptions that we might identify as theological: whereas some demons can be defeated by a well-placed kick in the groin, there's a different sort of power available from objects that have religious (and specifically Christian) origins.

The X-Files is well known (and loved) for its pairing of a cross-wearing skeptic with a true believer—only what the believer believed in was aliens. Dana Scully, who wears a cross necklace but only occasionally talks about her religious heritage, is an "unless I see it, I don't believe it" kind of person, while Fox Mulder has much more "faith" in things unseen. As Scully continues to encounter things that she had previously thought were impossibilities, she opens herself up to the idea that the cross around her neck might also mean something more. As a result, her optimism about the human spirit begins to rub off on her more pessimistic partner. A poster in Mulder's office (and the subtitle to one of the *X-Files* films) thus serves as a thematic summary of the show: "I want to believe." It's a prayer that Scully might voice about God as much as it is a faith statement by Mulder about aliens.

Television series like *The X-Files*, *Supernatural*, *Buffy the Vampire Slayer*, *Salem*, *Charmed*, *American Horror Story*, *Teen Wolf*, and any others that allow for the possibility of monsters or demons are already trafficking in theological categories and language whether they know it or not. Many TV narratives are completely grounded in the material world and therefore only allow room for what is empirically verifiable (Scully's "unless I see it, I don't believe it"). However, once a show suggests that there might be "other realms," it immediately opens a new register of meaning that allows the story-world to take seriously what the biblical author calls "the powers of this dark world and . . . the spiritual forces of evil in the heavenly realms" (Eph. 6:12). Any show that not only explicitly incorporates these "powers" into its diegetic world but also goes so far as to build "spiritual forces" (and even "heavenly realms") into its major plot lines is inviting theological (and even biblical) dialogue. It presses theology to consider new ways of engaging both these "spiritual but not religious" story-worlds and the fans who consume them with a fervent passion.

For example, *The Twilight Zone* tends to avoid being overtly (or even subtly) religious, but many of its recurring themes are no less spiritually charged. Whether it is showing the superficiality of physical beauty, examining the benefit of living in community, or using monsters as a stand-in for universal fears, the spirituality of this show—and the suggestion that we might live in a supernatural world, with monsters and aliens among us—presents its own style of spiritual-but-not-religious commentary from episode to episode.

HBO's *The Leftovers* takes place after a supernatural event that many of its characters believe was some version of what certain Christian groups call "the rapture." Some of the "leftovers" are themselves Christian, and they struggle with the idea that they were not taken, while many "sinners" were. As humanity struggles with the new reality (i.e., the realization that "the supernatural is real"), some begin to follow a cult-like leader, others seek out new forms of community, and others violently fend for themselves. Even though *The Leftovers* is operating according to the logics of its own story-world, it's not afraid to put theological issues front and center in a way that few shows ever have.

Of course, one key exception is the 2004 reboot of *Battlestar Galactica*, which not only created its own theology but also talked about it a lot. Characters continually try to figure out who they are, how they were created, and how they relate to the "gods." The series could easily be considered one of the most theologically oriented shows ever produced. There was actual talk of "doctrine" (as the show defined and developed it), as well as ongoing examinations of religious leaders, church communities, creation, and the afterlife. That the religion on *Battlestar* was an invented one (or, from the show's point of view, one that was in the process of being discovered) does not take away from the serious and eternal questions that were part of the show's DNA.[10]

These "spiritual but not religious" series (and there are countless others) demonstrate how theological understandings of life and the world emerge from shows that, on the surface, might have nothing to do with religion. Though they may or may not make specific statements about g/God(s), they all create room for the possibility of the supernatural, making the rather scandalous suggestion that "flesh and blood" might not compose the whole of reality. At the very least, they invite both skeptical believers like Mulder and believing skeptics like Scully to consider that the "truth" really might just be "out there."[11]

Religious Characters Navigating a Post-Religious World

It is not only on shows about religion (or those with an undercurrent of spirituality or the supernatural) that TV confronts audiences theologically. Many series feature characters with varying degrees of religious faith whose mere presence within the story-world means that religion will at least get a hearing, if not a full-blown trial. What is perhaps even more interesting is that these characters remain present and active even when the rest of the narrative is virtually devoid of any other religious pretense.

*M*A*S*H*'s Father Mulcahy was one of TV's most prominent Christian characters. Appearing over the entire course of the eleven-year series (and even on the short-lived sequel, *After MASH*), the priest is depicted as quite good. He is gentle, patient, and kind—a calm presence in the perpetual storm. He comforts those in need, laughs with those who laugh, and gives last rites to the dying. Even when a patient comes into the 4077th claiming to be Jesus Christ, it is Father Mulcahy who communes with him the most, offering him genuine compassion.

But it's hard to find one episode where the good Father interacts with another person of sincere religious devotion. Surely, amid all the doctors and nurses and enlisted men and women of that unit, there would have been some Christians, Jews, or Muslims. But no one in the *M*A*S*H* world other than Father Mulcahy seems to have any faith at all. To be fair, most everyone assigned to the unit attends church services, but that seems to be because, amid the redundancy of their lives, they just need something—anything—to do. It is rare (if it happens at all) to see anyone go to the priest for any of the sacraments central to Roman Catholic devotion (confession, baptism, or communion), and no one seeks out the priest's wisdom concerning what the Bible might say about war or asks him for prayer. In the end, those under his care seem to conceive of Father Mulcahy's vocation as a professional service—a kind of always-on-duty therapist.

Similarly, *The Waltons* and *Little House on the Prairie* both include ministers as recurring characters and show the families at the center of each series to be people of faith. A more recent example—Hallmark's *When Calls the Heart*—also includes church leaders and churchgoers as a part of daily life. But it's significant that the setting for all three of these shows is in the past. Implicitly, then, they are "historical" (even romanticized) takes on religious faith and practice, something that might have been important years ago but is now a distant and fading memory. In other words, to look back on this bygone era is also to recognize the degree to which modern society has come of age.

One family that did not outgrow its faith is the Reagans of *Blue Bloods*. The family of New York cops is shown to be faithful, churchgoing Catholics. They gather together just about every Sunday for a family meal and routinely pray before they eat. But it's notable to observe that, in the first season, their prayers are decidedly (and some would say awkwardly) nondenominational. With their hands folded, the Reagans recite a prayer that many who were raised in the Roman Catholic tradition would know by heart:

> Bless us, oh Lord,
> And these, Thy gifts,
> Which we are about to receive,
> From Thy bounty,
> Through Christ our Lord, Amen.

Only that's not what they say. In the early episodes, the Reagans leave out the "through Christ our Lord" part. And later episodes depict Tom Selleck's character highlighting where he differs from the Catholic Church on points of doctrine. The Reagans certainly practice their faith in terms of how they care for one another and the world around them, but they seem to pick and choose which part of their Catholicism they are going to embrace—and whether "Christ" has anything to do with the bounty they are about to receive when they pray. In this way, the series offers what is surely a sympathetic (although not uncomplicated) read of the religiously devout, even recognizing the many ways in which modern people wrestle with the very tradition of which they are a part.

The first episode of *Friday Night Lights* made it seem as if the show might be picking up where *7th Heaven* left off. Because it is set in Texas, churchgoing is as much a part of the cultural backdrop as football, and characters are seen going to and from church in between football practices, football fund-raisers, and football games. When one of the players needs money for school, it's the people with whom he worships who pitch in. And when the team prays before a game, the prayer is made "in Jesus's name."[12] It is simply taken for granted that faith is a part of the show and an ever-present part of the characters' lives.

In a later season, though, *Friday Night Lights* dives even deeper into religion. Lyla (played by Minka Kelly), a teenage girl who had not taken her religious convictions very seriously, suddenly becomes "born again"—or, at least, viewers were informed that that's what happened, since her actual conversion happens between seasons. Her journey even leads her inside a church (with contemporary worship music being played in the background) and to a budding romantic relationship with another Christian character.

But her piety was short-lived. After little more than a season, the writers set aside Lyla's conversion as if it had never happened. They instead chose to focus on reigniting her relationship with the football player Tim Riggins, played by Taylor Kitsch, failing to see that they already had a complicated romantic situation right in front of them that they could have explored. Lyla was in love with both Jesus and Tim Riggins. But such a love triangle was never meant to be.

The Good Wife and *The Americans* both feature teen characters who believe in God—specifically Jesus—and their beliefs are routinely woven into the show. The daughter on *The Good Wife* is shown studying the Bible, and sometimes she challenges her mother about the mom's behavior. The mom, in return, seeks advice (some might even call it "counsel") on issues relating to Scripture and the Christian life. It's clear that the mother respects her child's beliefs, is intrigued by her religious devotion, and even admires her for her growing faith.[13]

The parents on *The Americans* (which takes place in the 1980s) are not so pleased with their daughter's interest in Jesus, but that's mostly because they are Russian spies, and at least from their perspective, no Soviet parent would ever want a daughter adhering to any religion, much less Christianity. At one point, the mom bemoans the fact that they have tried to raise their daughter, Paige, right, but then she brings "this" into the house (the "this" being "religion").

The show presents a unique look at how tumultuous religious devotion can be for a family. In some ways it even echoes Jesus's words that whoever risked acknowledging him before others would turn "a man against his father, a daughter against her mother" (Matt. 10:35). Also, Paige's relationship with a youth pastor complicates matters, as he counsels her to follow the directives of Jesus, while her parents are more interested in her learning the ways of Stalin. Here again is a depiction of a devout character, but in this case she is not simply navigating a post-religious environment. Instead, her convictions have placed her in a constant state of conflict with her surroundings.

The world of *Grey's Anatomy*, though, is far more reflective of a post-Christian context that simply hasn't the time for religion. Dr. April Kepner, played by Sarah Drew, is a Christian, and the actress has stated that her own faith inspired the show's writers to incorporate this element into the show. Likewise, various characters on *Law and Order*, *Boomtown*, *St. Elsewhere*, *Oz*, *Judging Amy*, and *The Middle* have also identified themselves as Christians, and they mostly portray people of faith in a positive light. Television series as varied as *The Andy Griffith Show*; *Firefly*; *Thirtysomething*; *Walker, Texas Ranger*; *Marvel's Daredevil*; and *King of the Hill* (to name just a few more) have all presented either story lines or characters or both that represent at least a slice of what it means to be a person of faith in the modern world—that is, a world where religious practice is the exception rather than the norm.

Of course, it is asking too much to expect any one show (let alone one character) to represent an entire group of people, especially a group as broad and diverse as the Christian community. The Huxtables on *The Cosby Show* did not represent every African American family, just as Will on *Will and Grace* did not represent every gay man. But their presence—and an attempt by the writers and producers to portray these characters in all their complexity—contributed to Americans' understanding of and ability to empathize with people and cultures that had been historically underrepresented on TV. So the fact that there are more religious characters than ever on television is at least some form of progress (especially when compared to their absence), and certain shows are more than willing to dive quite deeply into what it means to believe (or not believe).

For example, the Sundance series *Rectify* features religion as a central theme (and sometimes a central conflict) of the show. The series centers on a character, Daniel, who is released from prison after serving fourteen years for a rape and murder that he may or may not have committed. Set in Georgia, the show is permeated by the religious culture of the American South. Many of the characters are churchgoers or at least were brought up in the church. Daniel's sister-in-law Tawney is quite vocal about her faith and takes it very seriously. As she struggles with her own feelings about him, she seeks advice and input from her own prayer group. Her discussions with Daniel—she's very concerned about his immortal soul—lead him to be baptized, and while he doesn't come out of the water praising God and singing hymns, it is this ritual act of devotion that initially motivates him to become a different kind of person.

There is something unique about how *Rectify* deals with religious faith and practice and how it depicts its characters as people who are trying to become something "other" than who they currently are. It's as if the implied narrator is presenting these characters not merely as the broken and flawed souls that we see on-screen but as a far more textured and complicated creatures. Daniel is always in the process of becoming and, as a consequence, is filled to the brim with potential. The narrative thus offers a rather optimistic portrayal not just of religious people but of humanity. Tawney, the vocal Christian, seems to intuit Daniel's human potential by approaching her brother-in-law as if to say at one and the same time, "neither do I condemn you" and "leave your life of sin" (John 8:11).

Although it is not unique to television, this kind of hard-won optimism might be more present in episodic TV stories than in other forms of storytelling. On TV, we are able to see the same characters from so many different angles, in so many different situations, over the course of so many hours and seasons and years. And because television characters exist in our lives for so long, we empathize with them in different ways and on different levels than we do with characters in film or novels. Our hearts ache when they make mistakes, and we celebrate their victories. We want them to be better than they are and hope that they'll become everything they were created to be. And even when they are prevented from flourishing for any number of reasons, television provides us with space and time to understand why they are being held back. In other words, we experience these characters as broken and incomplete yet moving toward a kind of wholeness that has its source beyond the narrative world.

For example, the third season of *Damages* explores how a key incident in the main character's life—the loss of her unborn child from a miscarriage that was the result of her purposeful, self-induced actions—helped to create the harsh, unloving (and very damaged) woman she had become. Years later, at her father's deathbed, even more of her backstory is revealed, showing how these numerous "damages" continue to shape her in the present. There is no mention of God and no discussion of theology. But when these episodic recollections of her trauma are located within an overarching narrative of her life as a whole, *Damages* is able to create space for a different level of understanding and empathy not just for her but for others who have experienced similar incidents in their past.

NYPD Blue offers a similar example. As discussed in chapter 4, the show's creator described the story as being about "the redemption of Andy Sipowicz." As a result, Andy was told to "talk through me" by a character who, in a dream, was presented as being Jesus. In addition, his relationship with the police receptionist who was both a churchgoer and a gay man challenged Andy's homophobia. Even his ex-wife—after going through rehab—reappeared in his life with the news that she was a born-again Christian. Given all these key moments, the Christian viewers who had protested the show when it first aired failed to notice that the series gradually morphed into one of the more "Christian" shows to have ever been on TV.

That Andy was becoming a better human being—partly from his life experiences and at least a little bit because of the influence of the religious people around him—simply affirms the notion that he was being redeemed. This person who was so brash and even vile at the beginning of the series was becoming less and less so and a lot easier for the audience to like. But he was also becoming different. Better. We might even say that, over the course of 211 episodes and eleven years, Detective Sipowicz was made new.

Jewish characters are present on television too, but it is rare for them to be religiously observant. The fact that certain characters on *Seinfeld*, *Northern Exposure*, *Friends*, and *Entourage* are Jewish is sometimes brought to the foreground, but they are rarely if ever depicted observing Jewish religious rituals (which is not to say that their Jewishness doesn't affect who they are as characters). The animated *Phineas and Ferb* features Isabella Garcia-Shapiro, who speaks (and sings) of her Mexican-Jewish heritage ("When we break into a chorus of 'ole' and 'oy, vey'!"), and the TV show *Thirtysomething*'s Jewish characters took tradition seriously enough for the episode "Prelude to a Bris" to move beyond the prelude to the actual bris. But the takeaway about Jews from watching only scripted TV could easily be that they approach their religious tradition as casually as the Christian characters on *7th Heaven*.[14] Faithful representations of religiously devout Muslim and Buddhist characters are even harder to find. Muslims especially, but Buddhists too, are often reduced to easy stereotypes like "terrorist" (e.g., *24*) or "monk" (e.g., *CSI*, *Kung Fu*).

When characters of the Christian faith appear to take their faith seriously on TV, they are sometimes mocked for it, which has less to do with Christianity per se than with the notion that belief systems in general are something to be avoided. Michelle Williams's character on *Dawson's Creek* has a fundamentalist Christian grandmother whom she lives with (and who also causes her to frequently roll her eyes). *The Big Bang Theory* has Sheldon's mother, a devout Christian whose statements are almost always met with biting responses from the more "rational" characters who make up the show, Sheldon being the primary culprit. *That '70s Show*'s Fez, an exchange student from an unknown country, refers to the family he first lived with as his "Bible-thumping host parents," and that description alone has the capacity to produce laughs from the audience. *The Office* and *30 Rock* present their Christian characters as rigid or woefully naive, respectively, and *Justified* shows more than one person of faith to be hypercritical (although it does balance things out with more positive portrayals as well). But if one were to add things up based on shows like these, it would be easy to conclude that most religious adherents are judgmental, joyless, and not very smart.

That being said, no discussion about religious characters on television would be complete without mentioning the *longest*-running character, on one of TV's longest-running series. This character has existed in the background (and sometimes foreground) of nearly six hundred episodes of TV, demonstrating patience, kindness, and peace by not letting any of his neighbors' antics get too far under his bright yellow skin. The character is of course Ned Flanders, and the show is *The Simpsons*.

That a Christian character exists on a show as subversive and irreverent as *The Simpsons* is as surprising as it is significant. Indeed, it's easy to see why Ned Flanders serves as a great representation of who a Christian is supposed to be. He is nonjudgmental, a faithful friend, full of joy, and never abandons his faith (even in times of crisis, like the death of his wife).

But it might also be said that Ned Flanders represents the picture that many people in the broader culture have in mind when they think of Christians—a literal cartoon whose children play with New Testament action figures and say, "Dang-darn-diddly" when they slam their thumbs with hammers. It's a shallow stereotype, but in the world of *The Simpsons*, nothing is sacred, and everything is mocked, so it's hard to get too worked up about a show that is an equal-opportunity offender. Taken as a whole, an alien observer who was learning about the Christian community by watching nothing other than the animated residents of Springfield would likely come to the conclusion that Ned is the most admirable character of them all. As a father, husband, and citizen, he's no Homer, but in some important respects, that's a darn-digedy-do good thing.

How (Not) to Talk about God

In addition to the explicit references to religion and religious people, the absence of God on TV—and those who believe in this God—is equally significant. During her job interview on the first episode of *The Mary Tyler Moore Show*, Mary Richards informs Lou Grant that it is illegal to ask about a job applicant's religion. But when asked, "How old are you?" Mary quickly replies, "Presbyterian." So we discover that Ms. Richards has at least some sort of religious identity. But viewers wouldn't have known it by watching the rest of the series. There is the requisite man of the cloth presiding at the funeral when Chuckles the Clown bites the dust, but other than that, religion simply doesn't come up. Mary might very well have been in church every Sunday, but the narrative focuses only on what she does the other six days of the week.

To place any sort of theological expectations on a half-hour comedy is a bit of a trap though. Of course God doesn't feature prominently; that's neither the purpose nor the function of a sitcom. Yet some sitcoms have presented their characters as churchgoers to various levels of comedic effect. *Everybody Loves*

Raymond, *King of Queens*, *The Middle*, and *That '70s Show* (when not referencing Fez's Bible-thumping host parents) each provided insight into the Sunday-morning habits of their characters, and even *Seinfeld* revealed that Elaine's boyfriend, Puddy, was a Christian (when she turned on the radio in his car and heard contemporary Christian music blaring from the speakers). So it's not that "churchgoers can't be funny." It's simply that the writers—for various reasons—generally choose to tell stories about something else.

It's one thing to avoid the nitty-gritty details about a character's religious practices. It's another to create a narrative world where God doesn't exist at all. If there was one setting where we might not expect God to be avoided, it would be a hospital, where characters routinely encounter death, life, joy, and suffering—experiences that generally require the presence of some kind of spiritual advisor. Yet one of the most successful hospital shows of all time, *ER*, did not feature a chaplain as a recurring character until its fourteenth (!) season—and even then it was difficult to decipher what the character actually believed. *Chicago Hope* was regularly chaplain-less, as was Princeton-Plainsboro (the hospital on *House*). Police procedurals like *Hill Street Blues* or any of the *CSIs* could have featured the department-hired chaplains that are on staff in nearly every big city, but none were found there either. On these and other shows, clergy might be seen officiating at weddings, funerals, and the occasional baptism or bris, but they are almost never presented as being a normal part of everyday life.

Certain shows, while not keeping God out of the conversation entirely, seem to go out of their way to move quickly past the topic. They make a big deal about a character's faith in the beginning (or for a certain moment) but then set these religious concerns aside as if the issue no longer has any bearing on the narrative. *The West Wing* tells the story of President Josiah Bartlett, a man known for his Catholic faith. In the pilot, he demonstrates his knowledge of the Bible during a discussion with one of the Christian "experts" who had come to see him. What is more, Bartlett frequently considers how his decisions line up with his Catholic faith. He is a thoughtful (if not quite devout) believer.

Until God makes him angry. In a season 2 episode titled "The Two Cathedrals," Bartlett is reeling from the death of his secretary, along with the day-to-day struggles of being president. He decides to take his frustrations out on God and, in a very powerful scene, stands at the altar in a church spewing his justified anger—some of it in Latin. (The series had already established that the Jesuit-educated Bartlett knew the language.) Bartlett's Latin rants are not subtitled; his rage is clear enough. His frame of mind is further amplified when he lights a cigarette and smokes it right there in the sanctuary. Then, in a final act of disgust, Bartlett drops his cigarette, snuffs it out on the altar, turns, and walks away.

The symbolism of turning his back on God was not at all subtle, and the episode might have served as a powerful setup for a journey of a man wrestling with God. But in terms of the series' narrative flow, the match was over. Bartlett was done, and from that point on it was almost as if God didn't exist at all. The president's faith would occasionally be referenced but rarely utilized. God had been all but snuffed out, like the cigarette under Bartlett's foot.

House of Cards received a great deal of attention when internet outlets screamed out clickbait headlines about Hollywood "spitting on Jesus."[15] The scene involves Frank Underwood going into a church and conversing with a priest. Frank admits that he understands the idea of a powerful "Old Testament" God who rules through fear, but he is flummoxed by the idea of Jesus. He asks to be left alone for a moment and moves to talk to the figure of Jesus hanging above the pulpit. "Love. That's what you're selling?" Frank sneers at the concept: "Well, I don't buy it." He then spits on the symbol of that unconditional love that he so powerfully rejects.[16]

Frank then wipes his spit off the crucifix, which causes the whole thing to fall to the floor. The figure of Jesus is shattered, and the pieces scatter on the floor. Frank picks up a broken ear and quips, "Well, I've got God's ear now." It's a powerful depiction of a man choosing the way of power over the way of grace. It would not be out of the question (nor out of line with the tenor of the show) for Frank to pick up the heated conversation with God at a later date. But for the moment, another character had declared God irrelevant to his life. The *House of Cards* universe—for the time being, at least—would be a godless one.

Homicide: Life on the Street and *House* both present characters on similar journeys away from their previous relationships with God. Frank Pembleton started *Homicide* as a thoughtful (also Jesuit-educated) believer but made a point in later episodes to express how he didn't really believe what he used to believe. Dr. Robert Chase on *House* talked of having been a student in a seminary and—in the earlier days of the series—often challenged Dr. House on his atheist beliefs. But as the series went on, those seminary days were mentioned less and less, until they were eventually not mentioned at all. House's atheism, on the other hand, became even more pronounced, and he never passed up an opportunity to mock (and sometimes berate) anyone who believed in anything beyond material reality.

Like *House*, *The West Wing* and *House of Cards* don't entirely ignore the question of God, but the very notion of the divine (and in these two cases, Jesus) is narrated as something that most people outgrow or eventually toss aside—snuffed out or spit upon. Maintaining complete self-reliance and developing one's personal moral framework (whatever that might be) seem to be the highest of goods.

A similar kind of vision serves as the apparent backdrop for the first season of *True Detective*. The eight-hour journey is less a story and more an exploration of nihilism, presenting two characters whose personal struggles had led them to believe in hardly anything at all. Matthew McConaughey's Rust Cohle speaks mostly in philosophical diatribes, and along the way it is difficult to tell exactly where the series is going or what it is going to add up to.

But if one were to ask the writer, the journey was clear. Nic Pizzolatto, who wrote all eight episodes, said that he saw his two main characters as men who were not able to "admit the possibility of grace."[17] Pizzolatto suggested, "If someone needs a book to read along with season one of *True Detective*, I would recommend the King James Old Testament."[18] And when the final line of the series presents its startling end point (which is, really, a starting point) for Rust's journey, the basic orientation of the entire series shifts. It becomes a journey not into but out of nihilism. The darkness that had simply permeated the series gives way, as Rust has what can only be described as a religious experience, or at least a mysterious, supernatural one. It leads him—along with the viewer—to reevaluate everything that has come before. When Rust, who seems to have been stuck wandering in darkness for so long, proclaims (as the last words of the season), "Seems to me, the light's winning," he is, in the words of Pizzolatto, admitting the possibility of grace—even in the darkest of nights.

True Detective thus embodies a subtle shift in the current televisual landscape. Its story-world, like many TV narratives before it, is one that is largely bereft of the transcendent. God is dead, and we have killed him—snuffing the divine out of existence like Frank Underwood or Josiah Bartlett. Yet at least for the characters in *True Detective*, grace remains a possibility, even in the face of God's palpable absence. It may seem fleeting or tragically inadequate at times. It may offer only a glimmer of hope. But the light is winning.

Real People, Real Life

Because this chapter started with a nonscripted show, we should also take at least a short look at how religion and religious people are represented in categories of television that fall outside fictional TV narratives—namely, news, sports, "reality," talk, and other awards shows. If these shows were our only source for theological reflection, what might it look like?

Well, one might think that God cares a lot about who wins sporting events, based on how many athletes work God into their interviews. And while it might seem odd to some that athletes mention how "blessed" they feel after a game or that they want to give glory to God for their win, those statements reveal that God is in some way a part of their everyday lives, regardless of how articulate they may be about it.

The people-on-the-street who are interviewed on the nightly news express similar sentiments, thanking God for protecting them from a natural disaster or praying for victims of tragedy. News coverage following these local or national tragedies often focuses on how communities of faith are responding to the hardships. Whether it's a hurricane that affects many or a crime that affects only one, people of faith sometimes startle reporters with a resilience that comes from a genuine sense of religious conviction. Religious communities are also frequently the subjects of news broadcasts when they work together to provide for others who are in need.

After the space shuttle *Challenger* explosion in 1986, President Ronald Reagan addressed the nation and quoted a poem to say that the astronauts had "slipped the surly bonds of earth" and "touched the face of God."[19] After the terrorist attacks on 9/11, political leaders gathered for a service at Washington National Cathedral. They sang hymns and talked freely of God. And after the shootings at a Charleston church in 2015, it was members of the church itself who spoke of their faith, their forgiveness, and their reliance on Jesus Christ. The first church service after the shooting was broadcast to the nation, and at the memorial service for one of the slain, President Obama sang an impromptu rendition of "Amazing Grace."

The funerals of Michael Jackson and Whitney Houston were filled with gospel music and Scripture, and both events were broadcast in their entirety on cable news outlets, with highlights shown on other channels throughout the day. Glimpses of church services show up on TV throughout the year—whether it's the pope's Christmas Eve mass from the Vatican, the president's family worshiping on Easter, or the Mormon Tabernacle Choir singing patriotic songs from its temple on the Fourth of July.

Of course, this kind of "reality" should not be confused with "reality television," which is an entirely different subject.[20] While it is fair to say that as soon as something is broadcast on TV it stops being "reality," there is a whole genre of TV that is classified under that title, and it is interesting to note how easily people of faith become integral parts of these story lines. *Survivor, The Biggest Loser, The Amazing Race*, and *The Voice* are just a few reality TV shows that seem to encourage participants to speak of their beliefs. Even *Big Brother* and MTV's *The Real World* tend to toss at least one religious representative into the mix (even if only to heighten the conflict and drama). And *Extreme Makeover: Home Edition* regularly showed churchgoing communities coming together to help those in need.

Contestants on *American Idol* talked openly about their religious commitments, and in 2008 all the contestants took to the stage to sing the popular worship song "Shout to the Lord" for a corporate moment of praise. Except they changed the words. One verse goes, "My Jesus, my savior . . ." But the idols-to-be sang, "*My shepherd*, my savior . . ." instead. Viewers who knew the song (and one can assume there were many of them; "Shout to the Lord" is an incredibly popular and well-worn song in many Christian churches) must have made their voices heard, because the next night, the contestants sang the song again, and this time the network executives allowed Jesus to be name-checked.

This incident is part of an odd pattern that seems to be indicative of all kinds of TV narratives—from those featuring Bob the Tomato and Larry the Cucumber to the family on *Blue Bloods* to the *American Idol* stage. Just as religious particularity is edited out of *VeggieTales* and away from the Reagans' dining-room table, the fact that network executives chose to remove "Jesus" from the lyrics of a song (a song, it can be assumed, that these executives did not realize millions of Americans knew by heart) is significant. So it's okay to sing about God on TV but only in the most generic of terms.

People did call God by name on two of the most popular reality shows airing in 2014: *Duck Dynasty* and *19 Kids and Counting*. Both shows feature families for whom their Christian faith is extremely important, even central to their lifestyle. But both of these shows present their subjects in a documentary, "Gorillas in the Mist" kind of way—as if these people represent a rare and fascinating species to be studied for their eccentricities. To be fair, both families *are* oddities: The average Christian in America doesn't know anyone with a busload of children, and has rarely, if ever, communed with overly bearded backwoods men who manufacture duck calls. But for those who either don't personally know any Christians or get their understanding of these "others" only from TV, or both, these two families both fit and define a stereotype of who and what a Christian is.[21]

Elisabeth Hasselbeck and Candace Cameron Bure might have added different layers to that understanding. While cohosts of *The View*, both spoke freely of their beliefs in God. They also spoke freely (and perhaps more ardently) about their beliefs in conservative Republicanism. Whether their theology or doctrinal views were articulate or thoughtful is a separate issue, but their presence on that panel—that two out of four of the regular hostesses were Christians—is significant in its own right.

The various talking heads that appear on cable news shows, talk shows, and entertainment shows are too numerous to count, but it does seem that our television culture is less religiously segregated than it is politically segregated. It is interesting to note, for example, that both Fox News and MSNBC have had shows hosted by preachers (Mike Huckabee and Al Sharpton, respectively). Authors of religious books frequently appear on mainstream talk shows like *The Today Show* and *Charlie Rose*, and *The Colbert Report* made a point of inviting religious figures onto that show, in part because Stephen Colbert is himself an articulate and outspoken person of religious conviction. And while *The Daily Show*—like *The Simpsons*—presents itself as an "equal opportunity offender," one might conclude from all these talk shows that religious adherents do in fact exist but remain unsure of whether they are simply the butts of comedic jokes, the victims of partisan attacks, or part of a more thoughtful cultural conversation.

As the Credits Roll . . .

Episodic TV serves as a bit of a cultural time capsule. To an outside observer (like our little green alien), a season of shows says, "These are the stories that mattered to us; these are the characters we chose to watch." As fiction, they are not a perfect representation of "This is who we actually are," but TV is still very much? "This is what/who represented us."

These representations don't always include religious people. And even when they do, they are more often a secondary concern. That there might be more characters with genuine religious commitments on TV today—and that they are more interesting, complex, and varied than ever before—is a good thing. But there is still a long way to go. This is not to say that the only way religion can be presented faithfully is by having characters speak in explicitly theological terms. Nevertheless, it is telling when they don't, for richer conversations inevitably take place when the whole gamut of our lived experience is presented in narrative form. And these are exactly the kinds of conversations that flesh-and-blood religious adherents need not only to join but to generate.

glossary of tv terms

accretion. A mode of drillable narrative complexity generated by the volume and duration of a particular narrative.

act break scenes. Scenes that come right before commercials on broadcast television.

affective music. Musical codes that provide viewers with interpretive access to that which is unseen—namely, a show's tone or mood, the inner workings of a character's psychology, and the audience's empathic bond with the narrative.

atmosphere. The element of a narrative that grapples with the unalterable givens in life—death, systemic injustices, and "otherness." Atmosphere raises the question of boundaries, of what is possible, and of what limits human beings.

authentic narrative space. The physical contours of a narrative's diegetic world, often fleshed out through sound.

beating out a story. Sketching out only the basic story points in their narrative order.

beat sheet. A brief, two- to four-page summary of an individual episode.

binary oppositions. The underlying narrative structure of many sitcom characterizations, leveraging binaries to create tension that can easily be diffused in thirty minutes.

breaking a story. The process in which the writers' room determines not simply what will happen within an episode or series but how it will happen.

centrifugal (narrative complexity). A form of serialization that creates narrative depth by spinning out into the larger world of other agents and structural forces.

centripetal (narrative complexity). A form of serialization that creates narrative depth by adding layers to the interior of a character's psychology.

cessation. An end to a series that serves as a stoppage or wrap-up without any indication that it will be the end of the series.

character. An aspect of story structure involving the characters and how they interact with one another and society at large. These stories address the question of human need and potential, thereby offering us paradigms for what it means to be human.

conclusion. A series that ends when a program's producers are able to craft a final episode knowing that it will be the end.

contextual music. A function of music/sound that involves both music's role in the context of a particular TV show and its ability to draw meaning from the viewer's broader musical-cultural context.

density. A mode of drillable narrative complexity that encourages audiences to "dig deeper" and discover hidden depths of meaning that go otherwise unnoticed.

diegesis. The self-contained universe that the characters inhabit in a story-world.

drillable. The manner in which a show encourages audiences to participate in its narrative structure, most often through "density" or "accretion."

editing. The process of cutting and remixing material and placing it into a dynamic relationship with other visual and aural elements.

episode. An individual installment of a TV series, either containing a complete narrative of its own or otherwise marked off from other episodes, usually by opening and end-credit sequences.

extra-diegetic. The level of narration that refers to the world of the narrator, whether that narrator is an actual agent in the story or an implied narrator.

finale. A conclusion with a going-away part. Finales are defined more by their surrounding discourse and hype than by any inherent properties of the narrative itself.

mise-en-scène. Literally "placing on stage." Most often used to describe the visual elements of theatrical or cinematic productions. When applied to television, it concerns anything that appears before the camera.

mockumentary. A fully scripted, fictional narrative leveraging the aesthetics of documentary filmmaking in a conscious and self-referential way.

montage. A series of discrete images or scenes placed together to form a narrative whole.

multi-camera setup. A method of filming a TV program that makes use of multiple cameras capturing a single "performance" from various angles. This setup is often found in sitcoms using a live studio audience.

musical other. Music that detaches itself from the narrative world and "speaks" from a location beyond the narrative.

narrative complexity. The particular manner in which a narrative creates depth, texture, and layers among its characters and settings.

narrative flow. The overarching spectrum of TV narratives within which all its segments exist, from the segment all the way to the corporation.

narrative world (or story-world). The various levels of narration implied by a given story.

network. The corporation responsible for broadcasting and financing TV programming.

non-diegetic. The narrative space where the audience sees, hears, reads, or otherwise encounters the story.

opening credits (or credit sequence or inter-title sequence). The segment of an episode that follows the teaser and precedes the narrative proper. It usually features a theme song, a title card, and a listing of the principal actors.

pitching. Suggesting various ideas about the setup or plot of a TV script.

plot. The manner in which a story moves through time. Plot is about the process by which a narrative moves from point A to point B.

point of view. Stories are told from a particular vantage point, which is often expressed through various narration techniques, both overt and implied.

proscenium theater. A stage or set designed for live productions, often featuring a "proscenium arch" that frames what is and is not a part of the production—that is, what the audience is meant to see. It often functions as the "fourth wall" in theater and in TV programs filmed on a set.

resurrection. The inverse of a cessation, a resurrection occurs when an already-concluded series returns, either on television or in another medium.

season. Generally following the broadcasting calendar, a season is a bounded set of TV episodes (usually from twelve to twenty-four) composing a self-contained narrative of its own.

segment. The smallest, usually self-contained unit of TV's narrative flow.

serial(ized). A form of episodic storytelling that assumes that the narrative accrues over time rather than "resetting" at the end of each episode.

series. The entirety of a program's episodes and seasons.

showrunner. The supervisor and head writer of a TV series.

stoppage. An abrupt, unplanned end to a series when a network pulls the plug midseason.

story beat. The most basic story point that serves as the central focus of a scene.

teaser. A brief, opening segment that runs prior to the credit sequence, usually designed to serve as a framing device or entry point into the episode.

trace. Our common object of inquiry more commonly known as a "TV show" and often referred to in TV studies as the "text."

wrap-up. A series ending that is neither fully arbitrary nor completely planned.

writers' room. The room in which television writers—as a group—spend most of their time. More commonly referred to simply as "the room," this is where ideas are "pitched," stories are "broken," notes are given, and punch-up is done.

notes

Acknowledgments

1. Edward John Carnell, *Television: Servant or Master?* (Eugene: Wipf & Stock, 2007), 99.

Introduction Turning Us On

1. And in fact, it turns out that they do not. Nearly seventeen months after the plane's disappearance, portions of it started washing up on shore.

2. Jacques Derrida, "Faith and Knowledge: The Two Sources of Religion at the Limits of 'Reason' Alone," in *Religion: Cultural Memory in the Present* (Redwood City, CA: Stanford University Press, 1998).

3. Clifford Geertz, *The Interpretation of Cultures* (New York: Basic Books, 1977).

4. Caryn James, "To Get the Best View of Television, Try Using a Wide Lens," *New York Times*, October 1, 2000, sec. 2, 39.

5. As it has been for a number of years, the Sundance Film Festival is on the leading edge of this phenomenon. See Brooks Barnes, "Small Screen Is Big Player at Sundance: Television Becomes a Force at Sundance Film Festival," *New York Times*, January 22, 2015, http://www.ny times.com/2015/01/22/arts/television-becomes-a-force-at-sundance-film-festival.html?smid=tw -nytimes&_r=1&referrer=.

6. "'Content is king-er than it has ever been' . . . 'Nobody watches crap anymore.' This is partially due to a new desire by top flight actors to work in TV and, of course, on-demand viewing" (Alex Kantrowitz, "Eight Developments That Are Disrupting the TV Industry," *Advertising Age*, February 11, 2015, http://adage.com/article/media/developments-disrupting-tv-industry/29708 6/?utm_campaign=SocialFlow&utm_source=Twitter&utm_medium=Social.

7. "This account of narrative complexity suggests that a new paradigm of television storytelling has emerged over the past two decades, redefining the boundary between episodic and serial forms, with a heightened degree of self-consciousness in storytelling mechanics, and demanding intensified viewer engagement focused on both diegetic pleasures and formal awareness" (Jason Mittell, *Complex TV: The Poetics of Contemporary Television Storytelling* [New York: New York University Press, 2015], 53).

8. Bill Dyrness, *Poetic Theology: God and the Poetics of Everyday Life* (Grand Rapids: Eerdmans, 2011), 10.

9. Robert K. Johnston, *Reel Spirituality: Theology and Film in Dialogue*, 2nd ed. (Grand Rapids: Baker Academic, 2006), 22.

10. Sarah Cardwell, "Television Aesthetics: Stylistic Analysis and Beyond," in *Television Aesthetics and Style*, ed. Jason Jacobs and Steven Peacock (New York: Bloomsbury, 2013), 24.

11. I owe the notion of a "trace" to Maeve Louise Heaney, who employs the term in her musical analysis of Arvo Pärt's *Spiegel im Spiegel*. See Maeve Louise Heaney, "Can Music 'Mirror' God? A Theological-Hermeneutical Exploration of Music in the Light of Arvo Pärt's *Spiegel im Spiegel*," *Religions* 5 (2014): 361–84.

12. The concept of culture as a "matrix of meanings" is taken from Craig Detweiler and Barry Taylor, who address TV as a site for theological exploration in one of their chapters in *Matrix of Meanings: Finding God in Pop Culture* (Grand Rapids: Baker Academic, 2003).

13. It is significant that Americans' viewing habits have remained relatively consistent for some time. A study from 1991 states, "The average American now watches more than four hours of TV each day, and the average household keeps a set on more than seven hours a day. The full force of television's impact is rarely felt in a single program or even a single season. It is the long-term result of exposure to an artificial reality so pervasive it has become a major part of the social environment" (S. Robert Lichter, Linda S. Lichter, and Stanley Rothman, *Watching America: What Television Tells Us about Our Lives* [New York: Prentice Hall, 1991], 3). Current statistics shift slightly depending upon the date of the study and the kind of viewing habits included in the study. Some studies, for example, do not include the hours spent on a personal computer streaming shows that were originally broadcast on television networks. Significantly, though, what has remained remarkably consistent is that Americans continue to consume between four and five hours of TV programming per day.

14. For an extended discussion of theology's dialogical nature and how this applies to cultural engagement, see Johnston, *Reel Spirituality*, 111.

15. Ibid., 114.

16. This is how Bernard Lonergan describes theological method. See Bernard Lonergan, *Method in Theology* (Toronto: University of Toronto Press, 1971).

17. William Romanowski and Jennifer L. Vander Heide, "Easier Said Than Done: On Reversing the Hermeneutical Flow in the Theology and Film Dialogue," *Journal of Communication and Religion* 30 (March 2007): 40–64.

18. I find the phoropter used by ophthalmologists to be a helpful metaphor for thinking about theological method and its relationship to how we "view" the world. As Caroline J. Simon notes in her elegant book on sexual integrity, clarity of vision does not come about by finding a single perfectly attuned lens that delivers 20/20 vision. Rather, it comes about through a convergence of lenses. She notes, "Orthodoxy is too often assumed to preclude multiplicity. If views are lenses, however, . . . multiplicity plus convergence yields clarity" (Caroline J. Simon, *Bringing Sex into Focus: The Quest for Sexual Integrity* [Downers Grove, IL: InterVarsity, 2012], 29).

19. Some would even argue that friendship is the central defining characteristic of Christianity. Rather than suggesting we "do good" to strangers, thinkers like Jean Vanier challenge the Christian community to enter into friendship with them. We must walk with others as friends, recognizing that we are their companions because we need them. See Jean Vanier, *Befriending the Stranger* (Mahwah, NJ: Paulist Press, 2010).

20. Noting that more than thirty-five hundred hours of new TV are now produced each season, one critic was particularly insightful: "We have access to greater, more varied stories than ever, and to the great stories of the past. But the golden age is also a Midas age, with the paralyzing promise of riches everywhere you touch. To enjoy any of it, you must acknowledge that you will never be able to enjoy all of it. Even a videophile sometimes needs to say a little prayer: God, grant me the serenity to accept the TV I can't see, the wisdom to know the TV I must see and the courage to change the channel" (James Poniewozik, "The Paradox of Television's New Golden Age: Now, You Don't Have Time to Watch It," *Time*, June 11, 2015, http://time.com/3917707/the-paradox-of-televisions-new-golden-age-you-dont-have-time-to-watch-it/).

21. As Mittell has recently noted, "I do not know how someone could manage to write a book like this without being selective in what programs to cover, and it is far better to be up-front about

why I have focused on these particular programs than to bury the hidden rationale in pseudo-objectivity" (Mittell, *Complex TV*, 207).

22. I have borrowed this phrase from Mark Labberton in his excellent *The Dangerous Act of Loving Your Neighbor: Seeing Others through the Eyes of Jesus* (Downers Grove, IL: InterVarsity, 2010).

Chapter 1 The Pilot Episode: What Is TV?

1. PR Newswire, "Netflix Declares Binge Watching Is the New Normal," December 13, 2013, http://www.prnewswire.com/news-releases/netflix-declares-binge-watching-is-the-new-normal-235713431.html.

2. Netflix, "Overview," http://ir.netflix.com/https://pr.netflix.com/WebClient/loginPageSales NetWorksAction.do?contentGroupId=10476&contentGroup=Company+Facts.

3. Ian Crouch, "Come Binge with Me," *New Yorker*, December 18, 2013, http://www.new yorker.com/online/blogs/culture/2013/12/come-binge-with-me.html.

4. Jonathan Bignell, *An Introduction to Television Studies*, 3rd ed. (New York: Routledge, 2013), 13.

5. Henry Jenkins uses the term "convergence culture" to identify the cultural shifts that have been brought about by the interaction between new and old media. This culture comprises highly active and participatory consumers who share a much more dynamic relationship with the producers of content than they did during the era of network control. See Henry Jenkins, *Convergence Culture: Where Old and New Media Collide* (New York: New York University Press, 2008).

6. Gary R. Edgerton, *The Columbia History of American Television* (New York: Columbia University Press, 2007), xvii–xviii.

7. Writing in the early 1990s, George Gilder rightly identified the coming technological revolution but perhaps underestimated TV's capacity to adapt to new technologies. "By all measures, TV was a superb technology for its time. Indeed, its presence and properties defined the time. But now its time is over. The television age is giving way to the much richer, interactive technologies of the computer age" (George Gilder, *Life after Television: The Coming Transformation of Media and American Life* [Knoxville: Whittle Direct, 1990], 10).

8. Pete Hammond, "EMMYS: As Television Landscape Shifts, Categories Split," May 31, 2014, http://www.deadline.com/2014/05/emmy-nomination-categories-split-changing-tv-landscape/.

9. Bignell, *Introduction to Television Studies*, 35.

10. Edgerton, *Columbia History of American Television*, 23.

11. Ibid., 14.

12. Here and elsewhere I am indebted to Gary Edgerton's insightful and imminently readable history of American television. For a more detailed analysis of the historical development of television technologies, see ibid.

13. Barbara Klinger, *Beyond the Multiplex: Cinema, New Technologies, and the Home* (Berkeley: University of California Press, 2006), 2–3.

14. Tobey Grumet Segal, "Kicking and Screening," *Sports Illustrated*, March 10, 2014, 20.

15. Marshall McLuhan, *Understanding Media: The Extensions of Man* (Cambridge, MA: MIT Press, 1964), 441.

16. Ibid., 23.

17. "Television tells stories, just as novels and plays and movies do. Indeed, it demands stories, on a fixed schedule, day in and day out. The endless flow of plots and characters, always available at the flick of a switch, is what differentiates this from all other forms of mass entertainment. It creates an alternate reality that is effortlessly accessible to the rich and the poor, the attentive and the passive, the learned and illiterate alike" (S. Robert Lichter, Linda S. Lichter, and Stanley Rothman, *Watching America: What Television Tells Us about Our Lives* [New York: Prentice Hall, 1991], 288).

18. This "seasonal" approach to TV programming does not hold up in other hemispheres, so this is a decidedly Western, even US phenomenon.

19. Henry Jenkins, Sam Ford, and Joshua Green, *Spreadable Media: Creating Value and Meaning in a Networked Culture* (New York: New York University Press, 2013), 132.

20. Ibid., 136.

21. Bignell, *Introduction to Television Studies*, 19.

22. Space will not allow for a full exploration of the technical use of this term. However, given all the pronouncements regarding the "collapse of the meta-narrative" in postmodern philosophy, it is indeed interesting that the most consumed product in our late capitalist society (i.e., TV) is structured not just by a meta-narrative but by a totalizing one. It would seem, then, that the resistance to meta-narratives among actual postmodern persons is related not so much to the notion that there is or could be a "grand" or "all-encompassing" story as to the real fear that meta-narratives are often the most invisible and thus present no option for critique or revision.

23. Lichter, Lichter, and Rothman, *Watching America*, 292.

24. We are indebted here to the work of Paul Ricoeur, which has shaped our notions of narrative as a fundamental resource for meaning-making. Mark I. Wallace encapsulates well Ricoeur's notion of how narratives shape human identity: "Everyone needs a story to live by in order to make sense of the pastiche of one's life. Without a narrative a person's life is merely a random sequence of unrelated events; birth and death are inscrutable, temporality is a terror and a burden, and suffering and loss remain mute and unintelligible" (Mark I. Wallace, introduction to *Figuring the Sacred: Religion, Narrative, and Imagination*, by Paul Ricoeur (Minneapolis: Augsburg Fortress, 1995), 11.

25. Edward John Carnell, *Television: Servant or Master?* (Eugene: Wipf & Stock, 2007), 80–81 (emphasis in original).

26. Alex Sherman, "NBC Gets $4 Million for Super Bowl Ads, Sells Out Inventory," Bloomberg Technology, January 3, 2012, http://www.bloomberg.com/news/2012-01-03/nbc-gets-4m-on -super-bowls-ad-slots-sells-out.html.

27. "New technology helped propel the [economic] boom. Industries such as automobiles, road construction, movies, radio, and home appliances helped create the world's first consumer economy" (Nathan Miller, *New World Coming: The 1920s and the Making of Modern America* [New York: Scribner, 2003], 150). As quoted in Edgerton, *Columbia History of American Television*, 38.

28. Bignell, *Introduction to Television Studies*, 25.

29. This is true at both the popular level and in academic writing. For an example of the former, see Jeff Wright, *God's Vision or Television? How Television Influences What We Believe* (Chicago: Urban Ministries, 2004). For an example of the latter, see Walter T. Davis Jr., Teresa Blythe, Gary Dreibelbis, Mark Scalese, SJ, Elizabeth Winans Winslea, and Donald L. Ashburn, *Watching What We Watch: Prime-Time Television through the Lens of Faith* (Louisville: Geneva Press, 2001), xiii.

30. I owe this insight to Klinger, *Beyond the Multiplex*, 19.

31. I am borrowing this language and this concept from George Lakoff and Mark Johnson, *Metaphors We Live By*, 2nd ed. (Chicago: University of Chicago Press, 2003).

32. "We actually live mythically and integrally, as it were, but we continue to think in the old, fragmented space and time patterns of the pre-electric age" (McLuhan, *Understanding Media*, 6).

Chapter 2 Becoming TV Literate: Formal Analysis

1. Until very recently, the notion of offering any kind of judgment or evaluation in art criticism was disparaged. However, both within and outside the realm of theology, scholars are recognizing that any act of assessment, analysis, or interpretation involves by its very nature some manner of evaluation. Evaluative criticism still has its detractors, but we are consciously developing our approach in conversation with those who see evaluation as an integral part of the hermeneutical process.

2. Jason Mittell, "The Qualities of Complexity: Vast versus Dense Seriality in Contemporary Television," in *Television Aesthetics and Style*, ed. Jason Jacobs and Steven Peacock (New York: Bloomsbury, 2013), 54–55.

3. Robert K. Johnston, *Reel Spirituality: Theology and Film in Dialogue*, 2nd ed. (Grand Rapids: Baker Academic, 2006), 185.

4. Jason Jacobs and Steven Peacock, introduction to *Television Aesthetics and Style*, 13.

5. Mittell, "Qualities of Complexity," 55.

6. Ibid., 45.

7. Cf. Aristotle, *Poetics* (New York: Penguin Classics, 1997).

8. There is not total agreement within TV studies concerning which should take priority—the discrete unit or the flow. We are taking up the position that, for analytical purposes, it is helpful to consider TV traces as both a "particle" and a "wave." But the concrete reality is that it is always already both at one and the same time. Our final interpretation must take into consideration the individual units in light of the whole, and vice versa.

9. John Ellis, *Visible Fictions: Cinema, Television, Video* (London: Routledge, 2000), 116–26. As quoted in Alex Clayton, "Why Comedy Is at Home on Television," in Jacobs and Peacock, *Television Aesthetics and Style*, 86.

10. I owe the notion of centrifugal and centripetal serialization to Jason Mittell, who also uses *Breaking Bad* and *The Wire* as exemplars of this type of televisual storytelling (Mittell, "Qualities of Complexity," 46).

11. Ibid., 50.

12. Ibid., 49.

13. Henry Jenkins, Sam Ford, and Joshua Green, *Spreadable Media: Creating Value and Meaning in a Networked Culture* (New York: New York University Press, 2013), 132–36.

14. Mittell, "Qualities of Complexity," 52.

15. These categories are taken from Rob Johnston's work in theology and film. He appropriates the literary paradigm from Wesley Kort as a critical tool for engaging with film stories.

16. I owe this insight to Jonathan Bignell, *An Introduction to Television Studies*, 3rd ed. (New York: Routledge, 2013), 101.

17. Andrew Levan, *Film Performance: From Achievement to Appreciation* (London: Wallflower, 2005), 71.

18. G. K. Chesterton, *Orthodoxy* (Chicago: Moody, 2013), 72.

19. Timotheus Vermeulen and James Whitfield, "Arrested Developments: Towards an Aesthetic of the Contemporary US Sitcom," in Jacobs and Peacock, *Television Aesthetics and Style*, 105.

20. There is also a hint of the Shakespearean here, which is indicative of *House of Cards* as a series. We are indebted to Richard Goodwin for this notion, who noted to us that Frank Underwood is like Iago as he addresses the audience, which raises the question of whether Frank is an antagonist or an antihero, or both.

21. As Sergio Dias Branco notes in his analysis of sitcoms, even static sets "present a limited sphere, but a porous one that let [sic] us see what lies behind its limits" (Sergio Dias Branco, "Situating Comedy: Inhabitation and Duration in Classical American Sitcoms," in Jacobs and Peacock, *Television Aesthetics and Style*, 96).

22. See, for example, John Thornton Caldwell, *Televisuality: Style, Crisis, and Authority in American Television* (New Brunswick, NJ: Rutgers University Press, 1995).

23. Mitchell Stephens, *The Rise of the Image, the Fall of the Word* (New York: Oxford University Press, 1998).

24. "The content and order of these words often matters less than their 'feel.' Instead of worrying whether a word is apt, the question may be whether it is sufficiently colorful, playful and concise" (ibid., 191).

25. Although its focus is on music in film, a helpful study of the religious significance of sound in audiovisual media is Kutter Callaway, *Scoring Transcendence: Contemporary Film Music as Religious Experience* (Waco: Baylor University Press, 2013).

26. All three of these categories have been appropriated from ibid., 77–92.

27. Aaron Sorkin, "How to Write an Aaron Sorkin Script, by Aaron Sorkin," *GQ*, June 20, 2012.

28. Ibid.

29. Jacob Smith, *Vocal Tracks: Performance and Sound Media* (Berkeley: University of California Press, 2008), 30.

30. Ibid., 36.

31. Ibid., 34.

Chapter 3 Becoming TV Literate: Process and Practice

1. Ryan Murphy, Brad Falchuk, and Ian Brennan, "The Quarterback," *Glee*, season 5, episode 3, directed by Brad Falchuk, aired October 10, 2013, 20th Century Fox Television.

2. By positioning our exploration in this way, we are attempting to chart a middle ground between reader-response criticism, on the one hand, and authorial intent, on the other. We are by no means the first to approach a popular cultural form in this way. Many working in the field of theology and popular culture have taken a cue from the work of Paul Ricoeur by approaching cultural artifacts in terms of the interaction between the "author," the "text," and the "reception" of an artifact. Excellent examples in this regard are Kevin J. Vanhoozer, *Everyday Theology: How to Read Cultural Texts and Interpret Trends* (Grand Rapids: Baker Academic, 2007); and Gordon Lynch, *Understanding Theology and Popular Culture* (Hoboken, NJ: Wiley-Blackwell, 2005). Outside theology, those working in philosophical aesthetics understand the aesthetic experience similarly. Matthew Kieran suggests that the subject matter of aesthetics and the philosophy of art is "The Aesthetic Triad," which "interrelates (a) the aesthetic object, its nature and identity, (b) its creator/ conditions of creation, and (c) our appreciation, and the conditions of that appreciation" (Matthew Kieran, *Contemporary Debates in Aesthetics and the Philosophy of Art* [Oxford: Blackwell, 2006], 6, as quoted in Sarah Cardwell, "Television Aesthetics: Stylistic Analysis and Beyond," in *Television Aesthetics and Style*, ed. Jason Jacobs and Steven Peacock [New York: Bloomsbury, 2013], 36).

3. The process can often start with a simple "what if" or "how about" pitch: "What if one of the characters loses his wallet?" or "How about an episode where the power goes out?" or "Maybe Ellen should get a puppy." That last one is a significant footnote to television history: the famous episode where Ellen DeGeneres comes out as a lesbian on her show *Ellen* (it originally aired in April 1997) is titled "The Puppy Episode," partly because the writers knew that the network executives had, for years, wanted to see Ellen's character start dating, which the writers vehemently did not want to make happen. But every year the writers would make a tongue-in-cheek suggestion that Ellen should get a puppy instead. When it was decided that the series was going to do the "coming out" episode, the writers taped a card to the wall in the room (next to the title of other episodes) that read "The Puppy Episode" as their "code" that they were going to eventually break that story—a story that they were certain was going to satisfy the network's long-term interest in seeing Ellen date. After writing the episode, they kept the title as it was. "The Puppy Episode" won the "Best Writing for a Comedy Series" Emmy Award that year. One more footnote: the character of Ellen never got a puppy.

4. Stuart Hall was one of the first to articulate this system of encoding and decoding. "Production and reception of the television message are not, therefore, identical, but they are related: they are differentiated moments within the totality formed by the social relations of the communicative process as a whole" (Stuart Hall, "Encoding/Decoding," in *Culture, Media, Language: Working Papers in Cultural Studies, 1927–1979*, ed. Stuart Hall, Dorothy Hobson, Andrew Lowe, and Paul Willis [Florence, KY: Routledge, 1980], 119).

5. This notion of a "power struggle" between the audience and the author is common in both cultural studies and media criticism and cuts across ideological lines. Cf. Chris Klassen, *Religion and Popular Culture: A Religious Studies Approach* (Oxford: Oxford University Press, 2014); and Robert H. Woods and Paul Patton, *Prophetically Incorrect: A Christian Introduction to Media Criticism* (Grand Rapids: Brazos, 2010). While we want to affirm the "negotiated" aspect of this interaction, we do not want to go so far as to say that all encounters between an author and an audience are entirely about power relations, nor does meaning always emerge from a kind of "violence" between the parties involved.

6. The notion of an "oppositional gaze" is taken from bell hooks, *Reel to Real: Race, Sex, and Class at the Movies* (New York: Routledge, 1996).

7. A focus on "lived religion" serves as the organizing framework for the collection of essays on television edited by Diane Winston. Although the contributors approach TV from the standpoint of communications theory rather than theology, Winston's volume is similar in spirit and tone to our own. She suggests that, because humans are symbolizing creatures, entertainment media are part of the cultural material that helps us make sense of our lives, our relationships, and our search for meaning. As a result, "television converts social concerns, cultural conundrums, and metaphysical questions into stories that explore and even shape notions of identity and destiny—the building blocks of religious speculation" (Diane Winston, introduction to *Small Screen, Big Picture: Television and Lived Religion*, ed. Diane Winston [Waco: Baylor University Press, 2009], 2).

8. Clive Marsh and Vaughan S. Roberts, *Personal Jesus: How Popular Music Shapes Our Souls* (Grand Rapids: Baker Academic, 2012), 7–13.

9. Staiger actually outlines four models: the education model, the reinforcement model, the mediation model, and the power relations model. Often, one or more of these models is used in conjunction with the others. See Janet Staiger, *Media Reception Studies* (New York: New York University Press, 2005).

10. For example, Pierre Boudrieu states that "the more you understand how things work, the more you come to understand that the people involved are manipulated as much as they manipulate. They manipulate even more effectively the more they are themselves manipulated and the more unconscious they are of this" (Pierre Boudrieu, *On Television* [New York: New Press, 1996], 17). And while the entire field of critical theory might be seen as parasitic on the prophetic tradition of the Hebrew Bible, it is sometimes difficult to discern when contemporary Christian media critics are borrowing from prophetic categories and when they are actually borrowing from neo-Marxist categories. For example, while Woods and Patton use language like "justification systems" rather than "super-structures," they are still talking about the ways that institutional structures work to protect the status quo by rendering the ideological workings of mass culture invisible. "All dominant framing stories, whether they are Christianity, Islam, Marxism, Freudian theory, or consumerism, require justification systems. By justification system, we mean the sum total of rationales available as evidence that the system is good and should remain dominant" (Woods and Patton, *Prophetically Incorrect*, 70).

11. Henry Jenkins suggests that the major shift that convergence culture has brought about concerns the relationship between producers and consumers. See Henry Jenkins, *Convergence Culture: Where Old and New Media Collide* (New York: New York University Press, 2008).

12. Referencing Baudrillard, Klassen applies the concept of the hyper-real to television to point out some of the potentially negative consequences of this cultural reality. "So, for example, we see television shows as more real than our real lives and, in fact, try to copy the simulacra of sitcoms, dramas, and 'reality' shows that are simulations without an actual referent. We become friends with digital characters—either in games or through chat rooms—with little or no tie to non-digital life. Actors not only play heroes, they become heroes, governors, or presidents" (Klassen, *Religion and Popular Culture*, 179).

13. Cf. Henry Jenkins, Sam Ford, and Joshua Green, *Spreadable Media: Creating Value and Meaning in a Networked Culture* (New York: New York University Press, 2013), 147.

14. Twitter, May 14, 2014, https://twitter.com/search?q=%23GleeSeasonFinale&src=tyah.

15. Ibid.

16. Both GLAAD and the AFA (the conservative American Family Association) say that the show is intentionally creating sympathies with and positive representations of gay and lesbian characters. Needless to say, representatives for these two organizations interpret the value of these depictions quite differently. And this in spite of the fact that Ryan Murphy, the lead writer and showrunner, and cast members deny that they are operating with any "Gayagenda" (Audrey

Barrick, "'Glee' Has No Gay Agenda, Actors Say," *The Christian Post*, August 3, 2011, http://www.christianpost.com/news/glee-has-no-gay-agenda-actors-say-53320/).

17. Twitter, September 27, 2013, https://twitter.com/glaad/status/383689582476136448.

18. Ibid.

19. Ibid.

20. Ibid.

21. We are helped here by Jenkins, Ford, and Green, who suggest that when consumers engage in the practice of analysis and interpretation, they are doing culturally significant work. In this sense, they are in fact "producing" the discourse in and through which we understand other media texts and, indeed, the world in which we live. See Jenkins, Ford, and Green, *Spreadable Media*.

22. This is the argument Graham Ward makes when addressing the value of interpreting cultural artifacts theologically. We will return to Ward's argument in a later chapter. See Graham Ward, *Cultural Transformation and Religious Practice* (Cambridge: Cambridge University Press, 2005).

23. Jenkins, *Convergence Culture*, 69.

24. Klassen, *Religion and Popular Culture*, 159.

25. Twitter, May 14, 2014, https://twitter.com/search?q=%23GleeSeasonFinale&src=tyah.

26. New developments in distribution practices have changed this distribution system in two ways. On the one hand, now that many seasons are made available in their entirety, the wait between episodes is eliminated through binge viewing. On the other hand, because these seasons are still released on a yearly basis, the wait between seasons is even longer (and perhaps more torturous) than before. So these shows tend to consume our attention more fully while we are watching/binging them but recede into the background as we wait for the next installment.

27. We owe this insight to Kate Wiebe, who is the executive director of the Institute for Congregational Trauma and Growth. See www.ictg.org/response-ndash-in-congregations.html.

28. Here and later in the discussion we are drawing from George Steiner, *Real Presences* (Chicago: University of Chicago Press, 1989), 155–65.

Chapter 4 The *Telos* of TV

1. "You Never Know Where You're Goin' till You Get There," lyrics by Sammy Cahn; music by Jule Styne. In *Cinderella Jones*, Warner Bros (1946).

2. Francis Davis, "Recognition Humor," *Atlantic* 275, no. 12 (December 1992): 135–38.

3. Though the *Seinfeld* episode that aired May 14, 1998, was in fact "The Finale" (that was the episode's title), the characters lived on in other formats. They reunited for what could be considered an "additional finale" on *Curb Your Enthusiasm* in 2009, and the characters of Jerry and George appeared in a 2014 commercial that aired during the Super Bowl. An extended version of that commercial was shown on Jerry Seinfeld's web series, *Comedians in Cars Getting Coffee*.

4. Jason Mittell identifies a few other descriptors for the kinds of narrative ends on TV. "Stoppage" is "an abrupt, unplanned end to a series when a network pulls the plug midseason. . . . A stoppage is always extratextually motivated" (*Complex TV: The Poetics of Contemporary Storytelling* [New York: New York University Press, 2015], 319).

5. The show also dealt with many serious subjects and featured Billy Crystal as one of prime-time TV's first openly gay characters.

6. Here it is helpful to recognize the various kinds of time that exist within TV storytelling. As Mittell helpfully suggests, we can think of time falling into three major categories. "*Story time* is the time frame of the diegesis, how time passes within the storyworld, and typically follows real-world conventions of straightforward chronology and linear progression from moment to moment, with exceptions of such as when characters time travel in *Lost* or *Heroes*. *Discourse Time* is the temporal structure and duration of the story as told within a given narrative, which almost always differs from story time via ellipses skipping over uneventful moments. . . . Finally, there is *narration time*, the temporal framework involved in telling and receiving the story. . . . For film and television, *screen time* is a better term for narration time, as it highlights the medium as part

of the narrative experience." All the "happily ever after" scenarios are actually taking place as an imagined extension of "story time" (Mittell, *Complex TV*, 26).

7. *Frasier* ran for eleven seasons.

8. The grown daughter was played by actress and comedian Janeane Garofalo, whose comedic persona contributed to the sardonic character that she portrayed.

9. We return to the way the church in particular responded to *NYPD Blue* in the next chapter.

10. Bill Keveney, "NYPD Blue: Looking Back at Its Colorful Moments," *USA Today*, September 14, 2004.

11. See https://thetommywestphall.wordpress.com/.

12. Whether one could develop the "Roseanne Universe" to rival Tommy Westphall's will have to be left to future scholars with too much time on their hands.

13. Many fans of the show were dissatisfied with the ending that aired, and the show's creators included an "alternative ending" (one in which the mother did not die) as part of the DVD boxed set of the series.

14. The series had also declined in the ratings, and it is intriguing to wonder what might have happened if *Lost* had attracted more viewers in its fourth year. There likely would have been no talk of bringing the series to closure two years hence, the powers-that-be would have wanted it to remain on the air as long as possible, and any number of more seasons would have been produced beyond the six seasons that aired. What might have happened in those (possibly several years of) episodes is anyone's guess, but it is a fact of television life that *Lost* could not sustain its initial popularity with viewers and was cut short as a result.

15. We will return to "The End" again in the conclusion.

16. Mark Lee, "Wise Guys: A Conversation between David Chase and Tom Fontana," *Written By* (May 2007), http://www.wga.org/writtenby/writtenbysub.aspx?id=2354.

17. Todd VanDerWerff, "David Chase Responds to Our *Sopranos* Piece," *Vox*, August 27, 2014, http://www.vox.com/2014/8/27/6076621/david-chase-responds-to-our-sopranos-piece.

18. Dan Snierson, "Breaking Bad: Creator Vince Gilligan Explains Series Finale," *Entertainment Weekly*, September 30, 2013, http://www.ew.com/article/2013/09/30/breaking-bad-finale-vince-gilligan.

19. Ibid.

20. Ibid.

21. Kristin Dos Santos, "Chills! Former Dexter Producer Clyde Phillips Reveals How He Planned to End the Series," *E! Online*, September 22, 2013, http://www.eonline.com/news/461558/chills-former-dexter-producer-clyde-phillips-reveals-how-he-planned-to-end-the-series.

22. Jennifer Vineyard, "Dexter Producer: Showtime Wouldn't Let Us Kill Dexter," *Vulture*, October 7, 2013, http://www.vulture.com/2013/10/dexter-writers-werent-allowed-to-kill-dexter.html.

23. Terence Winter, "To the Lost," *Boardwalk Empire*, season 2, episode 12, directed by Tim Van Patten, aired December 11, 2011, HBO.

24. Terence Winter and Howard Korder, "Eldorado," *Boardwalk Empire*, season 5, episode 8, directed by Tim Van Patten, aired October 26, 2014, HBO.

25. Using Mittell's categories, this would be a "wrap-up," which is a "series ending that is neither fully arbitrary nor completely planned. Typically wrap-ups come at the end of a season, when producers have come to a natural stopping point but without planned series finality" (Mittell, *Complex TV*, 320).

26. A "resurrection" is the inverse of a cessation. It occurs when "an already concluded series returns, either on television or in another medium" (ibid., 321).

27. At the time of publication, the series was not expected to air until 2017. A book about the lives of the characters during the quarter century between season 2 and season 3, written by Mark Frost, was scheduled to be released sometime before new episodes of *Twin Peaks* were broadcast.

28. A series "conclusion" is one of the less common endings. It is "when a program's producers are able to craft a final episode knowing that it will be the end. Sometimes a conclusion is planned in advance by the producers, and sometimes it is thrust on them" (Mittell, *Complex TV*, 320).

29. This movie was intended as a pilot for a series that never materialized. It was the era of *The Love Boat* and *Fantasy Island*, and the series would have featured the castaways hosting various guest stars each week at their island resort.

30. A "cessation" is an end to a series that serves as a "stoppage or wrap-up without a definite finality that it will be the end of the series" (Mittell, *Complex TV*, 321).

31. The character of Lou Grant continued on the air in his eponymous show—one of the only hour-long dramatic spin-offs of a half-hour comedy. Probably because of the producers' desire to separate the two shows tonally, almost no mention was made of the character's life back in Minnesota, and none of *The Mary Tyler Moore Show*'s regular characters ever appeared on his show.

32. Harry Castleman and Walter J. Podrazik, *Watching TV: Six Decades of American Television* (Syracuse: Syracuse University Press, 2010), 312. In comparison, 76 million people tuned in to say good-bye to *Seinfeld*, and nearly 53 million watched the *Friends* finale, ibid., 429. The final episode of *Lost*, when it aired, was seen by about 13.5 million viewers, though it has certainly been seen by many more people since then. See Jennifer Ross, "Lost Series Finale Somehow Only the 55th Most-Watched Ever," *Paste*, May 27, 2010, http://www.pastemagazine.com/articles /2010/05/thirteen-million-get-lost-in-series-finale.htm. The declining numbers for the finales of seminal shows reflect the ever-growing number of viewer choices, and the changing methods of television viewing.

33. It should be noted that the "Goodbye" in the finale's title wasn't completely "good-bye," as some of the characters went on to appear in a short-lived (and critically panned) spin-off. *After MASH*, featuring the characters of Colonel Potter, Father Mulcahy, and Klinger and his wife, aired from 1983 to 1985.

34. Mittell suggests that the true "finale" is the rarest of endings. Finales are "a conclusion with a going away party. Finales are defined more by their surrounding discourse and hype than any inherent properties of the narrative itself" (Mittell, *Complex TV*, 322).

35. Sometimes called "post-liberal" theology, narrative theology has its origins in the works of theologians such as George Lindbeck, Hans Frei, and Stanley Hauerwas. More recently, however, the concern for developing a "narrative" approach can be seen in the work of scholars from other disciplines such as biblical studies and homiletics. Cf. J. R. Daniel Kirk, *Jesus Have I Loved, but Paul? A Narrative Approach to the Problem of Pauline Christianity* (Grand Rapids: Baker Academic, 2012); and Eugene L. Lowry, *The Homiletical Beat: Why All Sermons Are Narrative* (Nashville: Abingdon, 2012). Narrative theology is even referenced in official doctrinal statements at the local church level. See "Narrative Theology," Mars Hill, http://marshill.org/about-us/about/narrative-theology.

Chapter 5 A Very Brief History of the Church and TV

1. Gerhard Friedrich, "*euangelion*," in *Theological Dictionary of the New Testament*, vol. 2, ed. Gerhard Kittel and Gerhard Friedrich, trans. Geoffrey W. Bromiley (Grand Rapids: Eerdmans, 1964–76), 707–37.

2. N. T. Wright, *Paul and the Faithfulness of God*, book 1 (Minneapolis: Fortress, 2013), 288–89.

3. Cf. Michele Rosenthal, *American Protestants and TV in the 1950s: Responses to a New Medium* (New York: Palgrave Macmillan, 2007).

4. In this way, we are simply following those historians who "eschew the reconstructive exhaustiveness characteristic of much professional historical scholarship as incompatible with its objective." See Brad S. Gregory, *The Unintended Reformation: How a Religious Revolution Secularized Society* (Cambridge, MA: Harvard University Press, 2012), 3.

5. Quentin J. Schultze, introduction to *American Evangelicals and the Mass Media*, ed. Quentin J. Schultze (Grand Rapids: Academie Books, 1990), 14.

6. Rosenthal, *American Protestants*, 63. Rosenthal also makes a compelling argument that "the use of mass media, particularly the use of the most modern and technologically sophisticated media—the radio and the television, would be an important symbolic touchstone in the early evangelical movement" (ibid., 67).

7. John P. Ferré, "Evangelical Television Criticism through a Half Century of *Christianity Today* Cartoons," in *Evangelical Christians and Popular Culture: Pop Goes the Gospel*, vol. 1, ed. Robert H. Woods (Santa Barbara: Praeger, 2013), 179.

8. Robert K. Johnston, *Reel Spirituality: Theology and Film in Dialogue*, 2nd ed. (Grand Rapids: Baker Academic, 2006), 55.

9. Ibid.

10. We owe the following reading of the history of mainline religious programming to Michele Rosenthal's *American Protestants*. Hers truly is a landmark study concerning the role that TV played in the cultural prominence (or lack thereof) of mainline and evangelical Protestants in the United States.

11. Albert Crews made this claim in his annual report to the BFC board in 1956. As quoted in Rosenthal, *American Protestants*, 47.

12. Here and earlier in the discussion, see Rosenthal, *American Protestants*, 37–61.

13. "Technique transforms everything it touches into a machine" (Jacques Ellul, *The Technological Society*, trans. John Wilkinson [New York: Vintage, 1964], 4). Significantly, Ellul identifies his Christian convictions as the primary impetus behind his critique of technological society. According to Ellul, the Christian's role is to stand uniquely at the point of intersection of this material world and the eternal world to come.

14. Malcolm Muggeridge, *Christ and the Media* (Vancouver: Regent College, 2003).

15. Virginia Stem Owens, *The Total Image: Or Selling Jesus in the Modern Age* (Grand Rapids: Eerdmans, 1980).

16. Quentin Schultze uses the term "videots" to describe the way TV tries to position the viewer. Schultze, *Redeeming Television: How TV Changes Christians—How Christians Can Change TV* (Downers Grove, IL: InterVarsity, 1992), 62.

17. Writing as late as 1992, Quentin Schultze, whom we will consider in more detail later, admits that critics like Ellul, Muggeridge, and Owens "are partly correct. Television's visual appeal can deceive viewers. It is not easy for most viewers to think about a program while they are being bombarded with images" (ibid., 25). In part, Schultze's response is rooted more in the model he employs to understand the relationship between media and audiences—something along the lines of the "power relations" model we discussed in chapter 3. But it is also because the thought of Ellul, Muggeridge, and Owens continues to exert a tremendous amount of influence on critics like Schultze.

18. "In the 1980s, Christian groups attacked the entertainment industry, often through boycotts on advertisers on shows. The Moral Majority and the Rev. Donald Wildmon's Coalition for Better Television led the way in boycotts" (Amanda Sturgill, "Evangelicalism," in *The Routledge Encyclopedia of Religion, Communication, and Media*, ed. D. A. Stout [New York: Routledge, 2010], 139).

19. Times Staff and Wire Reports, "Christian Group Calls for Boycott of Unilever," *Los Angeles Times*, June 13, 1995, http://articles.latimes.com/1995-06-13/business/fi-12784_1_boycott-unilever.

20. Richard D. Land, *Send a Message to Mickey: The ABC's of Making Your Voice Heard at Disney* (Nashville: Broadman & Holman, 1998), 68.

21. As John Ferré rightly notes, "Evangelical media critics have been more concerned with what television shows than with who is responsible for programming. Content is what we see when we watch television, after all, and it is content that inspires or offends" (Ferré, "Evangelical Television Criticism," 186).

22. Reflecting on this approach, Dean Batali states, "The [Christian viewers] who have gotten rid of their TVs or simply do not watch . . . are, essentially, just looking the other way. And you can ask the guy bleeding on the side of the road to Jericho how much good that does" ("Changing

the Channels," in *Behind the Screen: Hollywood Insiders of Faith, Film, and Culture*, ed. Spencer Lewerenz and Barbara Nicolosi [Grand Rapids: Baker Books, 2005], 14).

23. Neil Postman, *Amusing Ourselves to Death: Public Discourse in the Age of Show Business* (New York: Penguin Group, 2005), 157.

24. "Television . . . serves us most usefully when presenting junk entertainment; it serves us most ill when it co-opts serious modes of discourse . . . and turns them into entertainment packages" (ibid., 159).

25. Here and later in the discussion, see William F. Fore, *Television and Religion: The Shaping of Faith, Values, and Culture* (Minneapolis: Augsburg, 1987).

26. Ibid., 196.

27. Writing as an African American pastor for African American churches, Wright is particularly concerned about the statistics for TV consumption among the African American population. According to Wright, among certain age groups, African Americans are watching more than twice as much television as everyone else. See Jeff Wright, *God's Vision or Television? How Television Influences What We Believe* (Chicago: Urban Ministries, 2004), 1.

28. See Robert H. Woods and Paul Patton, *Prophetically Incorrect: A Christian Introduction to Media Criticism* (Grand Rapids: Brazos, 2010).

29. Ibid., 110–17.

30. Ibid., 114–19.

31. We are indebted to Mark Finney for bringing to our attention the significance of Walter Ong's work for understanding how the church has responded to TV technology.

32. "Our own age today . . . is marked by a new stress on the auditory" (Walter J. Ong, *The Presence of the Word: Some Prolegomena for Cultural and Religious History*, 2nd ed. [Albany: State University of New York Press, 2000], 9). According to Ong, there is great potential in this shift. "The present orality is . . . possessed of more reflectiveness, historical sense, and organized purposefulness than was possible in preliterate oral cultures" (ibid., 301–2).

33. "The fact is that the permanent correlative of human knowledge in the world of sense, as we have reiterated so often, is not primarily visual or tactile or gustatory or olfactory but auditory. . . . The picture must always be elucidated by the word more than the word by the picture" (ibid., 322).

34. By "prioritize" we do not mean "privilege." Our Christian theology is still the basic lens through which we understand all of life and the world—TV included. But dialogue requires all parties to allow space for the other to speak. We can do no better than Robert K. Johnston, whose work (on film) informs our understanding of theological dialogue: "To give movie viewing this epistemological priority in the dialogue between film and theology—to judge it advisable to first look at a movie on its own terms and let the images themselves suggest meaning and direction—is not to make theology of secondary importance. Religious faith is primary. In fact, I argue that the nature of both moviegoing and religious faith demands that film viewing be completed from a theological perspective. But such theologizing should follow, not precede, the aesthetic experience" (Johnston, *Reel Spirituality*, 64).

35. J. E. Eubanks Jr., "Why the Shift from Horror to Terror on 'CSI' Is a Problem," *Christianity Today*, January 16, 2015, http://www.christianitytoday.com/ct/2015/january-web-only/why-shift -from-horror-to-terror-on-csi-is-problem.html?start=2.

36. Ibid.

37. See Craig Detweiler, *iGods: How Technology Shapes Our Spiritual and Social Lives* (Grand Rapids: Brazos, 2013); Shane Hipps, *Flickering Pixels: How Technology Shapes Your Faith* (Grand Rapids: Zondervan, 2009); and Brent Laytham, *iPod, YouTube, Wii Play: Theological Engagements with Entertainment* (Eugene, OR: Wipf & Stock, 2012).

38. Craig Detweiler, "*The Wire*: Playing the Game," in *Small Screen, Big Picture: Television and Lived Religion*, ed. Diane Winston (Waco: Baylor University Press, 2009), 77.

39. Ibid., 79.

40. Ibid., 97.

41. Edward John Carnell, *Television: Servant or Master?* (Eugene, OR: Wipf & Stock, 2007).

42. "One would err . . . if he believed that television, another work of fallible men [sic], is an unmixed medium: wholly good or wholly bad" (ibid., 14–15).

43. "In no meaningful sense, thus, can we say that the TV set itself is our problem. Our problem is, was, and shall be, *man* [sic]. If man can control himself, television will take care of itself" (ibid., 17 [emphasis in original]).

44. Ibid., xiii.

45. "Carnell's reluctance to suggest a complete ban on television stood in contrast to both the fundamentalist position (which viewed TV as too worldly) and the mainline position (which encouraged people to just 'turn it off'), both of which were far more condemnatory of the new medium" (Rosenthal, *American Protestants*, 101).

46. Carnell himself acknowledged the somewhat anticipatory nature of his text: "All entries remain theoretical, of course, inasmuch as TV is too youthful and supple to lodge contained within ossified categories of finality" (Carnell, *Television*, xii).

47. It should be noted that, by grouping these three into the same category, we are not suggesting they are the same. In fact, while Detweiler is generally more appreciative of television in pursuing dialogue with contemporary media, Laytham is generally more cautious. Both, however, have recently taken small steps toward the others' perspective, with Detweiler demonstrating a bit more caution than in the past, and Laytham a bit more appreciation.

48. Paul Creasman, "Evangelicals Find God in *Lost*," in Woods, *Evangelical Christians and Popular Culture*, 214.

49. Ibid., 216.

50. See Schultze, *Redeeming Television*. Following closely the work of Schultze, Woods and Patton claim that the two primary properties of TV's "language" are its "immediacy" and "liveness," which "place limits on television's symbolic capacity, or the way it captures and presents reality to its audiences. Audiences, for better or worse, are affected by these biases as they interpret content and assign meaning to certain events" (Woods and Patton, *Prophetically Incorrect*, 113).

51. Ben Armstrong, *The Electric Church* (Nashville: Thomas Nelson, 1979), 8.

52. Mark I. Pinsky, *The Gospel according to* The Simpsons: *Bigger and Possibly Even Better! Edition* (Louisville: Westminster John Knox, 2007), i.

53. Ibid., vii.

54. Robert L. Short, "Praise for the First Edition of *The Gospel according to* The Simpsons," endorsement in Pinsky, *Gospel according to* The Simpsons.

55. See Chris Seay, *The Gospel according to* Lost (Nashville: Thomas Nelson, 2009); Tim Wesemann, *Jack Bauer's Having a Bad Day: An Unauthorized Investigation of Faith in "24": Season 1* (Colorado Springs: David C. Cook, 2006); and Jana Riess, *What Would Buffy Do? The Vampire Slayer as Spiritual Guide* (Hoboken, NJ: Jossey-Bass, 2004).

56. See Mark I. Pinsky, *The Gospel according to Disney: Faith, Trust, and Pixie Dust* (Louisville: Westminster John Knox, 2004); and Blake Atwood, *The Gospel according to* Breaking Bad (Dallas: AtWords Press, 2014).

57. Short, "Praise for the First Edition of *The Gospel according to* The Simpsons," in Pinsky, *The Gospel according to* The Simpsons.

58. Schultze, "Keeping the Faith," in *American Evangelicals and the Mass Media*, 32.

59. Fore, *Television and Religion*, 34.

60. This is the title of one of Osteen's best-selling works. See Joel Osteen, *Your Best Life Now: 7 Steps to Living at Your Full Potential* (New York: Time Warner, 2004).

61. "The fact that the electronic church has few major, measurable effects supports much social-scientific research about the impact of the mass media in general. The media have rarely been found to have important direct effects. At best, mass media have indirect and conditional

effects" (Stewart M. Hoover, "The Meaning of Religious Television: The '700 Club' in the Lives of Its Viewers," in Schultze, *American Evangelicals and the Mass Media*, 235).

62. Ibid., 236.

63. As Clifford Christians has suggested, "Evangelical broadcasters have typically based their scripts on straightforward, propositional claims about God and humankind. Nothing could be less effective on the small TV screen for communicating transcendence" (Clifford G. Christians, "Redemptive Media as the Evangelical's Cultural Task," in Schultze, *American Evangelicals and the Mass Media*, 353).

64. Creasman offers a helpful analysis of these texts, asking how they were put to use by evangelicals. Creasman, "Evangelicals Find God in *Lost*," in Woods, *Evangelical Christians and Popular Culture*, 213.

65. Christian Piatt, "*Lost*": A Search for Meaning (St. Louis: Chalice, 2006), 6.

66. Creasman, "Evangelicals Find God in *Lost*."

67. John Ankerberg and Dillon Burroughs, *What Can Be Found in "Lost": Insights on God and the Meaning of Life* (Eugene, OR: Harvest House, 2008).

68. Ibid., 10.

69. Walter Ong, "Voice as Summons for Belief: Literature, Faith, and the Divided Self," in *Literature and Religion*, ed. Giles Gunn (New York: Harper & Row, 1971), 72.

Chapter 6 Channeling Theology: TV and God's Wider Presence

1. See James K. A. Smith, *Imagining the Kingdom: How Worship Works* (Grand Rapids: Baker Academic, 2013), 172. We will return to Smith later in the discussion as one of our primary dialogue partners.

2. *Concerning the Teacher* (or *De magistro*) is written as a dialogue between Augustine and his son, Adeodatus. The question Augustine asks is a pedagogical one. That is, what is the role of the teacher when it comes to learning? What does it mean to communicate ideas? Is it all about conveying information from the teacher to the student? Or are there other factors in play? Augustine, *Concerning the Teacher (De magistro) and On the Immortality of the Soul (De immortalitate animae)*, trans. George G. Leckie (New York: Appleton-Century-Crofts, 1938) [hereafter *Concerning the Teacher*].

3. "We speak for the sake of teaching or reminding, since when we question we only do it that he who is asked may learn what we wish to hear; and that singing, which we seem to do for pleasure, is not properly speaking; that in praying to God whom we cannot suppose to be taught or reminded, words are for the purpose either of reminding ourselves or that others may be taught or reminded through us" (ibid., 7.19). It is interesting to note that, even at this stage, Augustine is emphasizing the centrality of language in the communicative process while, at the very same time, recognizing its inherent limitations.

4. "Indeed when things are discussed which we perceive through the mind, that is, by means of intellect and reason, these are said to be things which we see immediately in that interior light of truth by virtue of which he himself who is called the interior man is illumined, and upon this depends his joy. But then our hearer, if he also himself sees those things with his inner and pure eye, knows that of which I speak by means of his own contemplation, but not through my words. Accordingly, even though I speak about true things, I still do not teach him who beholds the true things, for he is taught not through my words but by means of the things themselves which God reveals within the soul" (ibid., 12.40).

5. "To give them as much credit as possible, words possess only sufficient efficacy to remind us in order that we may seek things, but not to exhibit the things so that we may know them" (ibid., 11.36). In other words, for Augustine, words could neither convey eternal truths nor "things-in-themselves." Their use and value was to focus the hearer's mind on the things themselves.

6. "What can be said to indicate that we learn anything by means of words beyond that sound which strikes the ear? For all things which we perceive are perceived either through a sense of the

body or by means of the mind. We call the former sensibles, the latter intelligibles; or to speak in the manner of our authorities, the former are carnal, the latter spiritual. . . . But if a question is not about things immediately sensed, although it is about things which we have sensed in the past, in this case we speak not of things themselves but of images impressed by things on the mind and committed to memory" (ibid., 12.39).

7. Augustine has the Master question the student: "And you have ventured to transfer the name which grammar taught you to that thing you admit does not belong to grammar? . . . And yet when you see a great many kinds of sound in which distinct measures can be observed, and we admit these kinds are not to be attributed to the art of grammar, don't you think there is some other discipline which contains whatever is numerable or artful in utterances of this sort? . . . What do you think its name is? For I don't believe it is news to you that a certain omnipotence in singing is usually granted to the Muses. If I am not mistaken, this is what is called Music" (Augustine, *De Musica* 1.1 [Washington, DC: Catholic University of America Press, 2002], 170).

8. We were very much helped in sorting out Augustine's thoughts on communication by Todd Johnson, who expounds upon Augustine's theory of communication to develop a theological method for worship and the arts in Todd E. Johnson, "Wisdom at the Confluence of Worship, Theology, and Arts," *Fuller Theology, News, and Notes* (Spring 2012): 4.

9. As a counterexample, he offers a vision at Ostia in *Confessions* in which he and Monica are in a space where they are able to overcome the distance of their mortal bodies. "We proceeded step by step through all bodily things up to that heaven whence shine the sun and the moon and the stars down upon the earth. We ascended higher yet by means of inward thought and discourse and admiration of your works, and we came up to our own minds. We transcended them, so that we attained to the region of abundance that never fails . . . and where life is that Wisdom by which all these things are made" (Augustine, *The Confessions of St. Augustine*, trans. John K. Ryan [New York: Image Books, 1960], 221 [hereafter *Confessions* 9.10.24]).

10. In Hebrew, the *neshamah*, or "breath (of God)." We will return to the Spirit of God again later in the discussion. For now, though, it is significant to note that the bodily, material, "enfleshed" nature of the first humans is emphasized in the text. In Genesis 2:23 (NIV) the man sings about his companion, "this is now bone of my bones and flesh of my flesh"—a poetic doubling to underscore the physicality of their relatedness.

11. As *LA Times* TV critic Robert Lloyd puts it, "Now I am inclined to define television as any moving picture—at all—watched on any sort of screen not located within a movie theater" ("How Should Television Be Defined Nowadays?," *Los Angeles Times*, November 21, 2014, http://www.latimes.com/entertainment/tv/la-et-st-ca-tv-section-critics-definition-20141123-column.html#page=1).

12. Or, as in the case of James K. A. Smith, TV constitutes the audience as an audience and thus changes the world into a TV. The primary criteria for life's meaning becomes "watchableness," thus rendering human worth as isomorphic. Instead of "being with" others, "to be is to be seen" (Smith, *Imagining the Kingdom*, 147).

13. Although her study is quite revealing in its own right and by no means takes a Luddite position, this is the base assumption of Sherry Turkle, *Alone Together: Why We Expect More from Technology and Less from Each Other* (New York: Basic Books, 2012). Turkle does not approach technology from a theological perspective but nevertheless explores the ways that communication at a distance might undermine genuine (i.e., face-to-face) human discourse.

14. We borrow the idea of technology as an "extension" of the human from Marshall McLuhan.

15. We owe this turn of phrase to Jaron Lanier, *You Are Not a Gadget: A Manifesto* (New York: Vintage, 2011).

16. This is a conclusion supported by research into the actual habits and practices of online communities. See, for example, Heidi Campbell, *Exploring Religious Community Online: We Are One in the Network* (New York: Peter Lang, 2005).

17. *Confessions* 1.1.1.

18. This is how William Dyrness articulates Augustine's notion of the journey of our affections in *On Christian Teaching*. See William A. Dyrness, *Poetic Theology: God and the Poetics of Everyday Life* (Grand Rapids: Eerdmans, 2011), 155–56.

19. "Augustine would say that the effect of sin on our love is not that we stop loving but that our love becomes disordered. It gets aimed at the wrong ends and finds 'enjoyment' in what it should merely be 'using.' Or, in other words, instead of being *caritas*, our love becomes *cupiditas*." See Augustine, *On Christian Teaching* 1.26.27–1.27.28. As cited in James K. A. Smith, *Desiring the Kingdom: Worship, Worldview, and Cultural Formation* (Grand Rapids: Baker Academic, 2009), 52n25.

20. Clive Marsh and Vaughan S. Roberts, *Personal Jesus: How Popular Music Shapes Our Souls* (Grand Rapids: Baker Academic, 2012), 9–10 (emphasis in original).

21. Marsh and Roberts rely on the work of James Carey to explicate the conditions of this shift toward a ritual view (ibid., 9–11).

22. Here and later in the discussion, see Smith, *Desiring the Kingdom*. In *Imagining the Kingdom*, he offers his own summary of the argument he makes in *Desiring the Kingdom*. "I make three intertwined proposals in *Desiring the Kingdom* that are at the heart of the Cultural Liturgies project and are all indebted to Saint Augustine, that patron saint of the Reformers: First, I sketch an alternative anthropology that emphasizes the primacy of love and the priority of the imagination in shaping our identity and governing our orientation to the world. Second, I emphasize that education is also about the formation ('aiming') of our love and desire, and that such formation happens through embodied, communal rituals we might call 'liturgies'—including a range of 'secular' liturgies that are pedagogies of desire. Third, given the formative priority of liturgical practices, I argue that the task of Christian education needs to be resituated within the ecclesial practices of Christian worship and liturgical formation" (Smith, *Imagining the Kingdom*, 7).

23. Smith, *Desiring the Kingdom*, 50.

24. Ibid., 83.

25. Ibid., 43.

26. Smith, *Imagining the Kingdom*, 14.

27. Ibid., 17 (emphasis in original).

28. Ibid., 137–38 (emphasis in original). We will discuss this further later, but it is interesting to note that it is at this point—where formative rituals result in action—that Smith becomes almost immediately suspicious of any ritual that takes place outside the walls of the church. The *telos* of these other "pedagogies of desire" is almost always interpreted as in opposition to the *telos* of the gospel.

29. See, for example, Mike Garafolo, "Stadium Innovations a Priority to NFL Owners," *USA Today*, May 20, 2013, http://www.usatoday.com/story/sports/nfl/2013/05/20/nfl-meeting-stadium -innovations-priority/2344803/.

30. Kutter Callaway, "In a TV World, NFL Is King," *Christianity Today*, January 22, 2015, http:// www.christianitytoday.com/ct/2015/january-web-only/in-tv-world-nfl-is-king.html.

31. Smith, *Desiring the Kingdom*, 74.

32. Ibid., 88.

33. "I have tended to emphasize the antithesis between the vision of the good life carried in secular liturgies and the vision of *shalom* that is performed in Christian worship. However, my antithetical account is not a 'total' critique. Following Augustine, I would advocate nuanced, ad hoc evaluations of particular cultural practices" (Smith, *Imagining the Kingdom*, 126n44).

34. Smith, *Desiring the Kingdom*, 88.

35. Smith, *Imagining the Kingdom*, 5.

36. Ibid., 168 (emphasis in original).

37. Ibid., 172.

38. Ibid., 169. It is important to note that Smith denies that his conception of worship is one in which the liturgy dropped down intact from heaven. Nevertheless, while Smith is a Protestant from the Reformed tradition, his conception of Christian worship is clearly indebted to

a stream of thought within liturgical theology that has been profoundly shaped by the thought of Alexander Schmemann, an Orthodox theologian who has done a masterful job of translating the value and insight of the Orthodox tradition for Western theology. One of his most significant contributions to the Protestant understanding of worship concerns the Orthodox conception of a divine "ordo," a particular form of worship that defines the basic structure of the church's liturgy because it actualizes the worship of the heavens. According to Schmemann, "The meaning of the Church's liturgical life must be contained within the Ordo, insofar as it defines the general structure or 'rite' of her worship. . . . To find the Ordo . . . to find the unchanging principle, to find the living norm or 'logos' of Christian worship as a whole . . . this is the primary task [of liturgical theology]" (Alexander Schmemann, *Introduction to Liturgical Theology*, trans. Asheleigh E. Moorehouse [New York: St. Vladimir's Seminary Press], 39). Although Smith does not cite Schmemann directly, he does draw upon the work of Frank Senn and others whose work has been deeply informed by Schmemann.

39. Smith, *Imagining the Kingdom*, 169n54.

40. This conception presupposes historical continuity with apostolic tradition and a level of liturgical uniformity during the patristic period. Ultimately, earlier liturgical forms and practices are considered more "authentic" and, therefore, superior to their historical accretions. However, theologians like Michael Aune have questioned these conceptions of the historical development of Christian liturgy. Quoting Max Johnson, he states, "There is probably no such thing as a pure ordo existing anywhere in some idealized form apart from its very concrete, cultural, ecclesial, and ritual linguistic expressions" (Michael B. Aune, "Liturgy and Theology: Rethinking the Relationship. Part 1, Setting the Stage," *Worship* 81, no. 1 [2007]: 58). Furthermore, Paul Bradshaw has challenged the notion of a historical, uniform ordo, suggesting earlier Christian practice was actually more diverse than later manifestations (Paul F. Bradshaw, "Difficulties in Doing Liturgical Theology," *Pacifica* 11, no. 2 [1998]: 181). These critiques point to classical liturgical theology's romantic conceptions of history as one of the many reasons for questioning its normative claims. If a pure ordo never truly existed, there is great difficulty in claiming it as the normative structure for Christian worship.

41. Interestingly, Smith seems to be moving toward a very different conclusion until the very last moment. "But we also need to recognize that this is how secular liturgies work: they, too, recruit our unconscious drives and desires through embodied stories that fuel our imagination and thus ultimately govern our action. And while Christian worship practices are distinguished by the presence of the Spirit and a very different story, not even secular liturgies are merely 'natural'; they can be fueled by the 'principalities and powers'" (*Imagining the Kingdom*, 15).

42. Dyrness, *Poetic Theology*, 5 (emphasis in original).

43. "Indeed, the genius of mall religion is that actually it operates with a more holistic, affective, embodied anthropology (or theory of the human person) than the Christian church tends to assume!" (Smith, *Desiring the Kingdom*, 24).

44. "The fact that we are 'liturgical animals'—and hence imaginative, narrative animals—is a structural feature of creaturehood that cannot be effaced or erased, even by sin" (Smith, *Imagining the Kingdom*, 140).

45. "Pursuing conversations about God today might not in the first instance be about the truth of Christianity, but about the presence and work of God in the contemporary situation and, especially, in the passions that move people to act, build, and create. It would proceed on the assumption that God is already deeply involved in their lives, and is already in conversation with them" (Dyrness, *Poetic Theology*, 5).

46. Smith, *Imagining the Kingdom*, 145.

47. Ibid.

48. Robert K. Johnston, *God's Wider Presence: Reconsidering General Revelation* (Grand Rapids: Baker Academic, 2014).

49. This is the impetus behind much of Augustine's writings in *Confessions*. Indeed, he frames the entire first book in the terms set forth by the question of God's pervasive presence in the world as seen in Scripture: "Since I do indeed exist, and yet would not be unless you were in me, why do I beg that you come to me? I am not now in hell, yet you are even there. For 'if I descend into hell, you are present' [Psalm 139:8]. Therefore, my God, I would not be, I would in no wise be, unless you were in me. Or rather, I would not be unless I were in you, 'from whom, by whom, and in whom are all things' [Romans 11:36]" (*Confessions* 1.1.2).

50. Johnston, *God's Wider Presence*, 92. Readers are strongly encouraged to consult Johnston's book (especially chapters 4 and 5) for a fully explicated engagement with these and numerous other biblical texts. For our purposes, it is enough to make reference to them, but Johnston engages in important exegetical work that is central to the validity of our argument.

51. Ibid., 117.

52. Ibid., 127–28.

53. Lanier, *You Are Not a Gadget*, 136.

54. George Steiner, *Real Presences* (Chicago: University of Chicago Press, 1989), 152.

55. In this way too we are following Steiner's lead: "These immediacies are familiar to anyone who has entered into personal relation with a poem, painting, piece of music at anything beyond the most trivial or casually enforced level. Yet they are very difficult to put into words" (ibid., 179).

56. Mary McNamara, "'Parenthood,' Ever the Adult," *Los Angeles Times*, January 29, 2015.

57. Steiner, *Real Presences*, 178.

58. Again, readers are directed toward Johnston's work in *God's Wider Presence* for a more detailed exposition of these categories. However, the concept of God's "immanent transcendence" has also been explored in depth by Jürgen Moltmann, especially in his *The Spirit of Life: A Universal Affirmation*, trans. Margaret Kohl (Minneapolis: Fortress, 1991). Interestingly, though, this same concept is not restricted to theology alone. Theodor Adorno too employed the concept of an "immanent transcendence" in his analysis of Mahler's music. See Theodor W. Adorno, *Mahler: A Musical Physiognomy* (Chicago: University of Chicago Press, 1992).

59. "All good art and literature begin in immanence. But they do not stop there. . . . The questions: 'What is poetry, music, art?', 'How can they not be?', 'How do they act upon us and how do we interpret their action?', are, ultimately, theological questions" (Steiner, *Real Presences*, 227).

60. We owe this insight to Smith in both *Desiring the Kingdom* and *Imagining the Kingdom*.

61. We have been greatly helped in thinking through the role of Sabbath-keeping in relationship to consumer culture by Walter Brueggemann, *Sabbath as Resistance: Saying No to the Culture of Now* (Louisville: Westminster John Knox, 2014). However, it is important to note that Brueggemann would likely not share our optimism regarding how people of faith might consume in constructive ways.

Chapter 7 Ethics: Is There Anything Good on TV?

1. Robert K. Johnston, *Reel Spirituality: Theology and Film in Dialogue*, 2nd ed. (Grand Rapids: Baker Academic, 2006), 222.

2. Recall once again Smith's insightful comment about the relationship between poetic, embodied practices and human action: "What's ultimately at stake in a liturgical anthropology is a philosophy of action. Liturgical formation is a way of describing the intense formative dynamic that shapes our imagination and forms our background horizons, which in turn affect how we constitute our world and thus what we feel ourselves *called* to in the world" (James K. A. Smith, *Imagining the Kingdom: How Worship Works* [Grand Rapids: Baker Academic, 2013], 137–38 [emphasis in original]).

3. Caroline J. Simon, *Bringing Sex into Focus: The Quest for Sexual Integrity* (Downers Grove, IL: InterVarsity, 2012), 23 (emphasis in original).

4. This is one of the basic claims that Roberto Goizueta makes in his brilliant book on Latino theology, *Caminemos con Jesus: Toward a Hispanic/Latino Theology of Accompaniment* (Maryknoll, NY: Orbis, 1995).

5. Gordon Lynch, *Understanding Theology and Popular Culture* (Oxford: Blackwell, 2005), ix.

6. Recall our brief discussion of George Steiner's work in chapter 3. For Steiner, listening to cultural stories is an act of hospitality. It isn't that we are unconcerned with what the biblical text says or what its "worldview" might be. Rather, we are simply attempting to engage TV stories from the position of Christian hospitality.

7. See "The TV Parental Guidelines," http://www.tvguidelines.org.

8. Robert Woods and Paul Patton make this claim regarding the need for evangelicals to move beyond the "big three" of language, sex, and violence, in Robert H. Woods and Paul Patton, *Prophetically Incorrect: A Christian Introduction to Media Criticism* (Grand Rapids: Brazos, 2010).

9. S. Robert Lichter, Linda S. Lichter, and Stanley Rothman, *Watching America: What Television Tells Us about Our Lives* (New York: Prentice Hall, 1991), 3–17.

10. Most often, the argument that content does affect viewers is prefaced by an acknowledgment that this claim cannot be demonstrated using empirical research. For example, while making the point that TV violence is bad for viewers, William Fore claims that, even though "it is technically impossible to show a cause-and-effect relationship . . . the vast majority of such studies demonstrates a positive association between exposure to media violence and aggressiveness" (William F. Fore, *Television and Religion: The Shaping of Faith, Values, and Culture* [Minneapolis: Augsburg, 1987], 143).

11. Jolyon Mitchell, *Media Violence and Christian Ethics* (New York: Cambridge University Press, 2007), 3–4. For readers wanting to pursue the full literature, Mitchell helpfully identifies a number of salient pieces, including a collection of essays in C. Kay Weaver and Cynthia Carter, eds., *Critical Readings: Violence and the Media* (Buckingham, UK: Open University Press, 2006). For alternative views, see W. James Potter, *On Media Violence* (Thousand Oaks, CA: Sage, 1999); and Cynthia Carter and C. Kay Weaver, *Media Violence* (Buckingham, UK: Open University Press, 2003). For a series of conflicting views on a variety of forms of media content, see Roman Espejo, ed., *Opposing Viewpoints: Mass Media* (Farmington Hills, MI: Greenhaven Press, 2010).

12. We have borrowed the categories of "witness," "hospitality," and "friendship" from Jolyon Mitchell, whose insightful work on Christian ethics and media violence informs much of this chapter. See Mitchell, *Media Violence and Christian Ethics*.

13. Neil Postman, *Amusing Ourselves to Death: Public Discourse in the Age of Show Business* (New York: Penguin, 2005), 87.

14. From Robert McChesney to Henry Jenkins to Robert Woods and Paul Patton, a variety of critics representing numerous areas of expertise and interest agree that the centralization of media ownership is the key ethical problem facing the contemporary world. As Robert McChesney suggests, "The U.S. media system is not the result of the 'free market' or of natural laws, but of explicit governmental laws, regulations, and subsidies that have created the giants that rule the roost" (Robert McChesney, *Rich Media, Poor Democracy: Communication Politics in Dubious Times* [Champaign: University of Illinois Press, 2009], xxii–xxiii). See also Henry Jenkins, *Convergence Culture: Where Old and New Media Collide* (New York: New York University Press, 2008); and Woods and Patton, *Prophetically Incorrect*.

15. "Spreadability" is the term Henry Jenkins and his colleagues use to define media that is consumed, shared, and recycled in convergence culture. Like Jenkins, we use "spreadable" instead of the more common term "viral" because "viral" denotes an agent that "infects" an otherwise "passive" body, and this does not reflect how media is actually consumed and used. See Henry Jenkins, Sam Ford, and Joshua Green, *Spreadable Media: Creating Value and Meaning in a Networked Culture* (New York: New York University Press, 2013).

16. http://www.cc.com/shows/the-daily-show-with-trevor-noah/news-team.

17. Mitchell, *Media Violence and Christian Ethics*, 10.

18. James McClendon, who identified as a lowercase-*b* baptist, titled the third volume of his systematic theology *Witness*. It is not insignificant that, in fact, *Witness* functions as McClendon's theology of culture. It is how he understands the Christian presence in the world: "How is the convert to relate to the traditional world of his or her origin? The broad Christian answer is that each follower of the Way is now commissioned as a witness, in but not of his or her world. Witnessing requires a new sociality, a revised engagement with those still fixed in the culture of their origin" (James Wm. McClendon Jr., *Witness: Systematic Theology*, vol. 3 [Nashville: Abingdon, 2000], 21).

19. Mitchell, *Media Violence and Christian Ethics*, 39.

20. Thomas Jemielity, *Satire and the Hebrew Prophets* (Louisville: Westminster John Knox, 1992), 14. Although his focus is not only prophetic literature, Edwin M. Good makes a related point regarding the many forms of irony found throughout the whole of the Hebrew Bible in his *Irony in the Old Testament*, 2nd ed. (Sheffield: Sheffield Academic Press, 1981).

21. Jemielity, *Satire and the Hebrew Prophets*, 53.

22. Ibid., 74–75.

23. Diane Winston, introduction to *Small Screen, Big Picture: Television and Lived Religion*, ed. Diane Winston (Waco: Baylor University Press, 2009), 4. The history of the critical developments within television studies is less central to our argument, so readers who are interested in the topic will find Winston's summary in her introduction to *Small Screen, Big Picture* a helpful place to start.

24. "All this illustrates the problematic nature of calls for more 'realism' on television, on the one hand, and for positive role models, on the other. Organized complaints helped doom 'Amos and Andy' and its accompanying stereotypes, but another result was to deprive blacks of their only toehold on the tube for a decade" (Lichter, Lichter, and Rothman, *Watching America*, 249).

25. Ibid., 257.

26. Woods and Patton, *Prophetically Incorrect*, 117–18.

27. James Poniewozik, "Review: *Fresh Off the Boat* Has the Makings of an American Original," *Time*, February 4, 2015, http://time.com/3694113/review-fresh-off-the-boat/.

28. Eddie Huang, "Bamboo-Ceiling TV," *Vulture*, February 4, 2015, http://www.vulture.com/2015/01/eddie-huang-fresh-off-the-boat-abc.html. Huang goes on to say, "This show isn't about me, nor is it about Asian America. The network won't take that gamble right now. You can't flash an ad during THE GAME with some chubby Chinese kid running across the screen talking s--- about spaceships and Uncle Chans in 2014 because America has no reference. The only way they could even mention some of the stories in the book was by building a Trojan horse and feeding the pathogenic stereotypes that still define us to a lot of American cyclope [*sic*]. Randall was neutered, Constance was exoticized, and Young Eddie was urbanized so that the viewers got their mise-en-place. People watching these channels have never seen us, and the network's approach to pacifying them is to say we're all the same. Sell them pasteurized network television with East Asian faces until they wake up intolerant of their own lactose, and hit 'em with the soy. Baking soya, I got baking soya!"

29. Mitchell, *Media Violence and Christian Ethics*, 290.

30. Ibid., 294.

31. Jason Mittell, *Complex TV: The Poetics of Contemporary Storytelling* (New York: New York University Press, 2015), 133.

32. Mittell refers to this as "character elaboration." "Characters rarely shift significantly, but our understanding of them often does, a change of a somewhat different narrative order that we might call *character elaboration*. . . . This model of change exploits the serial form to gradually reveal aspects of a character over time so that these facets of the character feel new to the audience, even if they are consistent and unchanging character attributes" (ibid., 136 [emphasis in original]).

33. Christian Keysers, *The Empathic Brain* (Amsterdam: Social Brain Press, 2011), 11. We are indebted once again to Mark Finney for steering us down the road that connects narrative and neuroscience.

34. Ibid., 194.

35. Mitchell, *Media Violence and Christian Ethics*, 295.

36. Christopher Rosen, "Parks and Recreation: Like *The Office* but . . . Well, Just Like *The Office*," *New York Observer*, April 10, 2009, http://observer.com/2009/04/iparks-and-recreationi -like-ithe-officei-but-well-just-like-ithe-officei/.

37. Ibid.

Conclusion The Season Finale: To Be Continued

1. Jason Mittell, *Complex TV: The Poetics of Contemporary Storytelling* (New York: New York University Press, 2015), 117.

2. We are borrowing the term "infinite middle" from ibid., 321.

3. Recall that we discuss at length the various types of finales and how they affect a show's meaning in chapter 4.

4. Mittell, *Complex TV*, 321.

5. Tim Greiving, "A Wrong Note Sets the Right Mood in *House of Cards*," NPR, February 26, 2015, http://www.npr.org/2015/02/26/389045445/scoring-at-risk-how-the-house-of-cards -composer.

6. See Joseph Campbell, *The Hero with a Thousand Faces*, 2nd ed. (Princeton: Princeton University Press, 1972).

7. It is also interesting to note the placement of this editorial heading among different translations. One's read of the story changes if "The Good Samaritan" title comes just before verse 25 instead of just before verse 29. And this is to say nothing of the fact that the Samaritan character is simply "a Samaritan," and not a "good Samaritan."

8. Building upon the work of H. Richard Niebuhr, Glenn Stassen states, "Twelve times in *The Meaning of Revelation* Niebuhr uses the term *drama* to point to the knowable pattern of God's action that enables us to interpret our lives in a unified way—or to our false interpretation of life as a drama in which we, rather than God, are the protagonists" (Glenn H. Stassen, "Concrete Christological Norms for Transformation," in Glen H. Stassen, D. M. Yeager, and John Howard Yoder, *Authentic Transformation: A New Vision for Christ and Culture* [Nashville: Abingdon, 1996], 153).

9. An interesting connection between the theological discourse on justification and the question of character development in television can be found in Oliver Crisp's recent discussion of the Reformed views on "justification in eternity" and "justification from eternity." According to Crisp, for those who hold a justification *from* eternity view, the individual, in time, experiences an ontological change. The individual is *in fact* released from bondage and so, on both moral and legal levels, is transformed. For those who hold a justification *in* eternity view, the change brought about by justification through faith is merely epistemic, and not ontological. This does not mean the change is trivial. But it is nevertheless a revelation—an unveiling—of the eternal purposes of God in time, and not an actual change in the elect individual's moral or legal standing. This fits well with our earlier consideration of the development of TV characters as more of an "unveiling" or "elaboration" than a "transformation" per se. See Oliver D. Crisp, *Deviant Calvinism: Broadening Reformed Theology* (Minneapolis: Fortress, 2014), esp. chap. 2.

10. This is similar to the kind of "faithful presence" described by James Davison Hunter, *To Change the World: The Irony, Tragedy, and Possibility of Christianity in the Late Modern World* (New York: Oxford University Press, 2010).

11. For a specifically theological counter-voice to this ontological nominalism, see Hans Boersma, *Heavenly Participation: The Weaving of a Sacramental Tapestry* (Grand Rapids: Eerdmans, 2011). A similar argument that puts forward a critical-realist ontology from a sociological perspective is found in Christian Smith, *To Flourish or Destruct: A Personalist Theory of Human Goods, Motivations, Failure, and Evil* (Chicago: University of Chicago Press, 2015).

12. We are indebted here to Mittell, *Complex TV*, 323. Many of the following insights concerning *Lost* fandom emerged in dialogue with Mittell's work.

13. Henry Jenkins, Sam Ford, and Joshua Green, *Spreadable Media: Creating Value and Meaning in a Networked Culture* (New York: New York University Press, 2013), 134.

14. Jeffrey Lieber, J. J. Abrams, Damon Lindelof, and Carlton Cuse, "The End," *Lost*, season 6, episode 17, directed by Jack Bender, aired May 23, 2010 (Burbank: ABC Studios, 2010), DVD.

15. Mittell, *Complex TV*, 323–29.

16. Ibid., 116–17.

17. *Lost*, "The End."

18. For Augustine, time participates in the eternity of God's life. "It is now plain and clear that neither past nor future are existent, and that it is not properly stated that there are three times, past, present, and future. But perhaps it might properly be said that there are three times, the present of things past, the present of things present, and the present of things future" (Augustine, *The Confessions of St. Augustine*, trans. John K. Ryan [New York: Image Books, 1960], 292–93 [XI.20]).

19. Cf. Carl A. Raschke, *The Next Reformation: Why Evangelicals Must Embrace Postmodernity* (Grand Rapids: Baker Academic, 2004). See also Peter Rollins, *How (Not) to Speak of God* (Brewster, MA: Paraclete Press, 2006).

20. In addition to Boersma and Smith cited earlier, others who are advocating for some form of return to a pre-Enlightenment ontology are Tracey Rowland, *Culture and the Thomist Tradition after Vatican II* (London: Routledge, 2003) and, from the perspective of theological aesthetics, Alejandro R. Garcia-Rivera, *A Wounded Innocence: Sketches for a Theology of Art* (Collegeville, MN: Liturgical Press, 2003).

Appendix Theology from TV

1. Adam K. Raymond and Andrew Bouve, "And the Most Thanked Person in Oscar History Is . . ." *Vocativ*, February 19, 2015.

2. Dominic Patten, "History's 'The Bible' Finale Watched by 11.7 Viewers," *Deadline*, April 1, 2013.

3. *A.D.: The Bible Continues* was canceled by NBC after its first season.

4. In 2014, Stephen Collins, who played the father, admitted to inappropriate sexual contact with children, putting a stain on the show as well. Many stations pulled reruns of the show from their lineup, though the series can still easily be found on both broadcast and streaming TV.

5. The reasons for this absence of shows like *7th Heaven* are complicated. As previously explained, some of it has to do with the perceived audience for a "family" show and whether they are sought after by advertisers. But another factor is that television executives tend to put on shows that they themselves like or the kinds of shows that people they know would watch. And with *an arguable* disconnect between the people of Hollywood and the rest of the country, the idea of promoting a show as traditional, conservative, and "soft" as *7th Heaven* has little appeal. But the changing face of television, along with streaming services that allow broadcasters to be more targeted toward their audiences, could mean that programming for this audience could once again start to appear.

6. Meg James, "It's Out with the Old as CBS Cancels 4 Shows," *TV Guide*, May 19, 2005, http://articles.latimes.com/2005/may/19/business/fi-upfront19.

7. Dilshad D. Ali, "A Chance at Redemption," *Beliefnet*, 2007.

8. Associated Press, "Talking Veggies Stir Controversy at NBC," September 22, 2006, http://www.foxnews.com/story/2006/09/22/talking-veggies-stir-controversy-at-nbc.html.

9. Phil Vischer, the creator of *VeggieTales*, charts the rise and fall of his company, including its eventual bankruptcy and sale, in *Me, Myself, and Bob: A True Story about God, Dreams, and Talking Vegetables* (Nashville: Thomas Nelson, 2007).

10. A twist was put on how this theological discussion related to humans when, in the final episode, it was revealed that these characters—whom most viewers had assumed were a future version of us—were actually our ancient ancestors who colonized earth after leaving their own planet.

11. In this way, *X-Files* embodies the "buffered self" that is indicative in Charles Taylor's understanding of our "secular age." For Taylor, all belief in the modern world is shot through with the skepticism we have inherited from the now-failed Enlightenment project. At the same time, all doubters are haunted by the ghosts of a once-porous world shot through with the transcendent. See Charles Taylor, *A Secular Age* (Cambridge, MA: Belknap Press, 2007).

12. The same week that *Friday Night Lights* premiered, *Studio Sixty on the Sunset Strip* also began its one-season run. That series featured an evangelical Christian character as one of its stars, and in the pilot she also prayed "in Jesus's name." It was a significant but overlooked moment regarding religion on TV: two Jesus-centered prayers were part of scripted television in the same week.

13. *The Good Wife* also features a minister in a recurring role. In one story line, he refuses to be "used" by the main character's ex-husband, who is trying to be seen in a more positive light by the public, and challenges the man to be a better person. The minister comes off as a person of genuine integrity and conviction.

14. *Bridget Loves Bernie*, a series that lasted only one season (1972–73), could have been a unique addition to this discussion. The show portrayed the interfaith marriage between a Roman Catholic and a Jew and aired between *All in the Family* and *The Mary Tyler Moore Show*. CBS canceled the show after one season, citing hate mail from viewers as a key factor. It remains the highest-rated show (it was number five for the season) ever to have been canceled after only one season.

15. Robert Davi, "How Hollywood Spits on Christianity," *Breitbart*, March 2, 2015. See also Tim Graham, "Shame on Netflix: 'House of Cards' Spits in the Face of Jesus," *Newsbusters*, March 5, 2015.

16. Laura Eason, "Chapter 30," *House of Cards*, season 3, episode 4, directed by Tucker Gates, aired February 27, 2015, Netflix.

17. Alan Sepinwall, "'True Detective' Creator Looks Back at Season One," *Hitfix*, March 10, 2014.

18. Ibid.

19. John Gillespie Magee Jr., "High Flight," http://www.arlingtoncemetery.net/highflig.htm.

20. For those interested in further reading on the theological significance of reality TV, see Stephen Faller, *Reality TV: Theology in the Video Era* (St. Louis: Chalice, 209).

21. In 2015 revelations regarding sexual molestation charges against one of the Duggar children came to light. For those looking to brand the family as weird (or even dangerous), this was all the evidence that was needed. *19 Kids and Counting* was canceled in the summer of 2015.

index